RAISING GLOBAL TEENS

A Practical Handbook for
Parenting in the 21st Century

Anisha Abraham, MD, MPH

First Published in Great Britain by Summertime Publishing

ISBN: 978-1-9998808-4-2

Cover and internal pages designed by Cath Brew at drawntoastory.com

Disclaimer
Names have been changed to protect the identity of people involved. The author has made every effort to cite the source of all statistics and quotations and gain copyright permissions where appropriate. Any inadvertent omission is regretted.

Praise for

RAISING GLOBAL TEENS:
A Practical Handbook for Parenting in the 21st Century

"I highly, highly recommend this book to not only parents, but to all educators, social service professionals, medically related personnel, and anyone else who loves and works with this population. You will be glad you took the time to read it, I promise you!"

Ruth E Van Reken, Hon DLitt
Co-author, *Third Culture Kids, 3rd ed.*
Co-founder, Families in Global Transition, <u>figt.org</u>

...

"An empowering book underscoring critical elements of effective parenting while addressing how to effectively guide your children through that inherently adolescent question – "Who am I?" Global teens grapple with this question of identity along with added layers that come with navigating different cultures. Thanks to Dr. Abraham, however, you'll be better prepared to help your teen reap the many benefits of being raised in multiple cultures. This masterful work will enable you to build the resilience in your children that will prepare them to thrive in both good and challenging times."

Ken Ginsburg, MD, MS Ed
Author of *Building Resilience in Children and Teens*, and
Raising Kids to Thrive, <u>parentandteen.com</u>

...

"Raising Global Teens will enlighten all parents, regardless of their geography. Anisha uses her own international and multicultural life journey, plus her work as a pediatrician and educator, to shine a bright light on what it's like to grow up cross-culturally. It's the kind of book that you don't realize you need until you start reading it... and then it becomes suddenly indispensable."

Cara Natterson, MD
Author of *Decoding Boys* and
The Care and Keeping of You series, <u>worryproofmd.com</u>

■■■

"If you want to learn how to navigate the unique challenges of raising a global teen, this book is for you. Dr. Anisha Abraham, a pediatrician and adolescent medicine specialist, engagingly discusses issues like sex, drugs, social media, and depression in a cross-cultural context and explains how to maintain your (and your teen's) sanity in these difficult years."

Sandeep Jauhar
New York Times bestselling author of *Heart: A History,*
<u>sandeepjauhar.com</u>

■■■

"At the heart of this warm, insightful and practical book on parenting adolescents in the 21st century is the reminder that adolescence is a time of grappling with identity. Deftly weaving her cross-cultural background with decades of experience as an adolescent doctor, Dr. Abraham packages the universal challenges of adolescence into bite-sized pieces of parenting wisdom. While particularly focusing on the identity challenges for 'global citizens', this book is highly recommended for any parent, anywhere!"

Susan Sawyer, MD
Chair of Adolescent Health, Department of Paediatrics, The University of Melbourne, President, International Association for Adolescent Health, IAAH.org

■■■

"Outstanding insight, advice and hope for global teens and their parents! This book addresses the missing cross-cultural perspective on raising adolescents that is needed in today's world. Dr. Abraham has harnessed her personal and professional experience, capturing the essence and challenges faced by global families and she has given us a road map to acceptance and success."

Leslie R. Walker-Harding, MD
Chief Academic Officer, Seattle Children's Hospital, Former President, Society for Adolescent Health and Medicine, adolescenthealth.org

■■■

"Dr. Abraham writes not only from first-hand but also clinical experience, which she uses to provide incredible insight into what it takes to help raise global teens who will thrive in an ever-globalizing world – all with a compassionate and easy to follow approach. I am so excited that this book has been written; it's going to help so many people!"

Christopher O'Shaughnessy
International Speaker and author of *Arrivals, Departures and the Adventures In-Between*,
chris-o.com

···

"What an inspired book! Full of professional insights and first-hand experiences, it is sure to engage anyone dedicated to empowering soon-to-be adults with the valuable skills they'll need to succeed. At first glance, you might think this book is only for teens living outside their home country or whose parents have different cultural backgrounds. But in today's globally complex and highly connected world, Dr. Abraham's informed approach to parenting has much broader relevance. I believe that all teens, no matter who they are or where they live, will benefit from being raised as global teens!"

Laura Jana, MD
Pediatrician and author of *The Toddler Brain: Nurture the Skills Today that Will Shape Your Child's Tomorrow*,
drlaurajana.com

···

To all the teens I have worked with over the years and who have provided the foundation for this book.

May the future be yours.

CONTENTS

Part I - The Basics

Part II - The Big Stuff

Part III - The Future

FOREWORDS

It's happened at last! Now I find a book that should have been in my hands 40 years ago! My wife and I raised our own global teens while moving 16 times in 19 years during my pediatric residency, US Navy days, living in Liberia for nine of those years.

In this wonderful book, Dr. Abraham not only explains the many aspects of teen development that all young people go through, but how the normal challenges of adolescence can be intensified by global mobility in ways I wish I knew back then. She has made it easy to see how to apply important principles in practical ways through the use of a series of case studies and with key points summarized in her **Big Answers** section at the end of each unit.

But it is not only for the sake of our children that I wish I had read this book years earlier. I think back to the hundreds of adolescents growing up globally who came through the doors of my clinic and recognize how I could have nurtured them better had this book been available then. Medical school taught me about the normal physical and emotional changes adolescents experience. Professional education continues to remind me why I need to consider the impact of various psycho-social realities such as the death of a parent, abuse, divorce, or even bullying when those I see in my clinic have symptoms such as depression, eating disorders, suicidal ideation, or recent changes in behavior at school. Although written for parents, Dr. Abraham makes clear why global, and even local, cross-cultural mobility needs to be considered by all professionals when encountering these types of symptoms in their clientele.

But it's not too late! Ruth and I have 13 grandchildren who travel, including one attending university in Europe. I continue to see patients from around the world in my clinic almost daily. I plan to apply the tools and perspectives from this parents' guide as I interact with all of these global teens.

David Van Reken, MD
Professor of Clinical Pediatrics,
Indiana University School of Medicine, Indianapolis, IN

This is an amazing book whose time has come. Although written for parents of global teens, the information presented is useful for any parent raising children in our 21st-century world. I love how Anisha recognizes that children raised cross-culturally for any reason are, first and foremost, simply kids. They have all the usual developmental matters to deal with as others who never move. But Anisha is also clear on how the impact of a culturally changing landscape can intensify common adolescent characteristics, which adds extra challenges for both parents and teens. As you continue reading, you will be masterfully drawn into each topic through a vignette of her story. Before you know it, you will be learning about the larger principles that particular anecdote exemplifies in clear but concise ways. Then, before you are overwhelmed, you will come to the grand finale of each chapter: specific, concrete steps you can take to deal positively with the situation.

I highly, highly recommend this book to not only parents, but to all educators, social service professionals, medically related personnel, and anyone else who loves and works with this population. You will be glad you took the time to read it, I promise you!

Ruth E Van Reken, Hon DLitt
Co-author, *Third Culture Kids: Growing Up Among Worlds*, 3*rd* ed.
Co-founder, Families in Global Transition, www.figt.org

PREFACE

Do you remember the triumphs and challenges that shaped you as a teen? Looking back at your own teenage years will likely bring back memories of life-defining accomplishments, but also embarrassing, angst-filled moments. Adolescence is a fascinating time of change, exploration, and growth – first and foremost for teenagers but also for everyone living and working with them. The teen years are that critical time in our lives where soon-to-be adults develop their unique identity and independence. Going through this all-important process is challenging as it is. However, it is even more daunting when teens live outside of their home country, have parents from different cultural backgrounds, or must regularly adjust to new environments.

To be sure, a cross-cultural background is a wonderful gift, equipping teens with unique skills that will serve them well later in life. As they go through puberty, however, teenagers need to develop their identity while confronted by the fluid, multicultural world around them. Not only do they need to answer the question 'Who am I?' but also 'Who am I when I was born in one country but live in another, or when my parents come from another community, or my parents have two very different backgrounds?'

There is a strong link between adolescent and adult health. That's why empowering global teens (kids ages 10-21 years) and maximizing their health and well-being is so important. You, as a family member, mentor, or educator are critical to your teen's success in the future. *Raising Global Teens: A Practical Handbook for Parenting in the 21st Century* is written to help you, the parent or caregiver, to navigate this unique time of change and growth in a cross-cultural context in partnership with your teen. This is particularly important at times of heightened stress and uncertainty, such as during viral pandemics with social distancing and online schooling, and other global crises.

As an educator, researcher, and pediatrician specializing in teen health, I have had the privilege of working across continents, including the United States, the Netherlands, and China over the last 25 years. I am also the daughter of South Asian immigrants to the United States, have a German husband, and have moved five times across the world in the last decade with two sons in tow. Having worked and experienced multiple cultures as a teen, parent, and physician, I have a personal mission to help improve the lives of global teens and their families.

Adults often have questions about how to raise global teens, provide guidance, answer tough questions, and ensure their children are off to a good start. There are books about global kids on the move, in transition, and in different environments. However, few have a focus on understanding the many changes that happen during the cross-cultural adolescent years from a medical perspective.

My book combines real-world questions and practical examples with answers grounded in research and experience from a physician and teen specialist who has worked with young people around the globe. *Raising Global Teens: A Practical Handbook for Parenting in the 21st Century* is an **easy-to-read book for the busy, modern-day parent, family member, or educator of a global teen.** I hope you enjoy reading it.

Anisha Abraham, MD, MPH
Amsterdam, the Netherlands
May 2020

HOW TO USE THIS BOOK

Raising Global Teens: A Practical Handbook for Parenting in the 21st Century begins with an introduction to the concept of the global teen followed by discussions on communication, puberty, the teen brain, identity, belonging, and media use. Core teen health topics such as sexuality, substance use, stress, depression, and special educational needs are also explored. It ends on a practical note, outlining tools to build resilience and develop skills to live in a highly interconnected, globalized world.

This book presents a series of conversations on key issues. Chapters may be read in order and in their entirety or can be chosen by topic of interest and read individually. To make navigation easy, each chapter is laid out in the same way, and includes the following sections:

- *Overview*: What to expect in the chapter
- *Big Questions:* Common parent and teen queries drawn from my work in clinics, hospitals, schools, and universities
- *Strategies:* Key adolescent health issues and ways to tackle them
- *Lightbulbs*: Interesting side notes
- *Bottom Line*: Summary of the chapter discussion
- *Big Answers:* Responses to the Big Questions
- *Resources:* Compilation of the chapter sources in addition to recommended books, articles, and websites to access further information

In preparation for this book, I conducted an informal survey in 2019 among cross-cultural or global teens and their parents in several countries through the schools and community networks I worked with. In this survey I asked whether they had ever received information about what it meant to grow up cross-culturally, the strengths and challenges of leading a cross-cultural life, and their top concerns in a variety of areas. I have used this information in the book to provide background and context. Although the findings of my book are not representative of all socioeconomic, ethnic, or cultural groups, many of the core issues I describe are often experienced by Cross-Cultural Kids of diverse backgrounds.

Throughout the chapters, research, facts, and advice are interwoven with personal stories, case studies, vignettes, and interviews with both experts and adolescents. Names (and occasionally locations) have been changed to protect the identity of teens and their parents. Note: you can go to the end of each chapter if you are short on time and want a quick summary of the content plus the answers to common questions.

Raising Global Teens: A Practical Handbook for Parenting in the 21st Century will enable you to have important conversations on challenging topics with your global teens and equip you with powerful tools that will help them to thrive.

Let's get the conversation started!

INTRODUCTION

"A global soul is a person who has grown up in many cultures all at once – and so lived in the cracks between them."

Pico Iyer

I was born in Delaware, a tiny state on the East Coast of the United States. My parents are immigrants from Kerala, also a small coastal state, in the southern part of India, some 13,000 kilometers away. They came to the US for graduate studies, but also to pursue the 'American dream.' Like in many immigrant homes, when I was growing up, we had aunts, uncles, and cousins coming in and out all day long. The kitchen was the pulsating epicenter of our house. My mother or father would cook while regaling guests with the latest family adventures, politics, or scandals in rapid-fire Malayalam, their native language. Someone would be assigned to cut mounds of onions till their eyes welled with tears. The chatting and stirring continued as the air filled with the smell of hot, fragrant spices, putting our stove exhaust into overdrive. Typical Kerala dishes, like shrimp curry flecked with whole red chilis, would emerge to be devoured with rice, chutney, yogurt, and an endless parade of side dishes.

But it wasn't just all fun, food, and family. There was a strong emphasis on academics. I was encouraged to work hard, stay out of trouble, and to pursue one of the two quintessential Indian choices for a teenager's future: engineering or medicine – safe and stable vocations in my parents' view. I soon learned that an intercultural adolescence is anything but easy. I attended a private school on an academic scholarship, which was wonderful but also difficult. The American rituals of growing up – driving, high school parties, dating, proms – were foreign concepts to my parents and quite distinct from their own experience of having had an arranged marriage in India. To make matters even more complicated, I was the only South Asian-American in my high school class. As a brown-skinned teenager with long frizzy black hair, I badly wanted to be part of the mainstream suburban world around me into which I didn't quite seem to fit. I did my best to navigate between my Indian and American worlds, sometimes with confidence, mostly with bewilderment. Solving a teenager's most momentous task of figuring out who they are and where they belong was a real challenge. There just weren't many others like me.

Adolescence can be an exciting but also challenging time, especially for cross-cultural teens. Looking back, there were a lot of wonderful gifts I received as a result of my dual cultural upbringing, such as family connections and a vibrant community. Yet, compared to my classmates, I also had distinct challenges to contend with, particularly about race, appearance, and belonging. In many ways, I was confused, and it wasn't till my early 20s, when I met more fellow Indian Americans, that I developed a clearer sense of my own identity. I sometimes wonder what those teen years would have been like had I had some awareness of the cross-cultural challenges much earlier on.

WHO ARE CROSS-CULTURAL KIDS AND GLOBAL TEENS?

You may not think of your child or teen as a Cross-Cultural Kid. However, an increasing number of young people around the world are one.

Here are a few questions to consider:

- Has your child or teen been raised outside of your or your partner's home country?
- Are you and your partner from different backgrounds, religions, ethnicities, or communities?
- Did you move from one country to another with your child or teen?
- Did you move from one part of your country to another with your kid?
- Is your child or teen a refugee or immigrant?
- Is your kid an adoptee?

If you answered yes to any of these questions, you have a **Cross-Cultural Kid**. Cross-Cultural Kids (CCKs) are children or teens who have lived in, or interacted with, two or more cultural environments. The concept focuses not just on mobility and location but also on the many layers of cultural environments that can impact a child or teen.[1] They include multicultural kids, immigrants, migrants, expatriates, and kids with a cross-cultural lifestyle both physically and virtually.

Some of you may be more familiar with the traditional concept of **Third Culture Kids** (TCKs). Third Culture Kids are a subgroup of Cross-Cultural Kids. The term was first coined by sociologist Dr. Ruth Hill Useem while studying American families working in India in the 1950s. This term is based on the concept that kids who move to another country with their parents may develop their own third culture between their parents' culture and the host country culture. Examples of TCKs are military, missionary, and diplomatic families.[2]

However, the number of children and teens experiencing different cultures as bi-cultural kids, migrants, immigrants, or adoptees is growing exponentially. Therefore, in this book I will focus on the broader and more modern concept of **Cross-Cultural Kids** (which includes TCKs) over Third Culture Kids alone.

Raising Global Teens is all about teenagers. In this book, I define global teens as Cross-Cultural Kids that are ages 10 to 21 years as puberty can start by 10 years and brain maturation can continue till the mid-20s.

UNDERSTANDING GLOBAL TEENS

When I was about six months old, I took a road trip in our enormous Oldsmobile with my parents and grandparents to the Midwest to visit family friends. This was at a time when there were so few fellow Indian immigrants in the area that when we did see one, we would stop everything to introduce ourselves. It was also 1969. Astronaut Neil Armstrong had just walked on the moon and was a huge celebrity with almost everyone around the globe, and my family was no exception.

En route on the highway in Ohio, we saw a large sign announcing Wapakoneta, home of Neil Armstrong. In one of our zanier family moments, my mom and grandmother decided that since they were near his hometown, they must meet Mr. Armstrong. When we stopped to eat at a local diner, they asked for directions to the Armstrong home. In an amazing turn of events they soon ended up knocking on his front door in their bright billowy silk saris. Neil's parents were probably shocked to see two petite, determined South Asian women turn up on their doorstep. To them, my folks must have seemed to have landed from outer space. Still, they had the grace and presence to invite my folks in for tea. As it turns out, Neil Armstrong was indeed home, visiting his parents, and joined us all for an animated discussion about his historic trip to the moon and a more recent visit to India as part of his Giant Step Apollo Tour. This is one of the many wonderful cross-cultural experiences that I heard about growing up. To me it is also emblematic of what can be gained by mobility and globalization.

This is my tribe

There is no doubt that globalization has changed our world view. Ruth Van Reken is a world-renowned expert on Cross-Cultural Kids. She grew up in Nigeria and is the author of several popular books including *Third Culture Kids: Growing up Among Worlds.* According to Van Reken, prior to World War II, many people around the world grew up and lived in monocultural communities with little mobility, often living in the same neighborhood near family for much or all of their lives.

People had a strong sense of cultural balance due to a deep, intuitive understanding of how things operated in the place they called home. Teens growing up in such environments had a clear concept of personal identity and community. They were raised knowing *this is my tribe. It's where and to whom I belong.* For example, my own parents' families have been in the same part of Kerala for over five hundred years. I remember visits as a child where we could walk and visit one extended 'Sankarmangalam' (my maternal grandfather's family) member after another, all living within a one-kilometer radius of the same South Indian village.

With increased mobility and trade, many families now live in places where these cultural boundaries have become porous. Today, there are fewer and fewer truly monocultural communities left. While they still exist, of course (and some may hope for them to re-emerge), the traditional way a community defines itself as 'us versus them' is breaking down.[3]

With globalization, places that were once impossible to reach are now easier to access both physically and virtually. Resources like Google Maps make it much faster to find your way around a new city, and apps like Duolingo make foreign-language communication less challenging. What's more, the Internet allows today's youth near instant access to international news and norms. Teens can follow emerging geopolitics on Twitter, fashion trends on WeChat, and cutting-edge videos on global platforms like TikTok.

Overall, this is a positive development, but it also poses practical challenges. The distance a teen needs to travel to experience a switch in culture has become short, leaving little time for adjustment and adaptation. For some of our teens, diversity comes with a walk down the street. Others make the cross-cultural switch when they interact with their parents of different backgrounds or when they enter their schools, where different languages and norms exist. Cultural norms can also change within the space of a short flight.

The challenges of being a global teen

In a perfect world, family, community, and place are *anchors* of stability for adolescents. They act as *mirrors*, reflecting images or concepts to teens of who they are or where they belong. In cross-cultural teens, these anchors and mirrors are less stable or clear.[4] For example, I found my adolescent years more difficult as I didn't have many others around that looked or acted like my own family. Being cross-cultural can exaggerate the normal adolescent challenge of finding a clear sense of identity.[5] These challenges may include:

- Developing a personal identity and sense of belonging
- Uneven and possibly delayed maturity during adolescence
- Loss of friends
- Difficulties with conflict resolution
- Unresolved grief and loss

With each of the moves I experienced as an adult, I felt tremendous loss. It took me months (if not years) to accept what I had left behind personally and professionally and to embrace the new community that I was now part of. Often this feeling is magnified during childhood and adolescence, especially with the loss of connection to friends, family members, school, or home. It can also be traumatic to move suddenly without enough time to say goodbye or maintain connections.

Identity and belonging, loss and grief, missing friends and family, are all part of the challenges of being a global teen. What's more, cross-cultural teens who are part of a minority or surrounded by many different norms or expectations, may test, experiment, or push boundaries in a different way than youths in a more homogenous environment. Global teens may face stricter expectations to conform with the community around them or to avoid calling attention to themselves, particularly if they live in a tight-knit immigrant, expat, or military community. As a result, cross-cultural teens may rebel later in life, sometimes as a young or middle-aged adult. Because they are not testing and rebelling as other teens would, it can also lead to an uneven maturity or delayed adolescence.

The upsides of being a global teen

Of course, being a global teen comes with tremendous strengths and advantages.[6] For example, Cross-Cultural Kids are more geographically and socially aware. They are more likely to demonstrate qualities such as:

- Tolerance
- Cultural sensitivity
- Empathy
- Adaptability
- Openness to change
- Ability to speak different languages

Not too long ago, we invited our neighbors in Amsterdam to dinner. Femke, our neighbor's 16-year-old daughter, was born in Vietnam, adopted as a toddler, and has grown up in the Netherlands. Her mom is Dutch and her father French. Femke is an avid field hockey player, has babysat our own boys, and is full of life. As a global teen with parents from different backgrounds, it was a joy to watch her speak multiple languages with ease. At dinner, she would switch from English with me, to Dutch with her mom, and French with her dad. Speaking more than one language can be one of the many gifts of a cross-cultural upbringing.

Helping global teens to thrive

Why is the teenage phase of life so important? Issues that first surface during the teen years often continue well into adulthood. For example, half of all mental health disorders arise before the age of 14.[7] If left untreated, these can affect education, employment, and even parenting. So much of my work as a teen health specialist is trying to address teen health issues before they become chronic and persist through adulthood. What's more, young people today face challenges that did not exist in previous generations. The intense use of social media can affect self-esteem, personal interactions, and sleep – issues that many of us as parents and caregivers aren't fully equipped to address. The teen years are a turbo-charged transition. Important opportunities for growth occur, mostly related to a teen's move towards building their identity and establishing independence. The pulling away from family is also a key process, allowing teens to leave home.

Teens usually learn who they should become from having stable family, peers, and community. Cross-cultural teens may not have the same anchors of stability and mirrors of reflection as others. This adds to the complexity of defining themselves. *Global Teens experience unique challenges and acquire strengths at a crucial time – just as they are establishing their own identity and independence.* Parents and caregivers have an important role in understanding these unique issues.

Today's global teens have a bright future ahead of them. The more parents, mentors, and teachers understand their unique issues and support their care, the more likely they will have a successful, happy, and rewarding adulthood.

COMMUNICATING WITH GLOBAL TEENS

"The most important thing in communication
is hearing what isn't said."
Peter Drucker

IN THIS CHAPTER:
- Communicating with teens, including having quality conversations and handling conflicts.
- Dealing with lying, navigating independence, handling experimentation, finding the right crowd.
- Setting boundaries and finding your optimal parenting styles.

It was a pleasant, sunny Friday afternoon in Amsterdam, when our normally cheerful 12-year-old son, Nick, arrived back from school angry and annoyed. Flinging his backpack violently against our entry hallway wall, he exclaimed loudly, "I don't want to go on this stupid, idiotic father-son camping trip with Pappi tonight. I'd much rather be at my school soccer game with my teammates this weekend."

He continued, "My friends will all be playing and traveling together, and I'll be stuck in a tent in the middle of nowhere. That's it. I absolutely refuse to go!"

My crestfallen husband sighed loudly. He had been patiently gathering camping equipment, sleeping bags, and food over the last few days and was now preparing to pack it all into the car for a timely departure. Eyebrows raised quizzically, we both gazed at each other, unsure what to say next...

As our family story reveals, adolescence is a time of rapid change and emotional growth for teens (and parents). To be fair, teens may have different perspectives or experiment with things that we as adults may not always understand. As with my son's case, it is important to realize that teens are testing boundaries with their behavior and communication style as they are learning to be their own people. Teens are neither children nor mini adults. What's key is that we value each teen's budding individuality, show unconditional love, but also provide clear expectations and limits.

BIG QUESTIONS

Common parent questions on communication and boundaries

1. My son will not talk to me anymore, and it is hard to know what's happening at school. How can I get him to open up to me?

2. Every discussion I have with my teen ends in a fight. How can we have a peaceful conversation again?

3. How do I handle a teenager who isn't always honest?

4. My 16-year-old daughter wants to get a tattoo. I won't let her do it. She says she's old enough to make her own choices. How should I address this calmly with her?

Common teen questions on communication and boundaries

1. My parents are way too strict, and I'm not allowed to do anything my friends are doing. What can I say to them?

2. My parents are totally unfair with their rules. My brother gets away with everything. They are much more strict with me. What should I do?

3. I am almost 20 years old and my parents can't relate to anything I do or tell them. How can I talk to them?

4. All my mom does is constantly nag me about my homework, friends, going to bed too late, and using my phone. It's so annoying! What can I do to get her to back off?

HAVING QUALITY CONVERSATIONS

Let's face it: communicating effectively can be tough. As a parent, I encounter this regularly. Sometimes, we feel that preteens and teens aren't talking to us or we are talking past each other. However, kids equally tell me *they* don't feel their parents understand them and instead nag constantly.

Talking past each other

To learn more about how to maximize effective communication, I chatted with *New York Times* best-selling author and educator Rosalind Wiseman after attending her talk at an international school in Amsterdam. Rosalind wrote two important books: *Queen Bees and Wannabes* about helping girls to survive cliques and conflicts (which was the inspiration for the hit movie *Mean Girls*) and *Masterminds and Wingmen* about boys' social hierarchies and the effect on their well-being. Rosalind's advice to the diverse parent and educator audience on communicating with teens was simple: "We talk too much, and we all need to go on a verbal diet!" Wiseman's remarks made me think of some of the chats with my own boys after school. "So, how was math class? What homework do you have tonight?

Did you eat a snack? Where is your coat?" With each new question, my boys' response rate steadily diminishes. Sound familiar?

As parents, we often ask preteens and teens a lot of questions. Ironically, our constant barrage of questions (and demands) may lead kids to say less instead of more. Young people often want to decompress after a long day. Wiseman says that the times we are on fact-finding missions such as the ride home after school, the dinner meal, or the trip to the store, are all just moments, not a lifetime, and hence we don't need to overload them with too much import. Here are some strategies for improving our discussion with teens.

Strategies for having quality conversations

Apply the 50% rule
Wiseman's advice is to keep conversations to a minimum. Apply the 50% rule and say half of what you intend to say.

Stick to three points
In addition to shortening the discussion, Wiseman suggests keeping conversations to three main issues, especially if your kids are distracted easily.

Duct tape it
One of the premises of the book *Duct Tape Parenting* by Vicki Hoefle is that if you spend more than ten minutes nagging your child every day, it's time for a change. The author suggests that we apply virtual duct tape and refrain from talking and nagging. I love the visual of putting duct tape on my mouth and saying less, not more. On some challenging days at home with my kids, I wonder if I should use some real tape to keep from talking on and on...

Ask curious questions
If we do ask questions, they should be curious ones instead of focusing on the minute details of the day. In this way we are more likely to make connections and have meaningful conversations. For example, ask preteens and teens: "Who makes you laugh? What are you most worried about when it comes to leaving home for university? Who do you follow on Instagram? Can you tell me how you play this video game?"

Be attuned to body language
In clinic, if my teen patients are not looking me in the eye, are focused on their phone or book, are tapping their toes, or are rolling their eyes, I know I haven't engaged them. According to the book *Captivate: The Science of Succeeding with People* by Vanessa Van Edwards, an author whose initial work with adolescents developed into exploring the science of facial expressions, we need to be aware of our own body language and how we interact with others, but also how they respond to us.

HANDLING ARGUMENTS AND CONFLICTS

Conflict happens when people with different views live and work together. As uncomfortable as they are, occasional arguments are a normal part of teen development and boundary testing. However, daily conflicts and arguments will negatively affect a relationship, particularly if a teen (or parent) is constantly on the defensive or feels accused.

In my clinical experience, disagreement often occurs when a teen and an adult view the same issue very differently.

For example, a parent may see a teen not taking prescribed medications, doing their chores, or completing a school assignment as essential issues whereas a teen may simply see them as a matter of personal choice. According to the Positive Parenting Program (Triple P), rewarding undesirable behavior, using ineffective punishment, or negative communication can also perpetuate conflicts and arguments.[8]

Teens (and parents) may learn that increasing undesirable behavior is effective in getting what they want when their first request is turned down. Imagine your teen son wants to watch a TV show instead of finishing his homework and you say no. He complains loudly that he only wants to watch for a short time, that you are mean and unfair. He then runs around the house angrily and slams a few doors in the process. After several minutes of this, you give in and allow him to watch his show. This outcome increases the likelihood he will use this strategy again next time. Sound familiar? As adolescents get older, they will test limits more often. Parents and caregivers can become worn down by such behavior and give in just to have some peace and avoid another argument.[9]

Giving harsh criticism or just nagging can feed ongoing conflict. Often, adults don't recognize that they are engaging in negative communication. For example, a well-intentioned parent or coach may harshly criticize a teen because they simply want him or her to try harder or do better at a given task. However, negative communication may make teens and adults feel upset, frustrated, or rejected, and rarely resolves the issue. (Disclaimer: as a parent, I admit I too have resorted to nagging because I feel that I need to say or do something to create change.) Thankfully, there are a few ways to make our interactions more positive.

Strategies for handling arguments and conflicts

Offer positive feedback

We all too often focus on what's gone wrong. Provide positive feedback, especially when a teen communicates calmly or handles a situation well. For example, "Thanks for putting the dishes away," or, "Thanks for hanging up your coat when you got home." We often forget how important a small compliment or positive comment can be. Finally, remember that praise works best when we are genuinely enthusiastic and we mean what we say.

Use a behavior contract and hold family meetings

Using a contract with the ability to earn privileges may be a good strategy for introducing a behavior that you think is important (such as making their bed) and for avoiding nagging. Describe the behavior, agree on the reward and what level of behavior is expected, and make sure you reward improvement. Ensure the big reward is something you have control over, or offer a series of smaller rewards. Write down a contract so it is all in writing. Finally, consider having regular family meetings to discuss contracts, conflicts, and difficult behaviors. Also, try to set rules for the meeting, take turns speaking calmly, and set a limit to the meeting time.

React less and just listen

According to one of my favorite parenting books entitled *Scream-free Parenting,* you must learn to pause, so you can respond more and react less. Once you as a parent learn to control your own emotions and behavior, your teens will soon learn how to control theirs. An important part of my work is asking open-ended questions and allowing teens to be able to freely talk without interruptions. It is amazing how much a teen will share with you if they feel they are genuinely being listened to.

ADDRESSING LYING

Adolescence can be rough. Teens are trying to fit in with their peers, struggling with control of their lives or feeling unfairly judged by others. For some, lying can be a way to handle these challenges. Teens may lie because it seems to them the best decision at that time.[10] For parents, an occasional lie by their offspring is nothing to get too worried about, while regular lying should be addressed.

David and Susan are cross-cultural parents in London. I meet them after finishing a parent talk at a local school. Susan starts off enthusiastically about a family trip to Asia, but her expression and demeanor change when she mentions her 15-year-old son, Rob. She admits tearfully that they are having a hard time working with him at home. They are worried about his new set of friends. More importantly, they are upset because they feel that there have been several instances where he has not been honest with them – for example, playing video games when he is supposed to be doing his homework or going out to an upperclassman's late-night party when he was supposed to be spending the evening with a friend. Before their move, they felt he was reliable and trustworthy. They are tired of constantly arguing with him and wondering how to improve relationships at home.

If a teen is making a habit of lying, ask what they may be trying to solve. My suggestion for Rob's parents is that if he says he cleaned up his room or was at his friend's house but was really playing video games or at a party, it may help to understand why the lying happened in the first place. Is he trying to avoid certain consequences, or does he think it's easier to lie than disappoint someone or upset them? Does he need to feel that he has control or fit in with peers?

Strategies for addressing lying

Establish clear rules
Teens don't have to like the rules, but they need to stick to them. For example, in Rob's case, his parents could tell him, "If you say you are at your friend's home, then you need to be there. If you move to a party, then you need to tell us where you are and be back by the time of your curfew. We want to make sure you stay safe." More importantly, parents or adults need to enforce the consequences if these rules are broken, such as not allowing another outing or extended digital media time (see *Creating Boundaries* later in this chapter for more on this).

Avoid being over controlling
Being over-zealous with controls and monitoring can lead to lies. There is a middle ground.

Be mindful of lecturing
Remember when you were a teen and your parents lectured you? You probably were desperate for them to stop. Yet, as parents, we often come to use the same techniques that we despised. Avoiding lecturing prevents teens from tuning out.

NAVIGATING INDEPENDENCE

Global teens are trying to learn how to navigate the world on their own. From what they wear to what they eat to who they spend time with, they are trying to take control, especially if they are experiencing constant change or must adjust to new cultural norms. For adults, it can feel like a tricky balance between giving them too much independence and being overly controlling. It is important to understand why teenagers are making the choices that they are. Ask why they are listening to punk rock or prefer to eat only pasta or want a tattoo. Also, allow room for them to express themselves, but explain your core values and beliefs. This process can start early in a child's life.

My son Kai decided one year as a preteen that he would only wear clothes that were grey, blue, or black to school. After several days of questioning why he would not wear any of the other clothes in his closet (and with me wondering if I was missing something deeper), he remained steadfast in his choice. My husband reminded me it was probably just a phase, but also an important way for him to express himself. I finally agreed, just as long as his clothes were clean. After a year of the same shirts over and over, he decided to go back to wearing everything again, and I learned a valuable lesson in allowing independence.

Cross-cultural perspective

The age of acquiring independence can greatly vary from community to community. In the Netherlands, most kids take a cycling exam by age 12 and get a *Verkeersdiploma* or traffic certificate. From that point on (and often earlier), many parents let their children ride bikes alone to school or activities. By late adolescence, many Dutch teens live away from home, plan their own schedules, and manage their own finances.

In my own experience, my Asian parents were much more involved in supporting my decision-making (and finances) into early adulthood. There is no strict rule as to when independence must occur. However, among cross-cultural families, what parents consider the norm, and how much to be involved, may be at odds with what teens perceive or see among their peers and the larger community. As a result, there can be big differences in views between parents and teens on how much autonomy to allow and when, based on their own experiences and cultural beliefs. Again, the key is to have open discussions with teens as to how expectations may be different and what that may mean.

Strategies for addressing independence

Allow them to take on responsibilities and seek help on their own

Make teens responsible for household duties such as taking out the trash, cleaning the dishes, minding a younger sibling. Give adolescents the freedom to start choosing which extracurricular activities to pursue, and how to balance their schedule. Encourage them to start seeking help and making appointments for teachers and health providers. Teach them financial literacy skills, such as starting a bank account or handling purchases with an allowance. Of course, this varies based on your teen's age and your family setting but start small and build up.

Be aware of what you say *not* to do

Global teens remind me regularly that if an adult tells them *not* to do something (such as sexting or drinking alcohol) they are more likely to do it. They suggest having a more nuanced conversation about options, responsibilities, and why the behavior may be problematic instead of starting the conversation by saying, "Don't do it." My recommendation is to be careful about how you frame issues and allow teens the independence that empowers them to make smart, well-informed decisions.

Give them privacy
In addition to stepping back, teens increasingly need their own space and privacy. Show you respect that. For example, knock before you enter their room.

FINDING GOOD FRIENDS

Choosing or finding good friends is one of the toughest issues that global teens must navigate, especially those who are perceived as 'different' or outsiders. While parents may want them to hang out with a specific group of friends, teens may have different preferences. Making friends comes down to honing certain skills, such as engaging in conversations and listening to others. It is important to ask teens what they value in order to help them find friends who will be a good fit. Teens who struggle with making friends may latch onto the first person who shows them attention. This can lead to insecurity or jealousy when their supposed best friend gives the cold shoulder. They may also engage in unusual behaviors to maintain the friendship. As a parent, you should trust and respect who they may be spending time with and set boundaries about which behaviors, such as bullying, are and are not acceptable.

Strategies for finding good friends

Having differences is normal
Help teens realize that differences of opinion can occur, especially in a cross-cultural context, and that not every conflict means the end of a friendship. This can be particularly tricky with social media, where misunderstanding based on pictures and a few words of text can occur. Teach kids

the importance of having conversations and respecting their friend's opinion while calmly asserting their own beliefs or values.

Be aware of your own opinions and fears
If you don't like your teen's new friend and you believe your reasons are valid, be thoughtful about how you bring it up. It can backfire. Help teens to navigate unhealthy or difficult friendships in a calm, supportive way by allowing them to tell you what they find challenging and how they should navigate it. Also, be careful of not imposing your own unresolved fears and issues on your teens and their friendships.

HANDLING EXPERIMENTATION

Trying things out

Suzy is a 16-year-old teen patient. Her father is in the US army and she and her siblings have moved several times from one American military base to another. Suzy is a conscientious student and has generally had an easy time making new friends following each move. One evening Suzy downs several vodka/Red Bull mix drinks at a friend's party. After a few hours she is barely conscious, vomiting, and pale. Her scared friends drive her home and admit to her parents that she has been drinking heavily and may have tried drugs. In the early morning hours, her parents bring her to our military community emergency room. Suzy arrives very dehydrated and has a high blood alcohol level. Her urine drug screen comes back positive for amphetamines. She is admitted to the pediatric ward for intravenous fluids and supportive care. I meet her parents outside her hospital room. They are both frightened and shocked by the sudden turn of events.

Suzy's parents ask what they have done wrong and why this situation happened. Did they miss anything? Had they been poor parents? We discuss that, in fact, this situation could have happened to many teens and is a great opportunity to discuss safety and boundaries while providing love and support. With Suzy, I discuss how mixing energy drinks and vodka plus using stimulants is a powerful and unsafe combo. Also, she has been lucky that she had friends watching out for her and parents who are engaged and brought her into the hospital. In the end, Suzy's parents tell her that they love her, she is very important to them, and they always want to be there for her if there is an emergency. They also discuss how they have certain rules about drinking and using drugs to ensure that she is safe and healthy.

Suzy experimented with drinking and taking drugs. Is experimenting itself bad? Experimental behaviors help young people to form their own identity, handle challenges, and learn about the world. In fact, in the past, willingness to take risks was key to survival. If our ancestors had not been bold enough to try new foods or discover new places, we would not be here. Having said that, there are times when experimentation can put teens in vulnerable places. The key is allowing them to experiment while still providing a safety net in case they fail badly.

Of note, kids that have grown up in the military or as expatriates or in a small immigrant community where they may have a specific identity apart from others have an added burden when it comes to experimentation, as it may affect their family's status in the community. Drinking, being sexually active, or trying out other teen behaviors may be particularly frowned upon or discouraged (even though it may be the norm for other local teens).

Strategies for handling experimentation

Be a loving parent
Adolescence is a unique time when teens struggle with their changing sense of identity. Teens need to feel your love and forgiveness. Like Suzy's parents, tell your teens often how important they are to you, even if they make a mistake.

Make time together
Teenagers are often busy with their own lives, but make sure you make time to have a quick conversation with them over a meal, trip, or activity. Check in with what's happening in their lives and those of their friends.

CREATING BOUNDARIES

Along with independence and freedom come responsibilities and boundaries. Risky experimentation can put teens in vulnerable positions, and it is important to create reasonable rules and expectations at home. For example, decide what the right curfew time on a weekend night may be or when or where digital media can be used. Having contracts such as using a digital media plan or a driving contract can be helpful in establishing boundaries. Be prepared to negotiate rules with your teen.

In addition to creating boundaries, consider how best to monitor them. Pediatrician, teen health specialist and author, Dr. Ken Ginsburg, advises in a piece for the Center for Parent and Teen Communication that "effective monitoring is about being the kind of parent whose teen chooses to share what's going on in their life. The way we listen tells teens they are free to talk. Controlling our reactions and not being overly critical signals to them that they can talk without fear of being judged." Many teens still have a desire to please adults. However, they are very sensitive to our feelings and will shut down if they sense we are trying to overly control them. According to Dr. Ginsburg, when we help them to craft their own ideas, teens gain resilience and share and discuss more often.

Strategies for handling boundaries

Encourage personal safety
One of the main reasons for setting boundaries is to ensure personal safety. As such, it is important for parents to discuss issues like safe sex and consent. In Washington, DC, one mom's basic rule for her teen daughter is to never get into a car with a driver who has been drinking. She developed a clear way for her daughter to contact her to get a ride if she was ever at a party involving drinking. No questions asked. Discuss potential actions and direct consequences so teens can clearly see why a certain behavior may be unhealthy or harmful to them.

Try compromise over command
Have clear consequences in place before rules are broken. You can ask teens for help in developing fair consequences. Be firm with consequences but not overly commanding; otherwise teens may rebel more.

FINDING OPTIMAL PARENTING STYLES

Snowplow parents (or 'curling' *ouders*, as they are known in Dutch) are defined as machines chugging ahead, clearing any obstacles in their child's path to success, so they don't have to encounter failure, frustration, or lost opportunities. Helicopter parents hover overhead, while Tiger parents monitor tightly. There's a fine balance between being supportive and engaged versus being controlling or engineering outcomes.

 The concept of Dolphin Parenting, promoted by Harvard psychiatrist and author Dr. Shimi Kang, resonates as an antidote to Snowplow, Tiger, and Helicopter Parenting. Kang explains that dolphins are sociable animals. As such, Dolphin Parents have rules and expectations but also value autonomy, creative pursuits, communication skills, and critical thinking.

Kang says that Dolphin Parents focus on maintaining balance in their children's lives and gently yet authoritatively guide, as opposed to clearing obstacles out of the way. As children grow up, Dolphin Parents gradually encourage them to make decisions for themselves. As a result, the kids of Dolphin Parents tend to be more self-confident and self-motivated. Dolphin Parents tread a middle ground between authoritative and overly permissive parents. It's not always easy to achieve, but an exciting model to consider.

Strategies for finding the optimal parenting style

Be compassionate
Demonstrate understanding when your teen experiences a setback or failure. Talk about what could have been done differently and what a backup plan might look like. "So, you didn't make the swimming team. You can try again next season if you practice and work hard. How can I help?"

Don't always help
If your teen forgets their homework or sports gear, don't jump in by calling the school or rushing to practice (I admit this one is tough, having brought sports gear to soccer practice on more than one occasion). In other words, don't constantly solve challenges for them and instead let them cope with the small failures and work with you on improving their organizational skills. For example, at home, we have a short checklist of chores that must be done each day. It's not perfect, but it does help us a lot.

Step back
For older kids, try not to micromanage your teen's high school career with the single goal of getting them into a dream school or job. Be supportive and realistic about their achievements and ambitions and realize there's a wide range of choices.

Model behavior
I know this is hard but take time to apologize and set things right again when you are in the wrong. Teens watch how we handle our own mistakes. I tell my boys that I am constantly learning how to do things better as a parent.

WHEN TO GET HELP

Sometimes teens and parents can still not see eye to eye. Consider suggesting your teen chats with a trusted adult or mentor. Talk to your health provider about getting help with communication at home. Don't forget there are many resources available to parents and teens if you can't communicate clearly and positively on your own.

Back to my opening story. Our son Nick was not happy about missing a soccer match so he could attend a camping trip with his dad. My husband wasn't thrilled that he was cancelling either and started preparing to go without him. We decided to give Nick time to express his feelings of frustration and anger without reacting or interrupting. I then explained to him how much the trip meant to his dad as a time for family bonding and sharing. Also, that Nick would have more soccer matches in the upcoming season while, as kids get older and busier, it becomes harder to have these dedicated family experiences. In the end, he made the decision to go on the camping trip. More importantly, he gave the weekend two thumbs up and had many good stories to share about his time in the woods with his dad and brother.

THE BOTTOM LINE: COMMUNICATING WITH GLOBAL TEENS

- It is tough to be a parent these days and to have effective communication with your global teen 24/7. Consider using the 50% rule and say less instead of more.

- Handle arguments by offering positive feedback, creating a behavior contract, and having regular family meetings. When it comes to addressing lying, understand the root cause and enforce rules and consequences.

- As for navigating independence, ensure you give privacy, but also real-world responsibilities. When handling experimentation, try to allow failure and encourage compromise over command.

- When helping teens to navigate friendships, discuss personal values and ways to handle differences. In creating boundaries, discuss contracts and ways to monitor them.

- Finally, consider Dolphin and Duct Tape Parenting and help your teen to learn how to problem solve instead of problem solving for them.

BIG ANSWERS

Common parent questions on communication and boundaries

1. **My son will not talk to me anymore and it is hard to know what's happening at school. How can I get him to open up to me?**
   Communicating effectively can be tough. Try using everyday moments such as commuting to an event where potentially you can't see his face and you have uninterrupted time together. Alternatively, schedule time for

regular family events such as dinner time to have conversations. Ask open-ended questions about what his friends or peers are doing. Be prepared to listen and be attuned to your teen's body language. Finally, check for subtle signs of depression such as withdrawal from friends or activities, or changes in sleep and school performance.

2. **Every discussion I have with my teen ends in a fight. How can we have a peaceful conversation again?**
As uncomfortable as they are, occasional arguments are a normal part of teen development and boundary testing. However, daily conflicts and arguments will negatively affect a relationship, particularly if a teen (or parent) is constantly on the defensive or feels accused. Trying to understand the other perspective is key. Pick your battles and choose which issues you feel are important and which are less critical. Consider the power of pausing when things get heated to prevent overreacting. Finally, remember to provide positive feedback for things that your teen is doing right as too often adults focus on what's going wrong.

3. **How do I handle a teenager who isn't always honest?**
Many teens lie because it seems to them like the best decision at that time. For parents, an occasional lie by their offspring is nothing to get too worried about, while regular lying

should be addressed. Try to determine the root cause. If a teen is making a habit of lying, ask what they may be trying to solve. Clearly state the rules and consequences for breaking them. Also, remember that being over-zealous with controls and monitoring can lead to lies. There is a middle ground.

4. **My 16-year-old daughter wants to get a tattoo. I won't let her do it. She says she's old enough to make her own choices. How should I address this calmly with her**?
   Teens are trying to learn how to navigate the world on their own. For adults, it can feel like a tricky balance between giving them too much independence and exerting too much control. It is important to understand why teens are making the choices that they are. Allow your daughter to express her feelings fully, but also explain your core values and concerns. In this case, you may want to explain that a tattoo is hard to remove later. What seems like a great decision as a teen may be a choice she regrets or questions as an adult. If she insists on getting a tattoo, try to get her to defer till she is a little older. Review the risks of getting hepatitis and HIV from less than hygienic tattoo parlors and discuss what she plans to get tattooed and where on her body. Hopefully, with a discussion of the pros and cons, you can get her to make a more informed choice or even reconsider her decision for now.

Common teen questions on communication and boundaries

1. **My parents are way too strict, and I'm not allowed to do anything my friends are doing. What can I say to them?**
    Your parents are trying to create boundaries and rules that they think are important. Having said that, they may not be aware of what you value as important. Try to have a calm discussion with them on the things you prioritize and why they should trust you with your choices. Decide what the mutually agreed consequences are if you violate their trust or agreement.

2. **My parents are totally unfair with their rules. My brother gets away with everything. They are much more strict with me. What should I do?**
    It is important to discuss what the rules are and what you would like to be able to do. Also, tell them that you feel that there is a difference in how the rules are enforced. It is possible that your parents consciously or unconsciously have different expectations or levels of trust for you and your sibling. Having an open discussion about what you would like to see different and why may be the first steps in improving the situation.

3. **I am almost 20 years old and my parents can't relate to anything I do or tell them.**

How can I talk to them?

Believe it or not, parents often tell me the same thing about communicating with their kids, so it is possible that you are both equally ineffective in discussing issues. How are you expressing your concerns with each other? Is it done in an angry or hostile way? Do you avoid talking about anything at all? Do you feel that they are listening to you or understand your needs? Consider writing out your thoughts for them to read instead if discussing issues is not working. Better yet, consider getting a trusted adult or objective family member to be involved. Finally, if these routes fail, consider speaking to a counselor or health provider who can provide some positive strategies for improving the situation.

4. **All my mom does is constantly nag me about my homework, friends, going to bed too late, and using my phone. It's so annoying! What can I do to get her to back off?**

   Often, adults don't recognize that they are engaging in negative communication such as nagging. For example, a well-intentioned parent may suggest or give a reminder over and over simply because they want their kid to try harder or do better at something. However, nagging makes people feel upset, frustrated, or rejected and rarely resolves the issue. Try to understand what the reason for the nagging is. Remind your mom that constant nagging usually backfires, and it is better to say less than more. Come up with an agreed code word when you feel that she is nagging. Also, discuss better ways for your mom to help you achieve a specific goal or task.

RESOURCES

Books

Duct Tape Parenting, Vicki Hoefle, Routledge, 2012

Queen Bees and Wannabes: Helping Your Daughter Survive Cliques, Gossip, Boyfriends, and the New Realities of Girl World, Rosalind Wiseman, Harmony, 2009

How to Talk So Teens Will Listen and Listen So Teens Will Talk, Adele Faber and Elaine Mazlish, HarperCollins, 2011

Masterminds and Wingmen: Helping Our Boys Cope with Schoolyard Power, Locker-Room Tests, Girlfriends, and the New Rules of Boy World, Rosalind Wiseman, Harmony, 2014

Scream-free Parenting: How to Raise Amazing Adults by Learning to Pause More and React Less, Hal Runkel, Broadway, 2008

The Dolphin Way: A Parent's Guide to Raising Healthy, Happy, and Motivated Kids – Without Turning into a Tiger, Shimi K Kang, MD, Viking, 2014

Websites and articles

'7 Expert Tips for Talking with Teens', Ken Ginsburg, Center for Parent and Teen Communication, 2019: https://parentandteen.com/keep-teens-talking-learn-to-listen/

'Common Problems Between Parents and Teenagers', Jennifer L Betts, Love To Know, 2019: https://teens.lovetoknow.com/Parent_Teenager_Problems

'Positive Parenting for Parents with Teenagers', Alan Ralph, Mathew Sanders, Triple P International, 2001: https://www.triplep.net

IDENTITY AND BELONGING   **2**

"In the social jungle of human existence, there is no
feeling of being alive without a sense of identity."
Erik Erikson

IN THIS CHAPTER:

- Helping global teens to develop their unique
  sense of identity in a fluid and multicultural
  world.
- Enabling teens to create a sense of belonging
  and connectedness in their community.
- Supporting global teens to develop their
  unique sense of identity.
- Helping teens to foster friendships and
  navigate cliques.

The air is hot and sticky. As my red and white taxi speeds down a narrow bridge on Tai Tam Reservoir Road, I enjoy the brief view of the tranquil waters and lush hills around me. The taxi turns a bend, and we arrive at a modern open building overlooking the reservoir and surrounding tropical foliage.

"Mhgòi," I say while handing over a few bills, thanking the cabbie in Cantonese. A colorful scene is unfolding before me. Gathering the ends of my blue silk sari, I approach the grounds of my boys' international school with excitement and anticipation. Global Village Day is one of our favorite events of the school year. Students, teachers, and parents dress in their native outfits and celebrate the many traditions and cultures that the school represents.

This year in our home, the run up to Global Village Day is revealing. As I usually do in preparation for the event, I run down the list of countries we could represent.

"So," I ask Nick, eight years old at the time. "Do you want to wear Indian?" thinking of the long, ornate, red kurtas and white pajama-style pants that we bought recently in New Delhi. "We could also do German?" hoping that the lederhosen my mother-in-law bought in Bavaria a year back still fit. "Or maybe you could be American?" thinking of the baseball hats and USA T-shirts from our last trip to Washington, DC. When there is no response, I add, "We could even be Chinese?" knowing they could wear their traditional tunics from our Chinese New Year celebration.

"I don't want to be any of those countries," proclaims Nick defiantly.

"What do you mean?" I inquire. "I want... I want to be Korean," he says resolutely.

30

"Korean?" I ask tentatively, wondering how that identity got into the mix and how we were going to get an outfit. "Sweetie, um, we have a lot of nationalities covered in our family, but Korean isn't one of them."

"Joseph is and that's exactly what I want to be," he retorts, mentioning his best friend he spends most of his free time with.

This is going to be interesting, I think, questioning how our big-eyed, dark-haired boys had come to represent so many different places and wondering which nationality and identity they will end up embracing as they become teens.

Cross-Cultural Kids typically interact with many cultural communities as they move from one environment to another, sometimes within seconds. As illustrated by my own son, exposure to many different cultures can lead to some confusion as young people settle on an identity they will eventually call their own.

Identity is defined as one's unique personality, sense of purpose, abilities, and connection to others. It can be shaped by the perception of oneself within family, culture, and community. It also reflects physical appearance, race, ethnicity, religion, and nationality in addition to sexual and gender orientation. Adolescence is a key time to establish a sense of identity. According to the informal survey I conducted (see the *Appendix*), identity and belonging, followed by transition and loss, are consistently identified as areas of challenge for Cross-Cultural Kids. Teens in the survey also report that navigating friendships, peer group, and stereotypes can be tough.

BIG QUESTIONS

Common parent questions on identity and belonging

1. What impact does my own experience as an immigrant/ military member/ expatriate have on my child or teen?

2. Our teen is adopted from Asia. We have a Western background and don't look like her. Lately, she's been embarrassed when we come to school or meet her friends. How should we handle this?

3. We are planning a family move and have two young teenagers. Is there a 'right' age to move during the adolescent years?

4. Our kids are mixed race. They sometimes get teased at school because of their name or appearance. Should we switch to a school where kids look more like them?

Common teen questions on identity and belonging

1. I am 14 years old and I am having a hard time dealing with all the cliques in my class and making friends at school. Any tips?

2. I don't feel like I fit in with other kids around me where I live. When I go to my home country, I don't exactly fit in there either. I find it hard

to answer the question "where are you from?" or "where is home?" because I just don't know.

3. We are always moving from place to place for my father's work. I am tired of having to make new friends and I really miss my old friends. What should I do?

4. In university, I found that I ended up hanging out with other kids that had the same international background as me. We had more in common than other classmates that I met. Is that OK or should I try to make friends that are different than me?

ADDRESSING IDENTITY – WHO AM I?

Leila is a bubbly 15-year-old who loves singing both pop songs and classical music. She is wearing cut-off jeans, a dark top, and a polka dot bow in her hair when we meet at a sunny hotel terrace in Bodrum, Turkey. As a Jordanian Egyptian student who lives in Dubai, she counts teens who are Arabian, Indian, and Egyptian among her friends. When it comes to her identity she says, "I have been living in Dubai for 15 years and speak Arabic and English, but I don't feel Emirati. In fact, few people can classify themselves as one. I think identity is confusing. I don't have a home country." Her older sister, Nabila, nods in agreement. She is 18 years old with curly hair and dark glasses and is planning to go off to university in the UK in a few weeks. She agrees that having a clear sense of identity is challenging. "I just wish I was British." She sighs. "It would be a lot easier."

The iceberg model of culture

Culture is learned from those in the surrounding environment including parents, extended family, teachers, peers, and caregivers. Culture is made up of seemingly small things like how we collectively, as a community, dress, eat, speak, and act. It also defines systems of shared concepts, beliefs, and values. Anthropologist Gary Weaver suggests that we view culture as an iceberg. He says that we can easily visualize the part of the iceberg above the surface of the water, which he terms the 'surface culture.' This is what we can see or hear, and it includes language or traditions. However, as with most icebergs, there is a much larger chunk of ice below the waterline. This part that we can't see he terms the 'deep culture.' This includes beliefs and values.[11]

What is our take-home message from the iceberg model? Unfortunately, stereotypes and racism happen when we make assumptions about another person based on surface appearance alone. These are important issues to consider as our world becomes increasingly diverse.

Identities that teens assume based on exposure to a new culture

Culture provides a sense of belonging and identity, and by extension creates self-confidence. The diversity of experience that shapes Cross-Cultural Kids' lives and world views is not always readily apparent on the outside. Authors Van Reken and Pollock in their book *Third Culture Kids* suggest that some teens (and adults) may develop different identities based on the surrounding culture in which they find themselves.

Their identities may include:[12]

- **Foreigner**
  A teen who looks and acts differently. The teen and others know they are not from a certain place.

- **Hidden Immigrant**
  Looks like a native of the host country but thinks differently. Views culture through a different lens than expected.

- **Adoptee**
  Looks different than the locals but thinks alike. This applies to international adoptees and others who have lived in a country or community long enough to feel at home. When they return to the place they were born, they may experience themselves as a foreigner there.

- **Mirror**
  Looks like, speaks like, thinks like a local. Some cross-cultural teens may appear and think like kids in the dominant host culture because they have lived there for an extended period of time.

There are also common behaviors cross-cultural teens may adopt in finding an identity, particularly if they are in the 'hidden immigrant' or 'adoptee' categories.

These behaviors may include:

- **Chameleon**
  A teen who tries to blend in and have the 'same as' identity as others.

- **Screamer**
  A teen who sticks out and creates an identity that is 'different' from others.

- **Wallflower**
  Acts invisible and tries to maintain a 'non-identity.'

- **Adapter**
  A teen who is comfortable in his or her own skin. Neither super rebellious nor over conformist as adolescents.

Many of the teens I work with say they have never had a conversation with their parents, mentors, or educators about how they feel about their sense of belonging, who their tribe is, nor how to make sense of their identity and background. Parents may also be unaware of how difficult the experience of self-acculturalization is for their children and teens. Dr. Mychelle Farmer is an adolescent medicine physician who spent her childhood years living among the US military community in Japan and Hawaii before moving to France as a teen. She is currently Chief Medical Officer for Advancing Synergy and is based in Baltimore. "Cross-cultural life can be very difficult when parents are not insightful," says Dr. Farmer. "Kids then need to figure things out for themselves. I became resilient. I thrived, but I had to. The other options at the time weren't so good."

Strategies for addressing identity

Talk about it
Starting a conversation about the topic is the first step in supporting cross-cultural teens. In the survey I conducted of 361 teens and parents, nearly 45% of cross-cultural teens and 70% of parents had never discussed or received information about what it meant to be a cross-cultural child or kid. "Often teens don't realize the full extent of these identity issues till their 20s," says Tanya Crossman, an Australian Cross-Cultural Kid expert, based in Beijing. She is the author of *Misunderstood: The Impact of Growing Up Overseas in the 21st Century.* "And parents too do not completely understand how difficult a cross-cultural childhood can be." Therefore, talking and sharing can be therapeutic. Some questions to consider include:

- Who is your tribe? Who do you identify with and why?
- How many circles or groups are you in? What groups are your friends in?
- What places or communities do you connect with? Which are harder for you?
- What do you think of having a multicultural life? Are there some areas that you would like support in?

Understand that you will view life from a different lens than your teen
When kids move across cultures, parents need to accept that they are taking a risk. Cross-cultural children may eventually come to have a different perspective on how they view the world. Instead of being angry that children and teens are changing, author Ruth Van Reken tells me that parents need to understand where their kids are coming from. "Letting the child go toward the other world, yet still grounded in the absolute values of the family,

allows children the freedom to grow in THEIR way, not their parents'... and use the gifts they have received," she advises.

Celebrate unique roots

Exposure through family customs, travel, movies, and books are important ways to uphold heritage and culture and create personal identity. In our family, regardless of where we have lived, Christmas is a hodgepodge of accumulated traditions. We take out the German nativity figurines, advent wreath, and Christmas bread or *Stollen*. My husband, Hannfried, toils over the creation of homemade mulled wine and *Lebkuchen* cookies. This is alongside our more American rituals of sending an annual Christmas card, having a holiday open house for neighbors, and attending a candlelight service at church. At times, we also top it off with traditional South Indian holiday fare – fiery chicken curry and tangy coconut-rice pancakes called *appam*. It's a very exciting and sometimes crazy mix, but one that I know our kids look forward to every year.

Give the gift of language

Language is an important tool for creating identity. One of the parents I know is Chinese American; her husband is Dutch. They have lived with their kids in Asia for well over 10 years. Their teens are fluent in English, Dutch, and Mandarin and are currently taking German in school. They made languages a priority, sending their children to a Chinese school to learn Mandarin, having them attend Dutch school on the weekends, plus spending time with family in the Netherlands and the US. Their mom speaks to them in English and their father in Dutch. Language is a wonderful resource that teens can use to navigate cultures and stay connected to their many communities.

Make sure that language use is two-way
It is important that kids speak back the additional languages they are growing up with (not just understand them). When I grew up, the emphasis was on assimilating into the host culture as quickly as possible, and that often meant speaking English. While my parents did speak to me in their native language, Malayalam, they let me speak back in English. Today, I understand Malayalam, but my speaking abilities are rudimentary (and a source of amusement for some family members). My story shows that language abilities for global teens don't always come automatically. We need to encourage teens to speak back, watch shows, read books, take lessons, and be immersed with others who use the language in engaging ways, not just from hearing it spoken. There are many websites and books that discuss how best to acquire language. Also, make some decisions about which languages to focus on if there are multiple languages at play. Needless to say, understanding and speaking more than one language can be one of the many gifts of a cross-cultural experience, if done wisely.

Use story telling
We all have a story. My father came as a graduate student from southern India to New York City on a 6-week passage aboard a Spanish cargo ship. Then, in the late 1960s, he marched with Martin Luther King in Selma, Alabama. My German father-in-law was a teen at the end of World War II. He felt first-hand the terrible guilt and silence that gripped his homeland and family in the war's aftermath. Often, we don't take account of how our story affects us. Shared stories can inspire, entertain, resonate, and provide relief. Unexpressed stories can fester and cause suffering. Getting kids to share their own stories is a powerful and valuable exercise in developing their identity and expressing themselves. Whether it is writing, speaking, drawing,

dancing, or anything else, there are so many avenues for young people to tap into their own narrative.

 According to Jo Parfitt, the author of numerous books for expatriates, including *A Career in Your Suitcase* and *Monday Morning Emails*, the Japanese art of *kintsugi* pottery is an apt metaphor for our unique identity and life experiences. Adapting to new surroundings or cultures and leaving old ones can be challenging. Kintsugi is a type of porcelain that has been broken and put back together with golden glue. This type of china is highly valued in Japan because the many breaks and the glue that holds it together render it more valuable than the perfect original piece. We all have many cracks, fissures, and patched up areas in our lives. Parfitt sees each of the pieces in the broken kintsugi as the stories that make us who we are and suggests that we keep our stories sacred, but not secret. In other words, that our stories make us who we are and that we should tell and honor them.

CREATING BELONGING – WHERE IS HOME?

Whether a teen acts like a chameleon, screamer, wallflower, or adapter, being aware of these various reactions and supporting further understanding of belonging is important. Growing up, I wondered where I really belonged.

I recall visits to India, where despite looking like others, my poor command of my parents' mother tongue, Malayalam, and my lack of Hindi, prompted strangers to curiously ask, "Where are you from? You must not be Indian." Likewise, in our small American hometown in Delaware, I was on occasion asked, "Are you from India? You have really good English."

As mentioned, if a teen does not develop a clear sense of belonging, it can affect them significantly into adulthood. In my own work, when teens are unsure or vulnerable, they may look to others, such as their peers, for acceptance and to help them define who they should be, how they should look, and what they should do. For example, a poor sense of identity (and self-esteem) can put teens at risk for poor body image and eating disorders or using alcohol and drugs. In some places where I have worked such as in Washington, DC, teens have joined gangs to create a sense of belonging.

Research supports these observations. For example, a US-based study conducted by Raquel Hoersting examines the relationship between a cross-culturally mobile childhood, identity, and self-esteem.[13] The study indicates that those individuals reporting 'cultural homelessness' had lower self-esteem scores. On the other hand, those reporting a higher level of belonging/cross-cultural identity had higher self-esteem and lower cultural homelessness.

John is a 14-year-old boy whose parents are from Argentina and have been working as engineers in a multinational oil company. He speaks Spanish and English. His latest move was from Houston to Dubai. He has been moody, angry, and is having a hard time making friends at his new international school. His parents are not sure if he's depressed. He was previously a happy, fun-loving kid.

Research shows that teens on the move may experience unresolved grief from the loss of their home, school, and friends and this may manifest itself as denial, anger, depression, withdrawal, or rebellion. These kids, like John, may exhibit difficulties with their own identity formation because stable, 'anchoring' elements at home and school are missing during an important time in their life.

To explore these concepts further, I spoke to Third Culture Kid expert and author Chris O'Shaughnessy at the Families in Global Transition conference in Bangkok, Thailand. Chris grew up in a military family in the UK and moved multiple times as a child and young adult. "Teens who don't have a clear sense of belonging may lack connection or rootedness in their respective community which can lead to vulnerability," says O'Shaughnessy. "In some cases, such vulnerability may lead to marginalization and radicalization."

Chris adds, "We have seen this among some groups of adolescents around the world such as after the terror attacks of 2015 in Paris and 2016 in Brussels. A lot of attention was focused on the community of Molenbeek, a suburb of Brussels sometimes referred to as the 'jihadist capital of Europe' [the ringleader and three operatives in the Paris terror attacks grew up in Molenbeek]. The youth of Molenbeek were particularly vulnerable to radicalization because they have, in many ways, been marginalized by Belgian society. Young people complain that with a Molenbeek address it's harder to get a job, they are stigmatized, and excluded... yet they live in the 'heart of Europe' amidst constant reminders of the European Union's aim for tolerance, acceptance, and unity. This fractured reality leads to a lot of identity issues – which combined with the disillusionment and marginalization, makes them easy targets for radicalization which provided an outlet for anger, along with a solid sense of belonging [to the terrorist group]."

In sum, as parents and adults, helping kids to create a sense of identity, belonging, and rootedness is critical. The following are some strategies to help improve self-confidence and minimize cultural homelessness.

Strategies for addressing belonging

Realize that every child is unique when it comes to change

I spoke with a mother of four daughters in Washington, DC, who had moved multiple times due to a World Bank job. She mentioned that her oldest seemed to have the most difficult adjustments as she moved during her teen years. Moving during the teen years is significantly harder as this is a formative period. Having said that, many young people are extremely resilient and handle change well. Change and moving may be inevitable as is the case for immigrants, refugees, and expats. The bottom line is that you know your teen and need to assess the impact of transition and change during the formative period of adolescence. Take time to explore how they may be addressing change as each child or teen will handle it very differently.

Create belonging in the local community

Kids that feel connected to the local community feel more self-confident. Ensure yours have a good understanding of the culture by encouraging them to get involved with community service, be part of a local sports team, or engage in other activities with locals. For expats and military dependents in foreign countries, putting kids in a local school may be a great way for them to pick up languages and assimilate.

Use social communities to build language

Multilingualism can be hard to maintain, especially if there are more than two or three languages at play, believes Mariam Ottimofiore, author of *This Messy Mobile Life*, who has lived in nine countries with her two kids and husband and is currently based in Ghana. She recommends getting support from others to encourage the use of the local language to make it fun and exciting for kids. Think about joining clubs or camps where the additional language will be used or enrolling in a study-abroad experience for immersion. At the same time, realize that it is OK that your child may not be able to maintain all the languages they have been exposed to. You and your teen will need to prioritize what languages are important and how to continue learning them.

Maintain contact by travel (or virtual tools)

For some teens, visiting places that they have lived in before or have connections to is an important way to create a sense of belonging and understanding. As we have learned from COVID-19, using virtual tools such as Skype or Zoom are great ways for kids to stay in touch with family or community in other places.

Educate yourself and others

Encourage your teen to meet other kids and adults with cross-cultural backgrounds to help create connections in your own community. Look at ways to integrate their understanding of other cultures through games, food, or activities. Beyond your own family, discuss the importance of diversity programs and cross-cultural training for other students, educators, counselors, and parents.

Demonstrate healthy ways to grieve and get help if needed

Encourage healthy ways to address loss such as journaling, connecting via phone or a video call, exercising, meditating, and listening to music (even crying can be cathartic). If needed, look for a counselor or mentor to support your teen in identifying and dealing with loss directly.

Be aware that adults can struggle too

Adults from cross-cultural backgrounds may not have a clear sense of identity or struggle to find belonging, which can add to the challenge of their own child or teen. On the other hand, cross-cultural adults may also impart skills and values honed from their own experience. As an adult expatriate, I realized that each time I moved, it took me 2 to 3 years to settle down in my new environment. I now know that finding a community and creating a sense of identity and belonging have been crucial to my happiness and sense of well-being in each country we lived in. Having friends who have gone through similar experiences, online forums, and cross-cultural organizations such as Families in Global Transition (FIGT), have also been immensely helpful to me. Being aware of these issues may be important for my teens as they navigate change and uncertainty in the future.

FOSTERING HEALTHY FRIENDSHIPS

Having strong friendships is an important part of cross-cultural teens' development as they create their identity and develop a sense of belonging. Friends help them become independent and prepare them for building trusting relationships that can continue into adulthood. In many cases, friendships are based on common interests like music, arts, sports, community, or clubs. A good indication that teens are in a healthy friendship is when they can spend time with their friends without fear of being teased, bullied, or alienated.[14] Often, adolescents may want to spend more of their time with friends over family (which for some parents may seem challenging), but it's a completely normal and healthy part of development.

Strategies for fostering healthy friendships

Uphold uniqueness
If your teen played chess or took Hebrew classes for years and dropped out because it was considered uncool, discuss why it may be OK to be unique or different and how to address this with friends.

Have diverse friends
It is important for teens to experience life from different perspectives. Support your adolescent in befriending people from different backgrounds and age groups (including an older mentor or confidante) and model this behavior as adults.

Discuss peer pressure
As parents, it is important to get teens to consider their ethics, morals, and values and how this relates to their friend group. This can relate to body image, social media, gaming, drugs, and alcohol, or other behaviors. The following are a few questions to discuss regarding friendships and peer pressure:

- What are some of the reasons you want to be part of this group of friends?
- Is there anything you may do with friends that would be against your values or beliefs?

- How would you handle it if your friends were mean to someone else or did something that you weren't comfortable with?
- What is the difference between joking and bullying?

NAVIGATING CLIQUES

Anka is an active 16-year-old. Fresh from a flight from Washington, DC, we chat over breakfast in Amsterdam. She is traveling before starting university in the fall. Her parents are Indian-German and Canadian, and she has lived in New Delhi, Washington, DC, and most recently Singapore. "One of the biggest challenges of moving to a new place is the lack of support when integrating into a new school," Anka tells me. She mentions how hard it can be to adjust to new scoring systems and standards. In addition to dealing with academic pressure and school challenges, she mentions that the social pressures can make life tough. "Managing cliques, particularly in middle school, was really difficult. It was hard to figure out friendships." Fiona, a thoughtful 13-year-old I meet after a school talk in London, agrees. "Being part of a group of girls is important to me. It is also stressful because I spend a lot of time worrying about who said what and if I will still be in the group. One day things are going great and the next day someone says or posts something negative about you and it's all downhill."

Unlike friendships, cliques are controlled by a 'leader' who decides who is in the group. Cliques involve rules and intense pressure to follow them. Members of the clique usually follow the leader's rules, whether it's wearing certain outfits or sitting in a specific place at lunch. Teens in cliques may worry about their popularity and whether they'll be dropped for doing or saying something wrong. In a clique, kids may be more easily pressured to try things like using alcohol or vaping.[15] Cliques are often at their most intense by ages 11-15, but problems with cliques can start as early as ages 8-10. Generally, by late adolescence, cliques are less of an issue and individual friendships take priority. Parents and adults can do a lot to support preteens and teens in navigating friendships and cliques and making good choices.

Strategies for navigating cliques

Put things in perspective
Sometimes, adults sharing their own experiences of growing up as a teen can be very helpful for young people in handling their rejection or fears. They learn that their experience is not unique and that relationships can change quickly at this age. Explain that if someone else is being unkind or judging them based on looks, dress, or accent, it is because they are insecure themselves. Finally, remind them that the true key to popularity is being fair, kind, and trustworthy.

Address behaviors
If your teen is part of a clique and is taking part in rejecting others, it's important to address this immediately. Discuss the role of power and control in friendships. Also, who may be 'in' or 'out' of the group, and what happens when kids feel ignored or bullied.

Find new friends
Get kids involved in activities that give them an opportunity to create friends outside of their current community or circle.

Address stereotypes and bullying

Unfortunately, teens who are viewed as different from the rest of their peers because of their race, appearance, name, or accent may be at risk for teasing and bullying. It is an issue that young people discuss with me regularly. If teens are being bullied, addressing it with peers, teachers, or coaches is essential. Ask what may be going on inside and outside of class. Find out if there are any programs available to address cliques and to help kids who are different in some way to get along with their peers. Although bullying and stereotyping should never occur, in some extreme cases, I know of families and teens who have chosen to relocate to schools and communities that are more accepting of multiculturalism and diversity.

THE BOTTOM LINE: IDENTITY AND BELONGING

- Adolescence is a key time to establish a sense of identity that reflects a teen's physical appearance, race, ethnicity, religion, and nationality plus sexual and gender orientation.

- Having a clear sense of cultural identity and belonging while handling transition and loss can be difficult for global teens. Create a clear sense of connection by encouraging involvement in local activities and being aware of the need for cross-cultural relationships in the community. When experiencing moves and transition, remember to address unresolved grief and loss.

- Build healthy friendships and navigate cliques by encouraging teens to find friends that are the right fit, not ones they have to work hard to fit in with or can't be themselves with. Also, discuss ways to handle peer pressure and address bullying and stereotypes.

- Finally, remember that parents and caregivers play an important role in helping global teens to develop their unique sense of identity and belonging.

BIG ANSWERS

Common parent questions on identity and belonging

1. **What impact does my own experience as an immigrant/ military member/ expatriate have on my child or teen?**

   Your own cross-cultural background may affect your sense of feeling fully connected and integrated, which in turn could influence the experience of your own child or teen. On a positive note, you also have important skills and values that you can impart to your family members. Be aware of how your experience affects you and be willing to talk to others, including your family about it. There are also wonderful groups, online forums, and books for adults to help explore the effects of their own cross-cultural experiences and get support if needed (see Resources).

2. **Our teen is adopted from Asia. We have a Western background and don't look like her. Lately, she's been embarrassed when we come to school or meet her friends. How should we handle this?**

   It is very normal for teens to want to be accepted by their peers. Parents may be unaware of how difficult this process is for their children and teens, especially if they look different from their family members. Perhaps starting a conversation about why she may be embarrassed and whether her peers have made any comments may be a good starting point. Also, try to highlight her unique roots and personal story. In some cases, accepting her embarrassment and realizing that this is a phase she will be going through (and will change as she matures) may also be helpful. Finally, if she's having a hard time with her perceived differences, consider consulting with other adoptees and mixed families, or talking to a school counselor or therapist.

3. **We are planning a family move and have two young teenagers. Is there a 'right' age to move during the adolescent years?**

   There's no simple answer as to how your teen will react to mobility and change. Moving during the teen years may be much harder for young people than at other times in their life for many reasons including that it is a formative period for developing a sense of identity. If there is a choice, perhaps it would be easier to stay in one place during early to middle adolescence. Having said that, many young people are resilient and handle change well. Know your teens, understand the culture of the community that you may be moving to, and decide whether the move is necessary. Also, take time to explore how your teens may handle a move and transition, and be willing to get support from the community or school if needed.

4. **Our kids are mixed race. They sometimes get teased at school because of their name or appearance. Should we move to a school where kids look more like them?**
   For some teens, feeling different can be difficult when they are trying to fit in and make friends. Discuss with your kids the value of their appearance and name. Encourage them to feel proud of their unique identity. Also, try to meet other kids and adults with cross-cultural backgrounds to help create connections. If possible, ask their school to discuss the issue of being teased and the importance of upholding diversity. Finally, remember that many teens tend to gravitate to others that look and act like them. It may be a reason to find a school that has a more diverse student body that is a better fit for them.

Common teen questions on identity and belonging

1. **I am 14 years old and I am having a hard time dealing with all the cliques in my class and making friends at school. Any tips?**
   Cliques can be hard to navigate, particularly at your age. The good news is that cliques tend to be less of an issue as you get older. Look for friends through common interests and activities. True friends respect others' appearance, opinions, and choices. Remember how important it is to be true to yourself, and question the importance of having to be in a specific group. Finally, if someone in a clique is being unkind or judging you based on looks, dress, or accent, it is because they are insecure themselves. Do tell your parents or a trusted adult if you are feeling bullied or pressured by peers.

2. **I don't feel like I fit in with other kids around me where I live. When I go to my home country, I don't exactly fit in there either. I find it hard to answer the question "where are you from?" or "where is home?" because I just don't know.**
   This is a common concern that many teens, especially cross-cultural ones, share. Having open conversations with your family and friends about identity and belonging may be a good starting point. Ask yourself, who do I feel comfortable with? Where do I feel that I belong

most? Try to create connections based on your culture, background, religion, or community to help create roots. Realize that the benefit of having cross-cultural experience also allows you to move from community to community in ways that others can't. Also, that there are many young people in the world just like you. If you want to learn more, there are great magazines, books, online resources, and chat groups for cross-cultural teens such as Denizen and I am a Triangle (see Resources section.)

3. **We are always moving from place to place for my father's work. I am tired of having to make new friends and I really miss my old friends. What should I do?**
You are not alone feeling this way. In fact, one of the top issues among cross-cultural teens is loss of friends due to moves. Let us not ignore that it is extremely painful to make and lose friendships. It is one of the hardest parts of being a global teen. Moving can help you to be more adaptable and make new friends in different situations. However, it is important to be true to yourself and your needs. Try to maintain contact either in person or virtually with your buddies. Also, consider talking to a family member, counselor, or mentor if you feel you need more support in creating new friendships and accepting changes in your old ones.

4. **In university, I found that I ended up hanging out with other kids that had the same international background as me. We had more in common than other classmates that I met. Is that OK or should I try to make friends that are different than me?**

Many cross-cultural students say that they feel most comfortable with other students that have had similar backgrounds. In fact, global teens often look for universities and colleges that have a diverse student body or have clubs and houses that support cross-cultural backgrounds to help with a sense of belonging and inclusion. It may be reassuring to have friends that share similar backgrounds and life experiences. Of course, part of the schooling experience is meeting folks that are different from you, so trying to join activities or groups that bring you into new circles is also important.

RESOURCES

Books

Arrivals, Departures and the Adventures In-Between, Chris O'Shaughnessy, Summertime Publishing, 2014

Bringing Up a Bilingual Child – How to Navigate the Seven Cs of Multilingual Parenting: Communication, Confidence, Commitment, Consistency, Creativity, Culture and Celebration, Rita Rosenback, Filament, 2014

Misunderstood: The Impact of Growing Up Overseas in the 21st Century, Tanya Crossman, Summertime Publishing, 2016

Safe Passage: How mobility affects people & what international schools should do about it, Douglas W Ota, Summertime Publishing, 2014

The Global Nomad's Guide to University Transition, Tina L Quick, Summertime Publishing, 2010

This Messy Mobile Life: How a Mola Can Help Globally Mobile Families Create a Life by Design, Mariam N Ottimofiore, Springtime Books, 2019

Websites and articles

'For Third Culture Kids', *Denizen*: http://denizenmag.com

Families in Global Transition: https://figt.org/

I am a Triangle: http://iamatriangle.com

'6 Ways to Help Your Teen Make and Keep Good Friends', Cheryl Somers, *Good Therapy*, 2016: https://www.goodtherapy.org/blog/6-ways-to-help-your-teen-make-keep-great-friends-0701164

Multicultural Kid Blogs: https://multiculturalkidblogs.com/resources-for-raising-global-citizens/

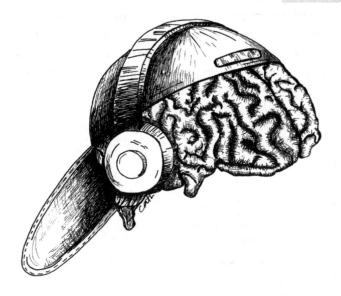

"The limbic system explodes during puberty, but the prefrontal cortex keeps maturing for another 10 years."
Robin Marantz Henig

IN THIS CHAPTER:
- Changes that occur during teen brain development.
- Effects of early exposure to stress, alcohol, and drugs.
- Important strategies for optimizing brain health.

When I was a doctor in training at our children's hospital in Washington, DC, there was an infamous story about a teenager who decided to take a poisonous snake from the local zoo because he thought it looked cool. He somehow managed to put it in a sack and get on a public bus to take it home. Everything was fine until the snake bit the teen before escaping on the bus, causing major panic. The teen was brought to the intensive care unit of our hospital for anti-venom treatment and thankfully survived. Why on earth, I wondered at the time, would a teen steal a poisonous snake from a zoo and... take it home in a bag?

The short answer is that there is a tremendous level of testing and experimentation during adolescence while the brain is still developing. The immature teen brain doesn't function in the same ways as in adults where its different parts work together to evaluate options, make choices, and coordinate actions. What's more, many of the known mental health issues such as anxiety, depression, and schizophrenia start in the teen years, reflecting the exquisite sensitivity of the developing brain.

BIG QUESTIONS

Common parent questions on teen brain development

1. Do teens' bodies and brains mature at different rates?

2. Can frequent transitions or changes cause changes in the adolescent brain?

3. What is the impact of binge drinking on the developing brain?

4. How can we support teens when they make questionable decisions?

Common teen questions on brain development

1. Is there a safe age to start vaping?

2. Do girl brains mature faster than boy brains?

3. How can I make sure my brain stays healthy?

4. Can stress or stressful events affect my brain?

UNDERSTANDING THE TEEN BRAIN

Imagine a new computer that hasn't been fully set up yet. There is software to be uploaded, data to be transferred, printers to be connected, and an anti-virus protection program to be installed. In some ways, the developing teen brain is like a new computer (except it comes without an owner's manual). It takes a little time and work to be fully set up and operational. Here is a quick roadmap of the process and what to expect along the way.

A developing system

The brain's prefrontal cortex is its command and control center – it takes care of planning, emotional regulation, decision-making, and self-awareness. The prefrontal cortex communicates with the other parts of the brain through synapses or connections. The synapses function like the wires of the computer system. Global teens experience a significant growth of synapses during adolescence. In fact, a young person's tremendous number of synapses accounts for a teen's incredible ability to learn several languages at once. This ability significantly decreases in adulthood (which some of us parents may already be experiencing). The brain starts pruning away the synapses that it doesn't need in order to make the remaining ones more efficient in communicating. As connections are trimmed, myelin, an insulating substance, coats the synapses to protect them and allow for effective communication. The insulation process starts at the back of the brain and slowly moves to the front. This process takes more than 10-12 years to complete.[16] What's the last part to be connected or plugged in? You guessed it, the command center or prefrontal cortex.

According to a study at the National Institute of Mental Health in Maryland, 'brain pruning' may explain why teens act the way they do. The pruning begins with the areas of the brain responsible for more basic motor functions, moves onto the language and spatial regions of the brain, and finally the area of the brain responsible for decision-making and impulse control. It is the pruning of the decision-making area that may explain a teen's moodiness, temper, and otherwise erratic behavior. As white matter replaces the lost grey matter, connections (and behavior) stabilize. The study indicates that while pruning stimulates learning in teens, it could also be the cause of the increased experimentation and risk taking behavior.[17]

One foot on the accelerator

Adults often complain about the constant need to make choices and weigh decisions. For teens, decision-making is even tougher. In part, this is because the developing brain's ability to seek pleasure through its limbic system is much stronger than its ability to regulate it. Imagine having your foot on the accelerator while driving and having a hard time braking. The example of the teen who took the snake from the zoo is an illustration of this process. Teenagers often try things because they have a heightened need to satisfy their reward center. In fact, they may need a higher level of risk to feel the same rush as adults. Because of the prolonged delay in rational decision-making, teens are also at risk for unsafe behaviors such as getting in fights, using drugs, or driving while using alcohol. Rental car companies in the US understand teen brain research and the risks of teen driving and as a result do not allow individuals under 21 years of age to rent vehicles. Based on the same research, most US states now have graduated driver license programs that ensure teens learn to drive over an extended period.

It takes time

The brain is the last organ in the body to mature. In fact, the teen brain is just 80% complete in structure and function during adolescence. It is only fully developed and connected to the frontal lobe by the mid-20s. It may seem ironic that the prefrontal cortex teaches the rest of the brain how the world works and yet takes the longest to mature. The delay, however, may serve an evolutionary purpose. By taking its time to grow, the prefrontal cortex stays open to learning and adaptation. Imaging studies of teens' brains have shown that most of the decision-making activity takes place at the back of the brain, while in adults it happens in the frontal lobe. By age 25, the brain is more capable of 'connecting the dots,' making plans, and resisting impulses. When I talk to young people, I tell them – tongue in cheek – that if they make an unwise decision, they may consider blaming it on their developing brain as it is still a work in progress.

In some countries and communities, global teens go to university, get married, have a family, and join the workforce much earlier (i.e. by the time they are 17-18 years old) than in other places. This shift to assuming adult responsibilities while still undergoing brain development is an important concept to be aware of. I believe cross-cultural teens are most likely to succeed if they have broad support from extended family, mentors, or a strong community network and awareness that their maturation process can be uneven. According to Dr. Jeffrey Hutchinson, an adolescent medicine doctor and former military physician based in Austin, Texas, "Parents can act like the tech support that most new computers offer."

Boys versus girls

As a parent of two boys, I have noticed differences in how my boys organize and plan compared to girls their age. As it turns out, there are true differences in brain development between boys and girls. The part of the brain that processes information reaches its peak expansion and development at 12-14 years old in girls and almost 2-3 years later for boys. Compared to boys, girls at ages 12-14 are also slightly better planners and more easily able to navigate complex scheduling.[18] What's more, scientists from Newcastle University in the UK have shown that the process of pruning (when the brain matures and starts storing information and focusing on what's important) occurs as early as age 10 years for girls, but closer to 15-20 years for boys, which is a sizable difference.[19]

The teen brain is vulnerable to stress

Cross-cultural teens may experience significant stress from global events like pandemics, transitions, change, grief, and loss. Research shows that the brains of children and adolescents are much more sensitive to stress than adults. Chronic stress is now known to damage the brain's hypothalamus as well as the pituitary and adrenal glands in the brain also known as the HPA-axis.[20] These brain areas control reactions to stress and regulate mood, growth, body temperature, and sexuality. The HPA-axis is also known to be an important area involved in schizophrenia and mood disorders. Researchers now believe that stress is likely to be an important risk factor in the development of schizophrenia and other mental illnesses.[21]

Regular stress also increases cortisol levels in the brain. In a 2018 study conducted at Harvard Medical School, researchers found that adult participants with high levels of cortisol had much poorer working memory. To further explore the connection, they did MRI imaging of a smaller group of the participants and found that those with high cortisol levels had lower brain volumes. In short, although some level of stress is beneficial and unavoidable, ongoing daily stress can cause changes to brain development and increase the risk of developing mental health issues.[22] As a result, it is wise to work on ways to address high levels of stress for developing teens, which I will explore more in *Chapter 8.*

Substance use and the brain

Drugs and alcohol can also have a serious impact on the teen brain. Recent studies show that the occasional use of marijuana can cause lingering memory problems even days after smoking, and that long-term use impacts the IQ.[23] Research also shows that young people are particularly vulnerable to addiction if exposed to drugs or alcohol at an early age. In fact, teens that start drinking or smoking before the age of 15 are more likely to become addicted and have a harder time stopping during adulthood.

Even one episode of binge drinking can cause subtle changes in teen brains. A recent study led by neuroscientist Susan Tapert of the University of California in San Diego compared the brain MRIs of teens who drink heavily with the scans of teens who don't. Drinking heavily was defined as consuming four or five drinks per occasion about two or three times a month. The team found damaged nerve tissue in the brains of the teens who drank. The researchers believe this damage negatively affects attention span in boys – and in girls the ability to comprehend and interpret visual information.[24] These changes may also be irreversible.

Getting teens to understand the importance of delaying the onset of drinking and avoiding binge drinking are important things to discuss with them. I often tell young people that they only have one brain and need to take care of it. If they can delay some behaviors, such as smoking, until they are just a little older and their brains are more developed, they will be less likely to get addicted and experience negative changes in their brain.

David is one of my teen patients. He is Italian-American and initially came to see me for a sports injury. As part of my routine screening, I asked about other common teen activities including drinking. At 18 years old he had recently started university in Washington, DC, and hanging out with a group of his dorm mates who liked to go to parties and drink alcohol regularly. On an average night, he may have 5-6 beers and be up till 3am. He told me he was at several parties where his buddies were so drunk they would pass out on the ground. It has also affected his school performance. However, he has enjoyed his new-found independence and being able to relax with his friends.

In talking to young people, I often ask them if they have a family member who is using alcohol or smoking cigarettes regularly. In David's case, we discussed that several of his family members, including his brother, had struggled with alcohol use. I told him that he may have a harder time stopping smoking or drinking than his friends. Also, that it may continue to affect his school performance and his developing brain.

Initially, David wasn't motivated to make a change in his drinking or even recognize it as an issue. With each of our follow up visits for his sports injury, we discussed his goals for university, ways to stay fit, his peer group, and alcohol use. After several months of having these conversations in clinic, he decided he needed to make a change and was concerned about the effects of his regular drinking on his grades, and his family history of alcohol use. He moved to a flat with a friend who didn't drink and a year after our first meeting confided he had stopped drinking himself. Although not all teens have such a significant change in their drinking behaviors, this story reveals the importance of getting teens motivated to make changes in their own behavior especially as it relates to the developing brain.

Sleep cycles shift

Ever wonder why many teens go to sleep and wake up later than younger kids? In teens, levels of melatonin, the hormone produced by the brain that induces sleep, typically increase later at night and decrease later in the morning compared to younger children or adults. Adults get a surge of melatonin around 8.30pm while with teens it happens closer to 11pm. As a result, waking up at 7am for a teen may feel like an adult getting up at 4am. This may also be why many teens stay up late and struggle with getting up in the morning (of course, late-night use of computers and phones doesn't help). Lack of sleep can also affect concentration, memory, and mood, and make teens grumpy and impulsive.

Plasticity is the key

Clearly, adolescents can acquire and retain more information than adults. Teens are better learners because their brain cells more readily 'build' memories. Plasticity, a term that denotes the ability to adapt, can help teens pick up new skills. The teenage years may be when budding singers or authors or scientists bloom. Before the brain is fully developed is the perfect time to learn a new language or take up an instrument. Teens are also early adopters of technology and new innovations. According to researchers, people also tend to remember more events from their teen years and early 20s than they do from other periods. This concept has been coined the 'reminiscence bump.'[25]

Self-conscious and egocentric

Hormones during puberty can have huge effects on the brain. One effect is to increase the receptors for oxytocin or the 'bonding hormone' which has been linked to feeling self-conscious (and which peaks around the age of 15).[26] Because of this effect, early adolescents are often described as focused on themselves and egocentric. Rest assured, with continued brain development and maturation, they gradually develop a broader view of their existence and the world around them.

Same but with some differences

Teen brain development is essentially the same across the world says psychologist Sarah-Jayne Blakemore. Blakemore is one of the foremost researchers on teen neuroscience and author of *Inventing Ourselves: The Secret Life of the Teenage Brain*. Speaking at an adolescent health conference in Ascot, UK, she reports that teen risk-taking peaks and declines at around the same ages around the world. Also, that scientists studying yearly MRIs of adolescents in several countries have found that brain maturation is relatively uniform. Researchers are continuing to explore what accounts for individual differences in brain growth, and how teens influence each other in risk taking behaviors.

 Experimental behaviors help young people form their own identity, handle challenges on their own, and learn about the world around them. Regardless of where they live, all teens go through the same crucial exploratory phase in their development.

According to Blakemore, risk taking is a good thing. She says, "If we didn't take risks, where would we be? On the other hand, it can be dangerous and can result in accidents or even death. If you look at mortality rates across the life span, the number one cause of death in adolescents is from risk taking: it's from accidents. That's not true at any other period of life." Adds Blakemore: "Risk taking is a good thing unless it goes too far. You need some constraints over risk taking, and that's where parents come in. That's probably evolutionarily important as well."

Strategies for optimal brain health

Protect the brain
Ensure teens eat foods that are good for the brain, including oily fish (such as salmon), nuts, chia seeds, flaxseed, blueberries, and drink lots of water. Make sure they get enough sleep. Communicate to teens the impact of early drinking or drug use on the teen brain and how they can address the pressure or need to drink or use drugs. Also, take steps to protect against head injury by using helmets for high-impact sports and seat belts in cars. Finally, ensure teens are screened for a possible concussion after a significant head injury and be aware of standardized guidelines for return to play in sports and activities.

Know your family history
A family history of substance use may predispose a teen to using drugs or alcohol and they may have a harder time stopping later. As mentioned with David, knowing your family history and discussing it openly with teens can be very useful.

Address stress
Challenging and stressful situations can affect teens more than adults as the developing brain is more vulnerable. In fact, significant stress during brain development has been shown to have permanent effects on the brain and future mental health. The rapid changes in the teen brain may

explain why the adolescent years are the period where mental health issues – such as anxiety, depression, bipolar disorder, self-injury, and eating disorders – often emerge. Help teens to handle stress by building in downtime, exercise, and other strategies as discussed in *Chapter 8*. Also, be aware of signs of emerging mental health issues as discussed in *Chapters 9* and *10*.

Be a sounding board

In adolescence, teens are trying to figure out who they are and where they belong. Global teens can add exposure to different cultures, languages, and communities to the mix. While these aspects can lead to powerful strengths and abilities later in life, they may also lead to confusion and turmoil during adolescence and the brain's extended development period. Teenagers face challenges, feelings, and temptations with brains that are not yet fully developed. By being informed about the workings of the teen brain, adults can serve as better sounding boards for teens.

Discuss future plans

Having an idea of what your teen wants to do for a career or accomplish in life (even if those plans still change) is a good marker for the prefrontal cortex functioning effectively and is a strong predictor of successful transitioning through adolescence. One of the questions I often ask teens is, "What are your plans or dreams for the future." I have heard a wide range of ideas, including wanting to be an astronaut, marine biologist, politician, or star soccer player. At times, though, I have met teens who have told me that they don't have a plan at all, or don't really care what will happen to them in the future. According to Dr. Jeffrey Hutchinson, not having a plan for the future "can be a reflection of stress, lack of role models or expectations, or not wanting to share dreams for fear of negativity." Bottom line, not caring about future goals can be a red flag and indicate the possibility of a difficult period and the need to have deeper discussions.

Understand the warning signs
Although all teens can be occasionally moody or impulsive, it is important to be aware of the warning signs of deeper emotional issues. Be attuned. Is your teen eating and sleeping normally and maintaining friends? It is during the teen years that mental illnesses such as depression or schizophrenia often first occur. If your teen is not sleeping properly, lashing out on a regular basis, or letting their grades drop or goals slip by, it may be time to get help.

THE BOTTOM LINE: THE TEEN BRAIN

- The teen brain is not fully developed until the mid-20s. Trying new things and taking risks are an important part of teens becoming independent.

- There is a constant tug of war between the brain's reward center and the prefrontal cortex which regulates logical thought and organization. As such, it may be difficult for teens to fully regulate their behavior and put on 'the brakes' when needed.

- Young people are more vulnerable to addiction or changes in brain development if they are exposed to drugs or alcohol at early ages. On a positive note, teens also have active and growing brains that allow them to acquire skills such as learning a new language quickly.

- Understanding the basics of brain development can give adults important insights into global teens' behavior and ways to support them.

BIG ANSWERS

Common parent questions on teen brain development

1. **Do teens' bodies and brains mature at different rates?**
   Yes. One of the great paradoxes of adolescence is that the brain and body finish development at different times. Whereas most teens are physically mature by the time they are 18 years old, the brain and emotional development continue till approximately 25 years of age.

2. **Can frequent transitions or changes cause changes in the adolescent brain?**
   Transition and change can cause increased stress levels. Stress in turn increases the cortisol level, which has been known to cause changes in memory and brain volume. Encourage teens to use coping strategies such as getting optimal sleep, food, exercise, and of course connecting with others either physically or virtually.

3. **What is the impact of binge drinking on the developing brain?**
   Binge drinking is common in many parts of the world among teens. However, one episode of binge drinking (4 or more servings of alcohol in a short period of time for a girl or 5 or more for a boy) can cause subtle changes to the brain as seen on MRIs. Regular binge drinking at an early age can also put teens at risk for alcohol

addiction and having a hard time stopping alcohol use when they get older. (For more on binge drinking, see Chapter 11 on Substance Use.)

4. **How can we support teens when they make questionable decisions?**

   Remind yourself that part of teen development is to try out new things. The ability to think about the consequences of actions may not come till later in adolescence. As described in Chapter 1 on communication, give teens boundaries. Provide information on issues before they occur. Consider role play to help young people address peer pressure and make smart choices. Finally, be there to support teens if they make choices that you don't think are wise. You are there to help them to learn better decision-making as they mature.

Common teen questions on brain development

1. **Is there a safe age to start vaping?**

   Starting vaping when you are 15 or younger makes it harder to stop as you get older and can cause changes in your developing brain. Vaping with marijuana has also been linked to lung injury and death among teens. Smoking (and perhaps vaping) has also been associated with increased risk of COVID-19. Bottom line, there is no safe age to start vaping as a teen. (For more on vaping see Chapter 11 on Substance Use.)

2. Do girl brains mature faster than boy brains?

Every kid is different. However, the part of the brain that processes information reaches its peak development at 12-14 years old in girls and almost 2-3 years later for most boys. Brain development seems to even out by late adolescence (around 18 years of age).

3. How can I make sure my brain stays healthy?

You only have one brain. Best ways to take care of it? Eat a balanced diet, drink lots of water, sleep well, wear helmets for recommended sports, stay calm, and avoid using alcohol and/or drugs, if possible. The younger you are when you start using alcohol and drugs the more likely it is to affect your developing brain. Also, you may have a harder time stopping when you are older.

4. Can stress or stressful events affect my brain?

Some stress is OK but having intense regular stress can be unhealthy. Stress can cause an increase in a hormone called cortisol which has been shown to affect memory and the size of the brain. Chronic stress can affect the parts of the brain that regulate mood, immunity, and growth. Try looking into ways to cut back on stress like talking to your parents, a friend, exercising, keeping a journal, or reaching out to a counselor. (For more tips, see Chapter 8 on Stress.)

RESOURCES

Books

Brainstorm: The Power and Purpose of the Teenage Brain,
Daniel Siegel, TarcherPerigee, 2014

Inventing Ourselves: The Secret Life of the Teenage Brain,
Sarah-Jayne Blakemore, PublicAffairs, 2018

*The Teenage Brain: A Neuroscientist's Survival Guide to
Raising Adolescents and Young Adults,* Frances Jensen,
Harper Paperbacks, 2016

Websites and articles

'Nurturing the Amazing Teen Brain', Anisha Abraham,
Center for Parent and Teen Communication, 2018: https://
parentandteen.com/nurture-teen-brain/

'The Mysterious Workings of the Adolescent Brain',
Sarah-Jayne Blakemore, *TEDGlobal,* 2012: https://www.
ted.com/talks/sarah_jayne_blakemore_the_mysterious_
workings_of_the_adolescent_brain

PUBERTY – PHYSICAL DEVELOPMENT

4

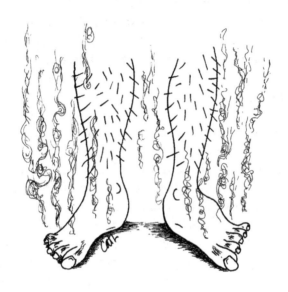

"Kids don't shuffle along in unison on the road to maturity. They slouch toward adulthood at an uneven, highly individual pace."
Robin Marantz Henig

IN THIS CHAPTER:
- Physical changes that occur among boys and girls during early, mid, and late adolescence.
- Signs of premature and delayed physical development and when to get help.
- Common teen concerns and issues related to physical pubertal development.

Puberty was baffling for me. I remember the hushed whispers and prolonged gazes when the first girl to develop significant breasts walked by. As one of the youngest kids in my grade, I was always worrying if I would ever catch up. Yet when I finally developed breast buds, I worried endlessly that one was much bigger than the other. We discussed lots of important issues at my home, but as far as I recall, developing breasts (let alone fears about unequal ones) was just not one of them.

If you are anything like me, puberty brings back memories of awkwardness and uncertainty. Many of us never had discussions with our parents or other adults on the topic at all. However, in a survey I conducted in 2019 with global teens, puberty is one of the top issues that concerned them. To ensure that teens have a solid understanding of the topic it is important that you know what to expect, when to start communicating, and how to answer questions candidly and without embarrassment. With good information (and a sense of humor), you and your teen will make it through puberty together.

BIG QUESTIONS

Common parent questions on teen physical development

1. How will I know if my teen is going through puberty?

2. What if my daughter is developing signs of puberty too early?

3. What if my son is late going through pubertal changes?

4. What should I do if my daughter doesn't get her period?

5. How can I help my daughter to manage menstrual pain?

6. Should I encourage my teen to get treated for their acne even though they are not worried about it?

Common teen questions on physical development

1. Why do I smell?

2. I am the shortest kid in the class. Will I ever grow?

3. How do I know if my periods are irregular?

4. Is it OK to masturbate? How much is too much?

5. Do you need to be circumcised as a boy?

6. Does the size of your penis matter?

PUBERTY

Puberty usually starts between the ages of 8 and 13. The word puberty comes from the Latin *pubescere,* which means 'to grow hairy.' The body makes hormones such as estrogen and testosterone, triggering important physical changes. These include an increase in weight and height, and new muscle and fat distribution. Hormones can have a tremendous impact on the developing brain which often leads to mood swings, but also to important cognitive and emotional changes.

The overall sequence of pubertal changes is generally the same among teens regardless of whether you live in Buenos Aires or Beirut. There is strong evidence that puberty is starting earlier among teens today than it did just 50 years ago. Also, the time at which teens are leaving home and become fully independent is happening later. Some wonder whether this new 'prolonged adolescence' and related emotional turbulence may account for the relative increase in anxiety and depression among young people. Although there is no clear answer as to why puberty is starting earlier, researchers cite obesity, a decrease in physical activity, changes in diet, and the presence of chemicals or endocrine disruptors in food and the environment as possible factors.

Timing varies

Puberty tends to start slightly earlier in girls than boys and lasts an average of three years for girls and four to five for boys. The exact timing of a young person's puberty and the amount of growth experienced also vary depending on factors such as maternal history, nutrition, and exercise.

For example, girls may have their menstrual cycles begin at the same age as their mothers. However, the start of menses can be delayed in girls who have a low body weight or engage in extreme levels of exercise.

Global teens

Teens may experience pubertal changes based on their distinct genetics and ethnic background. Cross-cultural teens may have an appearance, body type, and height that is different from their peers. This can serve as a source of stress and concern during adolescence. In Hong Kong, quite a few of the non-Asian expatriate teens I worked with felt much bigger compared to their more petite Asian classmates, which in some cases was a trigger for body image issues and disordered eating. I tell teens that everyone has a unique appearance and pathway through puberty.

The beginning signs

How do you know that puberty is starting? Just take a deep sniff. Believe it or not, stinky feet and increased body odor may be a subtle sign that teen hormones are kicking in. Parents may also notice that their teens are tripping more or appear awkward and less coordinated as they grow. There is a biological reason for this. Teens experience growth first in their extremities such as the hands and feet, followed by the arms and legs, and later the torso and shoulders. This unique growth pattern is one reason an adolescent's body may look clumsy and disproportionate. I remind my teen patients that they will experience growth in spurts and not uniformly, but that it will even out by the end of their adolescence.

For children that are transgender, the changes that occur during adolescence can be particularly confusing and difficult. It is important that the teen explores these issues as early as possible, as should their parents and health providers. If needed, physicians can prescribe hormone blockers that keep the body from releasing estrogen or testosterone at the first signs of the changes – around 10 years old for girls, and 11 for boys. This means the body won't go through the changes that occur during puberty, such as growing facial hair, breast growth, and the start of menstrual periods. The effects of the medication are reversible so teens can decide later to stop taking them and go through the complete changes of puberty.[27] Unfortunately, in some communities, because of lack of resources, cultural norms, and stigma, this may not be easy to do.

PHYSICAL PUBERTAL DEVELOPMENT FOR GIRLS

Changes for girls can be grouped by the early, middle, and late adolescent years. Here's what you as a parent need to be aware of and when you may need to seek further help:

The Early Adolescent Years (10-13)

Puberty for girls usually begins with the development of breast buds or tissue under the nipple. The breast bud may develop on only one side first and may appear as a hard, tender knot under the nipple. Buds can begin as early as age 9 or as late as age 12. Often, as was the case for me, one breast may be larger than the other and feel tender, which may be a cause for concern. The good news is that the tenderness tends to improve, and the breast size even out, within a few months. If your child is overweight, it may look like she is developing breasts. Her breasts may not be made up of real breast tissue yet, but of adipose or fatty tissue. Body odor and a clear vaginal discharge can also start around this time. The development of hair in the armpits and on the pubic area follows. Pubic hair starts as a few straight, dark hairs before it begins to curl and fill in the genital area.

Hair development

A common reason for parents to bring their daughters in for evaluation is when they notice hair on their legs or in their underarms and pubic region and are concerned it is starting too early. It is normal for preteen girls that are from an African American, Hispanic, Persian, or Indian background to develop dark underarm or leg hair alone. This is not a significant issue. However, if they are also developing breasts or pubic hair, they are likely to be in the early stages of puberty. If a child develops breasts or pubic hair before the age of 7 it is worth seeing a health provider as this may indicate a problem with early or precocious puberty.[28]

During puberty, girls may also experience an increase in body fat – around the hips and abdomen, for example – as part of normal physical development. However, in some cases it can be a trigger for body image issues, dieting, and disordered eating. It is important to discuss this with girls and reassure them that their new curves are a very normal and healthy part of puberty.

Menstrual cycles

As mentioned, many girls I work with want to know when their menstrual cycles or periods will come, how long it will last, whether it will hurt, and if it's OK to be irregular. Telling girls what to expect and providing reassurance goes a long way to reducing fears and concerns.

Girls may experience a rapid growth spurt after the development of their breasts and pubic hair. Approximately 2 to 3 years after their breast buds arrive and six months after their main growth spurt, most teen girls will start their periods. Typically, girls experience their first periods at around 12-13 years of age. It is also usually close to the age their mothers started their cycles. Periods may start with a bit of spotting, and cycles may be irregular for the first year.

In general, a menstrual cycle usually lasts from 3-10 days and occurs every 3-5 weeks. If your teen is 13 or older and has no breast development or if your teen is 15 or older and has no menses, it's important to ask your health provider for help. She may need lab tests to make sure that she is developing on schedule. It is normal to have a thin and sticky vaginal discharge at various times. However, if the discharge is thick and clumpy or smelly or causes significant itching or discomfort, it is important to have it checked out by a health provider.

 In clinic, my female patients often ask me when they will stop growing in height. Girls generally have their peak growth spurt before their menstrual cycles and tend to grow 1-2 inches (or 2.5-5 centimeters) after having their menstrual cycles. They usually finish their physical pubertal development about 2-3 years after having breast buds.

The Middle Adolescent Years (14-17)

Girls may experience continued growth of their trunk, legs, and breast shape but overall have a slow-down in the number of physical changes by the middle teen years. They may also start to look – alarmingly, to their parents – like adults at this time. Girls may also have increasing concerns about their body image and appearance.

 One helpful technique to encourage unwilling teens to discuss body changes is to ask them what they see when they view themselves in the mirror. It can be revealing to hear how they feel about their bodies and a useful way to check for body image issues.

The Late Adolescent Years (18-21 and beyond)

By the late teen years, most girls are fully adult in their physical appearance. Some issues related to body image and appearance may improve. However, the teen brain is continuing to develop. Changes in attitudes, interests, and moods are not just due to hormones, but also because of new connections and synapses being made in the brain, as discussed in *Chapter 2.*

PHYSICAL PUBERTAL DEVELOPMENT FOR BOYS

Like females, changes can be grouped into the early, middle, and late adolescent years. Here's what you as a parent need to be aware of and when you may need to seek further help.

The Early Adolescent Years (10-13)

Puberty may start between 9 and 10 years of age in boys. In addition to body odor and smelly feet, the first sign of pubertal changes is testicular enlargement. Often boys and their parents are not aware of these early pubertal changes compared to girls (who have more noticeable changes such as menstrual cycles and changes in breast size).

Along with their testicles getting bigger, boys may notice the appearance of soft hairs around the base of the penis. Over time, the hair will become curlier and coarse, and extend from the pubic area to the thighs. Boys will also develop hair on their underarms, legs, and facial area. At this age, boys may also experience the production of sperm, causing spontaneous ejaculation during sleep (known as nocturnal emissions). This can be embarrassing but is a normal part of development. I tell boys that having occasional sperm production at night is the body's way of ensuring all the hardware is working properly. Teens who are going through puberty at this stage may also start developing muscles. They can gradually begin weight training with supervision to improve posture and strength.

Breast enlargement (Gynecomastia)

Teen boys may also notice changes in their breasts which can be a source of alarm. Tom is a 13-year-old patient of mine in Washington, DC. His father is Peruvian and his mom is American. Tom has had a swelling at his left nipple for several months. At times it is painful. When we meet, he's worried. He tells me he has developed some hair under his arms, has a little acne, and has recently been using deodorant for body odor. When I examine him, he has a small, firm raised area on his left nipple that is slightly tender. He is otherwise in the early stages of puberty with some testicular and hair development.

Tom is likely experiencing breast growth, also known as gynecomastia, because of the conversion of the hormone testosterone to estrogen. In many cases, this will create a breast bud, often on one side alone. Although many of my male patients are worried that they are developing breasts or having cancer, this is usually a benign and a common occurrence in puberty for early to middle adolescent-aged boys. In normal pubertal gynecomastia, the breast development usually resolves in 1-2 years. In some cases, medications or marijuana use can also contribute to gynecomastia. I generally have teens come to see me to consider additional treatment if the breast enlargement has not resolved by late puberty (ages 17-18) or if the size is quite large.

 Obese and overweight boys may have the appearance of breasts, also known as pseudo-gynecomastia, due to excess fatty tissue. In my experience, many obese boys refuse to take off clothes at the gym or in front of others because they are embarrassed about their appearance. I tell obese teens with pseudo-gynecomastia that once their weight decreases, the fatty breast tissue generally will too. For many of my male patients, this is often a motivation to consider losing weight or changing their lifestyle.

The Middle Adolescent Years (14-17)

Teen boys in this age group may continue to notice growth in height, genitals, and weight, in addition to an increase in muscle mass. Facial hair, voice changes, and acne may also develop. Teens at this age may also notice an increased ability to perform sports and exercise.

As opposed to girls, boys tend to have their peak growth spurt closer to 14-15 years old and may continue to develop. They usually complete their physical development by 17 years of age. Teens often ask how tall they will be as adults. I tell them that height is a function of genetics coupled with nutrition and sleep. Also, that it is at night-time that the growth hormone is secreted, which is a good reason for them to turn off their screens and get some sleep.

 A quick rule of thumb to predict adult height for boys is this: Mom's height plus Dad's height + 13 cm (or 5 inches) divided by 2. For girls, subtract 13 cm (5 inches). Living among the Dutch, who are reported to be among the tallest in the world, a teen from a typically South Asian background may feel shorter. It's all relative. Overall, it's best to monitor individual height, weight, and Body Mass Index percentiles and reinforce that their growth pace and final height is truly unique for each teen.

The Late Adolescent Years (18-21 and beyond)

At this age, most young people are fully physically developed. However, there may still be concerns about physical appearance and body image. As noted in *Chapter 3*, although their body may be fully mature, their brains will continue to develop till the mid-20s.

Acne and body odor

Parents may notice that teens suddenly have pimples or strong body odor in adolescence. Glands in the skin are activated by hormones and produce more oil during the teen years which can lead to skin conditions such as acne. Sweat glands in the armpits and groin area are stimulated by pubertal hormones which can lead to increased body odor. Many teens have acne and are self-conscious of it but may not relay this to adults or providers. Be proactive by discussing the many products available to treat acne ranging from topical over the counter creams to prescription oral antibiotics. Note that it is important to treat acne in moderate to severe cases as it may lead to scarring in adulthood. However, if a teen is completely unwilling to use a treatment it is probably not worth forcing them to take medication. As they grow, they may change their awareness and perhaps consider getting treatment.

Strategies for addressing physical pubertal development in girls and boys

Discuss menstrual cycles

It is best to prepare girls by discussing what to expect and how to use pads or tampons. There are great books and online resources available. One parent I know created an emergency kit with a sanitary pad for her daughter to keep in a backpack in the event she had her first period at school.

Check on body image

Teens may put undue pressure on themselves to achieve an idealized and often unattainable appearance. For example, adolescents in many westernized countries often compare themselves to their peers and images they see online, on TV, and in magazines. Feeling occasionally unhappy or self-conscious about how you look is normal during adolescence. However, if your teen persistently feels unhappy about a specific body part, their size, or lack of muscle development, they may be at risk for a body image disturbance and possibly an eating disorder. Parents have an important role in helping teens to develop self-confidence and healthy body image as they grow. Consider counseling early on for teens who may identify persistent concerns with these issues (see *Chapter 10* on body image and eating disorders).

Talk about penile size

One of the more common questions I get from early to middle adolescent teen boys when I discuss pubertal changes in schools is whether penile size matters. Remind your teen that they will each have a unique shape or size and that size has little to do with function. In some cases, there may be teasing at school or other underlying issues. If your son is really worried, you can also see a provider who can do a full exam, review norms for penile size by age, exclude other conditions, and help alleviate concerns.

Reassure teens about development

During puberty, teens are also adjusting to their developing bodies and often compare themselves with their siblings and peers. Give reassurance that your teen is normal, that growth occurs in spurts and can feel awkward. Also, that all kids go through the same changes but at different times and that they will become healthy adults. Try to give straightforward explanations for their physical changes and help them to identify and redirect inaccurate beliefs. Also, encourage your teen to think about their unique strengths and assets that are not related to their appearance.

Model behavior

Although easier to say than do, use every opportunity to be a healthy and mature role model for teens and encourage good habits such as eating and sleeping. As parents you have a unique and supportive role in helping guide kids to feel good about themselves and to have a positive experience despite the many physical changes they may be experiencing during adolescence.

THE BOTTOM LINE: PHYSICAL DEVELOPMENT DURING PUBERTY

- The stages of teen physical development are generally similar for teens around the world, although the exact timing may vary based on genetics, nutrition, and lifestyle.

- Boys and girls will generally progress from the initial development of their genitalia to having growth spurts, an increase in body fat and muscle and, for girls, the start of their periods. Physical development is usually complete by late adolescence (18-21).

- Common concerns include progressing too slowly or too fast through puberty, irregular periods, and having breast development as a boy.

- Parents and caregivers play an important role in discussing normal development, reassuring teens about their concerns, helping them to get evaluations or support if problems occur, and modeling healthy behaviors.

BIG ANSWERS

Common parent questions on teen physical development

1. **How will I know if my teen is going through puberty?**
   The first physical changes in girls are often breast buds and in boys, testicular growth. However, the first general signs of puberty in boys and girls may be more subtle and include mood swings, acne, and body odor (such as smelly feet).

2. **What if my daughter is developing signs of puberty too early?**
   Any girl with pubic hair or breast development before the age of eight may have precocious puberty or puberty that is happening unusually early. It is important to see a health provider if you are concerned changes are happening too early. They will check to make sure there are no other issues, and in some cases stop hormonal changes from occurring till later. Studies show that some girls who develop too early may get teased and have body image concerns. It is important to check in and ask your daughter if she is feeling self-conscious or being teased and to help her feel comfortable with the changes that are happening.

3. **What if my son is late going through pubertal changes?**

    Puberty can be genetic. So, if you or your partner started puberty late, your teen may too. However, if a child is falling off the growth curve, not having intermittent growth spurts, or is not progressing in their pubertal changes, it may be an indication that they need to see a physician for further evaluation. Some teens who develop more slowly than their peers may feel self-conscious about their lack of physical development. According to some studies, this may be particularly an issue for boys. Take time to make sure their body image and self-esteem are doing OK.

4. **What should I do if my daughter doesn't get a period?**

    Pubertal changes can be genetic. However, if your teen is 15 or older and has no period yet, it's important to have your health provider check that she is developing on schedule and there are no underlying issues that could be affecting her menstrual cycles.

5. **How can I help my teen daughter to manage menstrual pain?**

    Pain that occurs during menstrual cycles is linked to a release of prostacyclin, the same substance that causes pain during maternal labor. Menstrual pain known as dysmenorrhea may last one to several days of a period and is relatively common among teen girls. It can usually be treated with over the counter ibuprofen or prescription dose anti-inflammatories. Other treatments may include increasing exercise, and calcium, magnesium, and omega-3 fatty acid supplementation. However, do seek further care from a health provider if the pain is persistent, not responsive to over the counter treatments, or leads to absences from school or work. There are excellent options available to manage dysmenorrhea. Providers can discuss these options, including regular medications to help ease the pain.

6. **Should I encourage my teen to get treated for their acne even though they are not worried about it?**

   Acne in the teen years is very common. It is important to treat acne in moderate to severe cases as it may lead to scarring in adulthood. However, if a teen is completely unwilling to use treatment it is probably not worth forcing them to take medication. As they grow, they may change their awareness and perhaps consider getting treatment. The acne itself could also resolve.

Common teen questions on physical development

1. **Why do I smell?**

   Sweat glands in the armpits and groin area are stimulated by hormones which, coupled with bacteria production, can cause body odor. The best way to handle this is to take regular baths and use deodorant. The good news is that body odor will decrease as you get older.

2. **I am the shortest kid in the class. Will I ever grow?**
Height is genetic. If your father or brother had a late growth spurt, so may you. If you have noticed other signs of puberty, then chances are your growth spurt is still going to happen. If you haven't noticed any changes at all, it may be time to talk to an expert. Either way, it is important to get advice and be confident of where you are in the growth process.

3. **How do I know if my periods are irregular?**
Periods usually happen every 3-5 weeks about a year after they first start. Your periods may be irregular if your cycles are occurring more often than every 3 weeks or less often than every 5 weeks. There are several reasons for periods to stop or to be less regular including weight loss, stress, pregnancy, polycystic ovarian syndrome, and low thyroid levels. If your periods are too frequent, you may also be at risk for irregular cycles and low iron levels. Bottom line, if you are concerned, keep track of your periods on your phone or a calendar for a month or two and discuss your cycles with an adult or your doctor.

4. **Is it OK to masturbate? How much is too much?**
Masturbating is a very normal part of pubertal

development and exploration (for guys and girls) that can be done in the privacy of your own room or bathroom. Although boys often ask me, you will NOT lose all your sperm by masturbating. There is no right amount of time to masturbate, although if you are spending hours doing it, you may want to explore why. You could be at risk for having some irritation and soreness too.

5. Do you need to be circumcised as a boy?

The practice of circumcision varies widely depending on country, culture, and religion. In the US, it is commonly done in the hospital during the first week of life. Likewise, among the Jewish and Muslim communities it is an important rite. However, in many other countries and communities it is not. If you are not circumcised, just be aware of keeping your foreskin clean by washing your penis with soap and water. Also, see a provider if you have any redness, swelling, or irritation.

6. Does the size of your penis matter?

Penises come in different sizes and shapes. Just like noses, hands, and feet, the size and shape of people's body parts vary widely. However, the size of your penis has nothing to do with function and should not be important. If you feel very uncomfortable or worried about your penis size, it may be time to talk to a parent or provider to ensure that everything is OK.

RESOURCES

Books

Guy Stuff: The Body Book for Boys, Cara Natterson, American Girl, 2017

Just the Facts: A Guy's Guide to Growing Up, Melissa Holmes, 3Leaf Press, 2017

The Care and Keeping of You Journal: for Younger Girls, Cara Natterson, American Girl, 2013

Websites and articles

'Common Concerns About Puberty', Anisha Abraham, Center for Parent and Teen Communication, 2018: https://parentandteen.com/concerns-physical-development/

Center for Young Women's Health: http://youngwomenshealth.org/

Young Men's Health: http://youngmenshealthsite.org/

Girlology: https://www.girlology.com/

PUBERTY – EMOTIONAL DEVELOPMENT

5

"Adolescence is a time in which you experience everything more intensely."

Edward Zwick

IN THIS CHAPTER:
- Changes that occur in normal teen behavioral/emotional development during early, mid, and late adolescence.
- Common issues that arise related to teen behavioral or emotional development.
- Tips for discussing puberty and related changes with your global teen by age group.

Pierre is a 12-year-old student from France who moved with his family to the Netherlands a few years back and attends my sons' international school in Amsterdam. I occasionally drive him to and from school activities with my boys as he lives nearby. When I first meet Pierre, he doesn't speak much English or Dutch. He appears shy and a bit reserved compared to his other classmates but is curious and keenly aware of what is going on around him. However, after a year of attending school, he is confident in his new language abilities, is a strong goalie for the school soccer team, and popular among his classmates. He is chatty and animated on our car rides home, discussing his weekly highlights and joining in our silly trivia games.

I don't see Pierre over the summer holidays, but when the school term restarts a few months later, it is obvious that there have been some changes both physically and emotionally. To begin with, Pierre has grown significantly and is nearly my height. He has a spattering of red pimples across his forehead and a hint of facial fuzz on his upper lip. After responding briefly to one or two of my questions about his summer on the car ride home, Pierre abruptly puts on large silver headphones. He then pulls the hoodie of his faded sweatshirt over his head and shifts his complete attention to a glowing laptop screen. The remainder of the ride occurs in semi-silence. The once chatty Pierre now seems aloof and distant. Once we reach his house, he grabs his backpack, mumbles a low "bye," and dashes out of the car without looking back. The sudden shift in Pierre's behavior takes me a bit by surprise. However, his enigmatic switch stands as a firm reminder of the many changes that adolescents go through both physically and emotionally as they age, particularly among boys.

Alongside the physical changes, the global teen may be going through intense emotional development and maturation during puberty. He or she may be questioning their identity, trying to figure out if they are normal, and slowly adjusting to their developing bodies. They may experience more extreme emotional highs and lows. Also, they may feel the need to be alone and exert their independence from adults. Parents in turn may find it awkward and difficult to have discussions with their teens about what they are experiencing during puberty.

BIG QUESTIONS

Common parent questions on teen emotional development

1. My teen is chatty and happy one moment, then angry and irritable the next. What accounts for such big shifts in mood and how should we as parents handle it?

2. How is emotional development different for boys versus girls?

3. When and how should I talk to my teen about the changes that occur during puberty?

4. My teen doesn't want to talk about puberty at all. He says it is all too weird. What should I do?

Common teen questions on emotional development

1. Is it normal to feel so self-conscious about everything?

2. My parents are always nagging me about spending too much time in my room alone or listening to my music too loud. What should I do?

3. Will my mood swings get better when I am older?

4. I am 12 years old and was born a girl but feel more comfortable as a boy. What should I do?

THE EARLY ADOLESCENT YEARS (10-13 YEARS)

During the early adolescent years, teens may be slowly acknowledging their developing body and may feel awkward or self-conscious. They more likely focus on themselves and perhaps their peer group and start to exert a need for independence and privacy, turning more inwards.

As illustrated by Pierre, some boys become quieter and less talkative during puberty. Dr. Cara Natterson is a pediatrician and author of the popular *The Care and Keeping of You* series and more recently of the book about boys and puberty called *Decoding Boys: The New Science Behind the Subtle Art of Raising Sons.* According to Dr. Natterson, puberty starts in boys long before any visible signs appear. However, changing temperaments during puberty can cause confusion for boys and parents alike.

In a phone interview from Los Angeles, California, Dr. Natterson tells me that "we need to talk to our boys about their body changes." Her recommendation, which I agree with, is to use teachable moments such as times when the ubiquitous sexy clothing advertisements on billboards are in view. She suggests that we discuss topics like pornography, sexting, consent, body image, and violence. She also recommends that we respect their 'need' for privacy, monosyllabic conversations, and alone time. Without doubt it is important to discuss with teens the changes they are going through.

Gender norms can affect emotional development starting at an early age. Dr. Bob Blum is a Professor of Public Health at Johns Hopkins University and helped lead a study on gender expectations and early adolescents in 15 countries around the world. According to Dr. Blum, "Even in the most liberal societies, children internalize the belief that boys are strong and independent, and girls are weak and dependent. Children receive these messages regularly from their peers, teachers, parents, religious leaders, and coaches." [29]

Researchers in the study found that in most cultures and countries, by the time girls are 10 years old, they have been taught that their main asset is their physical appearance. As a result, they are concerned about their bodies and other people's attitudes toward them. The authors suggest that these expectations may put girls at higher risk for being victims of violence and boys at increased risk for HIV and substance use. The authors conclude that to have healthier teens, we need to make changes in gender messaging early on. [30]

Concrete thinkers

In addition to turning more inward and needing more space, early adolescents are also more likely to think about their behaviors in present terms (concrete thinking) as opposed to thinking about the consequences of their behaviors (abstract thought). The ability to develop abstract thought occurs during middle adolescence although there are some adults (you may know them) that still think concretely. If your teen is a concrete thinker, ensure that your advice or counseling is presented in terms they can understand.

For example, in my practice, if I have an early adolescent who has tried smoking, I avoid discussing the odds of having lung cancer, which may be a very abstract thought. I do talk, however, about the fact they may have bad breath, their teeth may turn yellow, they could have premature wrinkles, or smoking may affect their peak sports performance. I also get them to calculate how much money they may be spending on cigarettes in a week or month and how much they could save to use for something else like shoes or music (or donating to a good cause).

Privacy please

By around 12-14 years old, teens will be continuing to experience pubertal changes including growth spurts, changes in fat and muscle distribution, acne, and body odor. They may also be more sensitive to social pressures and exclusion. Parents sometimes note there is more door slamming, screaming, and distancing from adults and the growing need for privacy during this time. Sources of conflict that parents and teens tell me about include:

- Homework
- Clothes
- Internet usage
- Music choices and volume
- Friends
- Bedroom
- Choice of leisure activities
- Transitions
- Alcohol and drug use

Mood swings

Hormonal changes may lead to frequent mood swings. Parents may notice that their teen is happy one moment and angry or sullen the next. It is important to realize that your teen may not always be aware of their emotions or be able to control them completely. You as a parent can help guide your teen to feel good about themselves and have a positive experience despite the many emotional changes that may be occurring. You can also provide support regarding optimal sleep, nutrition, and exercise, all of which affect their emotional health.

Sofia is a 13-year-old patient of mine. About a year ago, she moved to the East Coast of the US after living on the West Coast her whole life. During a routine visit, her mom mentions that Sofia is increasingly spending her time in her room on her phone, texting or emailing her friends, or sleeping in. She has been reluctant to participate in family events. In conversations at home, she often tells her parents, "You just don't understand," or, "Leave me alone," occasionally bursting into tears or dashing out of the room and slamming the door. Her parents are concerned about all the changes that are occurring and are wondering whether this is normal adolescence or something else.

When I meet Sofia, she tells me she misses her friends in Los Angeles, California. Also, she resents the family move and wants more independence. She tells me she is worried about her facial acne, recent changes in her body, including her breasts and hips, and navigating friendships at her new school. She denies trying to diet or purge to change her weight, feeling depressed, suicidal, or cutting. Sofia is probably experiencing normal emotional changes during puberty along with the challenges of transitioning to a new school and city. However, Sofia's parents are doing the right thing in talking to a health provider to ensure that there are no other issues that could be triggering the moodiness. They need to check that Sofia feels connected to her new school environment and community and is managing her transition well.

THE MIDDLE ADOLESCENT YEARS (14-17)

Trying things out

Global teens at this age may experience a slow-down in the number of physical changes they are having. In fact, many adolescents in this group may have close to an adult appearance. However, this is a common time, based on normal brain development, for thrill-seeking and experimentation. Some teens may try drinking alcohol, using drugs, or having sex. This is an important time to maintain open communication and to be aware of who your teen's friends are and what they are doing. Studies indicate that teens who maintain close relationships with parents at this age are less likely to engage in high risk taking. Your teen may also become stressed about grades and relationships and set high expectations for him or herself. They may also continue to be very concerned about their appearance. As teens begin to develop a sense of self, they may struggle to discover who they are as an individual. They may go back and forth from a know-it-all attitude or being rebellious, to feeling very unsure about themselves.

Understanding consequences

As teens get a little older, they will also move from concrete thinking to thinking more abstractly and understanding the consequences of their actions. For example, if I drink and drive, I may have a car accident. Not all teens develop abstract thought at the same time. As adults, it is important to assess where your teen may be in this process and how to provide advice and suggestions accordingly.

 Teens mature emotionally at different rates. In my practice, I have seen some teens who are very independent by middle to late adolescence. They're able to manage many of their responsibilities in school, work, and home on their own. Other adolescents have a harder time handling demands and can barely complete assignments or get to school on time without support. Teens with chronic illnesses may be delayed or regress in their psychological development. Know your teen, be their advocate, and work alongside them.

THE LATE ADOLESCENT YEARS (18-21 AND BEYOND)

At this age, most young people are fully physically developed. Teens can now also more easily put the brakes on risk taking and engage in strategic planning. Nevertheless, they may continue to engage in risky behaviors, such as unprotected sexual activity and binge drinking. In fact, I remember being deployed as an active duty US Army pediatrician for a training exercise and having to provide medical care for young soldiers that were in their early 20s in the hot Californian Mojave Desert. On the surface, they seemed very mature and responsible, but off duty they occasionally engaged in behaviors, like doing stunts and dares, akin to late adolescent experimentation. As discussed in *Chapter 3* on *The Teen Brain*, the developing brain often does not mature fully until the mid-20s.

Teens entering early adulthood may also have a stronger sense of their own individuality and can identify their own values. In this time frame, achieving future goals, such as having a job or getting into university, may be key. Friendships and romantic relationships may become more stable. In addition, teens may become more emotionally and physically separated from their family. On a positive note, many re-establish an 'adult' relationship with their parents, considering them more an equal from whom to ask advice and discuss mature topics with, rather than an authority figure. [31]

 There is evidence that Cross-Cultural Kids may be more sophisticated in working with individuals from other backgrounds and cultures. However, they may have a more prolonged adolescence and difficulties with conflict resolution and handling grief, which may affect their emotional development.

HOW TO TALK TO TEENS AND TWEENS ABOUT PUBERTY

Parents are often worried about when to start conversations about puberty, what to say, and who should say it. I remember being at a gathering in London and being begged by a mom (when she discovered I was a teen health doctor) to encourage her husband to talk to their son about puberty and to give him a few pointers on what to say. My advice? It is never too early to start, and conversations should be developmentally appropriate and led by whoever is most comfortable having the discussion. Here is a rough guide as to what to say:

- For 8-9 years old, don't forget to use the correct names for anatomical parts, such as 'penis' instead of 'the thing down there.' Discuss bodily changes that they may have noticed or that may be coming shortly, such as body odor, breast buds, pubic hair, and mood changes.

- For 10-13 years old, who are going through early changes, you may want to prepare them for menses, growth spurts, an increase in curves, acne, and mood swings.
- For 14-17 years old, the fact that they may continue to have body changes. Also, the importance of building positive self-esteem and developing independence.
- For 18-21 years old, the focus should be on their increasing autonomy and making healthy choices.

Keep the conversation open

For some parents, it is probably easiest not to have direct eye contact when discussing difficult or embarrassing topics and therefore having something else to look at may help. I know parents that find it easiest to speak to older teens when they are on a car ride or taking a trip (or for younger kids, when they are in bed and about to sleep). One strategy that I teach parents who are struggling to talk with their teen about a sensitive topic is to discuss those subjects as they occur in a TV show or to ask about their teen's friends instead of their teen themselves. By doing this, all the important issues and discussions come up, but it doesn't put the spotlight on your teen. Finally, it doesn't matter if you are the same gender as your teen or not. What's most important is that you are having the conversation!

Strategies for addressing teen emotional development

Family is key
Although it may not seem obvious, family support is a big buffer for many of the emotional issues experienced during adolescence. Be aware of your own anxieties and anger

when helping teens through conflict situations.

Maintain close bonds

Having regular connections either physically or virtually with extended family and friends can be grounding for global teens. Our kids have enjoyed doing summer camp with their cousins while visiting their grandparents. The multi-generational experience provides a fresh perspective on the issues they may be struggling with as well as a sense of support and validation for their unique abilities and strengths.

Build a village

Your goal as a parent of a teen is addressing the changes that are happening emotionally and providing a stabilizing force for your child. Build a small team of people in your life that your teen can chat with about puberty or adolescence. Examples might be a coach, a teacher, or a religious leader. Says Dr. Jonathan Fanburg, a pediatrician and adolescent health specialist in Portland, Maine: "Encourage extracurricular activities in your teen's life, so this village exists."

Address low self-esteem and perfectionism

Help your teen to develop self-confidence and a healthy body image as they grow. Encourage them to think about their unique strengths and assets that are not related to their appearance or physical power. Encourage them to become involved in activities that foster self-esteem. Also, address perfectionism and emphasize the need to be kind and compassionate to oneself in the face of self-induced pressure to accomplish a task or goal.

THE BOTTOM LINE: EMOTIONAL DEVELOPMENT DURING PUBERTY

- Global teens progress in stages in their emotional development. In early adolescence, teens (10-13 years) are slowly acknowledging their developing bodies and may feel awkward about all the changes. They are also more likely to be focused on themselves and their peer group.

- Middle adolescents (14-17 years) are more likely to engage in experimenting and risky behaviors but will also start to think about the consequences of that behavior.

- By late adolescence (18-21), teens may still be trying things out but are better at considering limits and consequences.

- Parents and caregivers provide a stabilizing force to global teens during all the emotional changes that are occurring in adolescence.

BIG ANSWERS

Common parent questions on teen emotional development

1. **My teen is chatty and happy one moment, then angry and irritable the next. What accounts for such big shifts in mood and how should we as parents handle it?**

   Try to not get on the roller coaster. Realize that your teen may not always be aware of their emotions or be able to control them completely. You as a parent can help guide your teen to feel good about themselves and have a positive experience despite the many emotional changes they may be experiencing. Parents can also provide coaching with sleep, nutrition, and exercise, which affect teen emotional and physical health.

2. **How is emotional development different for boys versus girls?**

   In some ways, development is not that different. Both girls and boys may experience mood changes and emotional highs and lows. However, some teens may also become less talkative during puberty, which may lead to a decrease in parent-teen communication. Use teachable moments and openly discuss topics like pornography, sexting, consent, body image, and violence.

3. **When and how should I talk to my teen about the changes that occur during puberty?**

   It is never too early to start. Use teachable moments and keep the conversation open and developmentally appropriate. For 7-9-year-olds, you can talk about the correct names for sexual body parts. You can also discuss changes that they may have noticed in their body or that may be developing such as odor, breast buds, pubic hair, and mood changes. For 10-13-year-olds, you may want to prepare them for menses, growth spurts, an increase in curves, and acne. For 14-17-year-olds, the fact that they may continue to have body changes and the need for more independence is worth discussing. Finally, for 18-21-year-olds, the focus may be on emotional issues and the continued need for independence.

4. **My teen doesn't want to talk about puberty at all. He says it is all too weird. What should I do?**

   Perhaps start by asking about what your teen's friends are doing or what they have observed around them. Have a conversation when you don't have to look directly at your teen, for example during a car ride or walk together. It can be less intimidating or awkward. Your teen may be facing issues with peers that he or she may not want to talk about. The need for privacy and independence may cause your teen to appear distant. If you push too hard, your teen might feel that you are asking too many questions and pull further away. If you give too much space, you may miss an opportunity to provide support and information. Try to balance privacy with knowing what's happening in their lives.

Common teen questions on emotional development

1. **Is it normal to feel so self-conscious about everything?**
   Believe it or not, brain changes in the teen years may make you feel more self-conscious than at other times. You (and your peers) may spend a lot of time thinking about appearance, abilities, friends, and fitting in. It is very important to have friends and family that accept you for who you are. If you are constantly worried, it may be time to reflect on your strengths and get involved in activities that build your self-confidence. If you like writing, try keeping a journal and keep track of what you are grateful for and what you are worried about. Finally, do also consider reaching out to a trusted adult or friend who can help you through this period.

2. **My parents are always nagging me about spending too much time in my room alone or listening to my music too loud. What should I do?**
   Listening to music and spending time in your room alone are top issues that teens clash with their parents over. However, being alone

and increasingly independent are important parts of becoming an adult. If this is a source of conflict for you, explain to your folks how important having 'alone time' is for you (and teens in general) as you grow. Also see if you can schedule some time with your parents or family so they feel connected.

3. **Will my mood swings get better when I am older?**
Some teens notice that they may feel more ups and downs during the teen years. Very happy one day and sad or irritable the next. The hormones that allow you to develop and grow also affect your emotions. The good news is that as you grow older, these mood swings will improve.

4. **I am 12 years old and was born a girl but feel more comfortable as a boy. What should I do?**
This is a big question and here are a few suggestions. You could try dressing in a more masculine way. You could discuss your feelings with a friend, family member, counselor, or doctor. You could also look for local support groups to help you with the next steps. Finally, there are hormonal supplements a doctor can prescribe that will help stop normal female pubertal changes like having breasts until you are ready to decide about your gender identity and what to do next. Remember, this can be a hard issue to deal with alone, especially if

you don't feel that your peers or family are supportive or if you live in a community where you may not be able to openly discuss these feelings. It is important that you try to talk about these feelings early on with adults that you can trust.

RESOURCES

Books

Decoding Boys: New Science Behind the Subtle Art of Raising Sons, Cara Natterson, Ballantine Books, 2020

Raising Cain: Protecting the Emotional Life of Boys, Michael Thompson and Dan Kindlon, Ballantine Books, 2000

The Care and Keeping of You 2: The Body Book for Older Girls, Cara Natterson, American Girl, 2013

Untangled: Guiding Teenage Girls Through the Seven Transitions into Adulthood, Lisa Damour, Ballantine Books, 2017

Websites and articles

'Support Emotional Development in Teens', Anisha Abraham, Center for Parent and Teen Communication, 2018: https://parentandteen.com/adolescent-emotional-development/

'Young Teens', Centers for Disease Control and Prevention, 2019: https://www.cdc.gov/ncbddd/childdevelopment/positiveparenting/adolescence.html

'Puberty Stages and Concerns', Barbara Poncelet, Very Well Family, 2019: https://www.verywellfamily.com/questions-about-teenage-puberty-3200887

'Teens Health', Kids Health, 2018: http://kidshealth.org/en/teens

6

"Sexuality is one of the biggest parts of who
we are."
Carla Gugino

IN THIS CHAPTER:
- Having a conversation about sexual health with your teen.
- Understanding what to discuss with your children between the ages of 2 and 21.
- Addressing hot topics including healthy relationships, gender and sexual orientation, sexually transmitted infections, contraception, and sexual assault.

We had just moved to the Netherlands from Hong Kong. One rainy summer morning my boys and I decided to set out by bike and explore the local science museum, NEMO. After cycling by the bustling main train station, we arrived at a rather futuristic-looking building overlooking the waterfront. The first three floors had a series of well-conceived exhibits involving subjects like gravity, chemistry, and space. However, it was on our visit to the 4th floor with the clear sign "All about the adolescent" where I was confronted first-hand by the Dutch approach to sexual health.

Here my boys were immediately drawn to a series of interactive exhibits about the teen brain and what happens during puberty. Moving on to the section entitled "Let's talk about sex" there were colorful displays on the science of sexual attraction, the various methods of contraception and (in one curtained off section for older kids) tiny mannequins in various sexual positions. To be honest, I was a bit shocked at the level of openness. Sex education in a children's science museum? *I wondered aloud. However, having now lived in the Netherlands for a few years, I can safely say the exhibit is part of a thoughtful effort to start the discussion about sex health early and make it a normal part of growing up. There is a lot we can learn from the Dutch model.*

Having a crush, relationship, or even breakup are all part of adolescence, together with becoming aware of your sexual or gender identity. Parents often worry about the effect these experiences may have on a teen. As discussed in earlier chapters, teens talking about sex and relationships can be awkward and challenging for parents and global teens. Many teens tell me that they haven't discussed the topic at home. As a physician, I respect that there are a wide range of views on the topic. However, parents play an important role in imparting their values and morals on sexuality to their teens. In a multicultural world, teens are exposed to diverse perspectives (and pressures) related to sexual identity and relationships. What Amsterdam's NEMO museum tells us is that there are always opportunities to have an open and positive discussion about sexual health with teens.

BIG QUESTIONS

Common parent questions on sexual health

1. At what age should I start talking about sexual health with my child?

2. I fear that my kid will learn about sex from their peers or through social media. How can I avoid this and if it does happen, how can I address it?

3. How should we educate our kids about the importance of consent in relationships?

4. When it comes to safe sex, what should we discuss with our college/university-bound teen?

Common teen questions on sexual health

1. When is the right time to have sex?

2. It seems everybody is in a relationship except me. Am I normal?

3. How do I tell my parents that I think I am gay or questioning my sexuality?

4. Can you get a sexually transmitted infection if you only have one partner?

5. What is the best way to prevent getting pregnant?

LET'S TALK ABOUT SEX

We all have different levels of comfort when it comes to discussing sexual health. These comfort zones are based on our own experiences growing up, our parents, family, culture, and community. I remember giving a workshop to a group of parents on "Talking to Your Kids About Puberty and Sex." It was a humid September evening and I arrived early at the auditorium of a school to set up. I noticed that there was a group of nervous looking fathers in suits and ties, huddled around the refreshment table, trying to make small talk. I introduced myself and asked what brought them to the lecture. "Our wives sent us so we can learn how to talk to our boys," was the unanimous response. "We were actually hoping that you could just talk to our kids in school about it so we didn't have to," one dad blurted out. "It's just too scary," announced another. "Please just tell us exactly what we need to say," added a third. We all had a good laugh over how nerve-wracking the topic can be.

What teens say

I get lots of questions from global teens about sexual health that range from the poignant to the funny to the unprintable – all of which reflect the natural curiosity they have on the topic. I often ask young people if they have talked to their parents about sex and, if so, what they discussed. A number say no. Quite a few tell me that they have had conversations at home.

Sometimes, the intentions of these discussions are spot on, but the timing or delivery is a bit off. One of my favorite stories is from a 13-year-old British teen, Chris, from London. He told me he had played football (soccer) for many years at a local club. He was on his way to play a match against a tough rival team on a clear fall evening when his dad pulled the car up next to a busy pub on a Wimbledon street and said, "Son, it is time to talk about the birds and the bees." Chris confided that he had never spoken to his father about the topic before and was absolutely horrified when his dad proceeded to describe in detail how babies are made and why he needed to use protection. Meanwhile, says Chris, "I kept wondering why my dad decided to have 'the talk' right then?" The finer points of the discussion seemed to be lost that evening. The only thing Chris says he could think about was getting to his football match on time.

One of my teen patients at an army base in North Carolina relayed that his father, a military officer, simply left a textbook on human reproduction on the kitchen table for him to read (but never actually talked to him about it).

A female Chinese high school student told me that her mom's only advice to her about sex was, "You are absolutely NOT allowed to consider it till you get into a good university..."

For all the awkward encounters described, there are of course teens who have had very open discussions at home. There are also adolescents who come into clinic with their parents or guardians to have conversations together about negotiating relationships, gender or sexual identity, starting contraception, getting the human papillomavirus (HPV) vaccine, or screening for and treating sexually transmitted infections (STIs). My hope is that all parents and global teens make these connections and have honest discussions about sex and relationships to improve their health and wellbeing.

The global teen context

To define the cross-cultural perspective of sexuality more I spoke to Dr. Maria Trent, a Professor of Pediatrics and an adolescent medicine specialist at Johns Hopkins University in Baltimore, Maryland. According to Dr. Trent, "A key developmental milestone of adolescence is developing a healthy sexuality." She adds that "cross-cultural youth may experience challenges when there are differences between a family's cultural values and expectations about sexuality and that of the culture in which they are now living. As with all things related to adolescence, it is vital for parents to start having conversations early and to understand the landscape of sexual health issues in their current context and how their cultural values are influencing adolescent development."

As Dr. Trent says, culture and community can affect the conversations global teens have with their parents. This can lead to mixed messages when parents are from different cultural or religious backgrounds or when community norms are remarkably different from a teen's own family's values. However, the responsibility to discuss sexual health starts with parents. Sex education may be covered in schools, but the curriculum and depth of teaching vary tremendously depending on where you live, the community's expectations, and local regulations.

I know parents that strongly believe sex should not occur till marriage and others that allow their teen daughter's boyfriend to spend the night. Modern teens need to be equipped with information to navigate the wide range of views on sex that they face while developing their own identity. The good news is that there is excellent evidence that young people whose parents discuss sex and sexual identity openly and honestly with them are more likely to delay having sex, avoid early pregnancy, have fewer partners, and have more positive relationships.

Spring Fever

Reproductive health experts consider the Dutch approach to sex education at school and at home one of the most successful. Here are a few reasons why. Dutch parents tend to openly discuss sexual health and their adolescents' romantic relationships at home. Moreover, since 2012, sex education has been mandatory in Dutch schools, with the Spring Fever curriculum starting at 4 or 5 years old.[32] Kids begin by discussing feelings, knowing what is meant by *good* rather than *bad* touch. At the age of 7, sessions include understanding respect and attraction. By 8 or 9 the curriculum includes same-sex attractions in the discussion (such as some of you may have two mommies). By the ages 10-11 years, Dutch kids learn about changes during puberty, love and dating, men and women in the media, and other topics.

Long Live Love

For teens in Dutch schools, the "Long Live Love" (*Lang Leve de Liefde*) curriculum helps students develop the skills to make their own decisions, form their own values, and consider not only the biological aspects of reproduction but also the value of negotiation skills. A big focus of the message is on having a positive sexual relationship and maintaining open communication.[33] This vastly differs from other countries, where the pervasive attitude is to avoid discussing sex or to tell teens to just say no. The open and early approach both at home and in schools certainly has distinct benefits.

Proof it works

According to the Dutch sexuality research institute, Rutgers, Dutch youth have one of the lowest teen pregnancy rates in the western world and Dutch kids choose to have sex later than teens elsewhere.[34] What's more, most Dutch teens say that their first sexual encounter was positive. By comparison, studies of teens in other countries show that their first experiences were neither positive nor consensual. In fact, in the United States, two-thirds of sexually active teens surveyed said they wished they had waited longer to have sex. Research also shows that most Dutch youths use some form of protection when having sex and have low rates of HIV infection and sexually transmitted diseases.[35] There is much we as parents can learn from the Dutch approach.

Strategies for discussing sexual health

Start early
As I have mentioned before, don't wait to have the conversation! Children are becoming aware of their

emerging sexuality at younger ages than their parents realize. Have an active ongoing dialogue so that your child feels comfortable discussing this topic with you. For example, discuss simple concepts regarding where babies come from with toddlers and progress to more specific and detailed discussions with school age children and teenagers.

Use correct terms

It is important to avoid using nicknames for your child's or teen's sexual anatomy, which may relay the message that these body parts should not be talked about or are embarrassing. I've had teens tell me that they have an issue with their 'chuchewawa' or 'that thing down there.' I've had to remind them there is a proper name for the body part such as their vagina or their penis. I also tell kids that they should be comfortable seeing or touching their own body and genital region, so they know what's normal. Finally, I remind them to tell their parents or doctor if something changes and is concerning.

Use daily experiences to talk about sex and relationships

When with school age kids, for example, if you see a pregnant woman, talk about how a baby grows inside a mother's body. With a preteen, if a couple is dating, talk about healthy relationships and falling in love. With teens, if you watch a movie with a racy or sexualized scene, talk about the importance of building intimacy slowly.

 Using examples from TV, movies, books, or advertising allows questions to develop naturally. In our house, we used a screening of the Bollywood movie *Padman* – about a man that creates inexpensive sanitary pads for low-income women in India – to kick-start the discussion with our early adolescents about where babies come from and the reproductive cycle.

Use transition times

"Times of transition may be great opportunities for conversations that are otherwise awkward but could in these situations come up more naturally," says Dr. Harshita Saxena, an adolescent medicine physician at the Walter Reed National Military Medical Center, in Bethesda, Maryland. "For example, use the time before sleep-away summer camps to discuss the importance of autonomy/ personal space and boundaries. Before middle school to discuss relationships as kids may be exposed to others 'dating' for the first time. Or prior to starting high school/ college to discuss ways to stay safe and engage in a positive relationship as teens may feel more pressure to be sexually active or consider being in a relationship."

Set the stage

Asking teens directly about sex and gender issues without appearing embarrassed or judgmental increases the likelihood that they are willing to discuss personal issues. Listen carefully without interrupting and try to understand your teen's concerns. Ask open-ended questions that allow them to discuss subjects they've been wondering about.

Ask about peers

Asking about what friends or peers are doing may be a less threatening way to start the conversation. For example, start with queries such as, "What do your friends say about sexting?" or, "Is anyone you know dating or having a relationship?" before progressing to more personal questions such as, "What do you think about being in a relationship?" or, "Do you feel pressure to sext, or be sexually active?"

Keep the conversation open

Lois van der Minnen is a medical student and president of a local chapter of Tienerwijs, a group that provides peer to peer sexual health education to secondary school students throughout the Netherlands. Lois is also a cross-cultural teen who was born in the Netherlands, raised in Switzerland and attended high school in the USA. "Keep the conversation open!" she advises. "Let your children or students know that they can come to you with questions about anything. Even if you feel like you've said it a thousand times or that your teen already knows it. It's important to repeat so that they know they can come to you with questions or concerns. They're still going to be embarrassed to talk about certain things so try to lower the barrier for them to seek advice. Furthermore, don't try to tackle all sexual health related topics with one huge loaded conversation. Having one big talk can often make children feel that they can't talk about it at any other time or ever again."

Consider the ABCDs

Sociologist Amy Schalet is author of *Not Under my Roof: Parents, Teens, and the Culture of Sex*. She recommends the ABCD model for approaching teens and sexual health based on her research and experiences living in both the

US and the Netherlands. According to Schalet:[36]

- **A is for Autonomy** or the ability for a teen to make individual choices, to plan, and to be aware of needs. She suggests we ask questions like, "What do you think 'being ready' for sex means?"
- **B is for Building** good, healthy relationships that help lead to positive sexual experiences. Questions we should ask include: "Among your friends, are there couples you admire? What makes that relationship special?" and "Are there couples whose relationship bothers you? What might improve their relationship?" (If romance is too hard to discuss, ask teens about their friendships, instead.)
- **C is for Connectedness.** By keeping that connection strong and the conversation open, parents can have more influence. She suggests parents say, "The most important thing to me is my relationship with you; even if you behave differently from what I want, I want you to feel that you can talk to me."
- **D is for Diversity** or differences. She states that sexuality is an area in which each person is unique. Teens need to acknowledge and respect that there are big differences in the rate of physical and emotional maturation, a wide range of sexual orientations, and a striking diversity of beliefs about sex based on religion and culture. Says Dr. Harshita Saxena: "It is OK for a teen to not be in a relationship, even if it seems like their entire peer group has coupled off. Just as a room full of 13-year-old kids will look incredibly varied in terms of growth and development, so too can their relationship status."

WHAT PARENTS SHOULD DISCUSS AND WHEN

I had a worried Spanish mom write me from Madrid to tell me that she had a 9-year-old son who had been playing video games and had inadvertently viewed pornographic content that popped up on the gaming site. It was a few days before he told her, and his actual description of the pornographic site was vague. She sensed he was very upset by what he saw but didn't have the language to express it. She wanted to know if his sex life would be forever 'damaged' by what he saw and how she could provide positive information about relationships. She also felt very guilty for not having a conversation about sexual health (and porn) with him earlier.

Although this mom is very concerned, her son's revelation could be a great moment to build on and to start having conversations about what he did see and how it affected him. Also, what pornography is and what positive relationships are about. If this seems daunting, here's a bit more to consider.

The layered approach

The 'sex ed' discussion should not be just one 'big talk,' but more of a layered approach with key concepts sprinkled into everyday conversations. It should start early in life, be built over time, and be based on the developmental level, maturity, peer group, and the prevalent culture experienced by your child. Have you ever made lasagna? There are many recipes, but they are all based on layers: pasta sheets followed by a sauce then cheese and more pasta and so on. The dish is not always easy to make and a bit time consuming to do from scratch, but it creates a substantial meal. Here are some tips for creating your own 'sex ed lasagna.' The age groups are approximate. Some kids may be mature enough to have certain conversations even earlier than the age range suggested.

Strategies for talking about sex by age group[37]

- **Ages 2 to 4**
  Kids this age should know the right words for private body parts, such as 'penis' and 'vagina.' Also, where a baby comes from. They won't understand all the details of reproduction – so keep it simple.

- **Ages 4 to 5**
  You could tell kids how a baby is born. For example, "When you were ready to be born, you came out through mom's vagina." A major focus at this age should be creating boundaries and discussing what is and isn't appropriate touch. Your discussion should make clear that kids have a say over their bodies – which helps them stay safe and lays the foundation for understanding consent.

- **Ages 5 to 6**
  You could provide a general idea of how babies are made. "Your mom and dad made you," or "A cell inside dad called a sperm joined together with a cell inside mom called an egg."

- **Ages 6 to 7**
  At this age, you can start to provide a basic explanation of intercourse and relationships. "Sex is one of the ways people show love for each other. When the penis and the vagina fit together, sperm moves through the penis to the egg." It's important to introduce kids of this age

group to the idea that families and relationships can be built in various ways. For example, some kids may have two moms or two dads or several co-parents and caregivers. Also, that gender can be fluid.

- **Ages 7 to 9**
  Kids should know that sex is important and should be positive but is something that you can wait for. According to Cory Silverberg, sex educator and author of *Sex is a Funny Word: A Book about Bodies, Feelings and YOU,* this is also a good time to mention masturbation as something that is normal but should be done in private. Also, that pornography is not a realistic portrayal of a healthy relationship, and to remind them that no one should be touching or hurting them.

- **Ages 9 to 12**
  At this age, talking about sex can go along with discussing puberty. It is important to check and ask how they are feeling about their bodies. Start to have conversations about sexual choices and reiterate your family views. Many kids may be increasingly aware of their gender and sexual orientation. Explain that there can be a range of identities and that it is important to respect other people's choices. This is an age where kids may be online or getting a phone. Remember to discuss Internet safety and digital citizenship. For example, the consequences of sharing nude images by phone, whether they are your own or someone else's.

- **Ages 12 to 14**
  By now, kids are developing their own values, so check in regularly. Discuss the responsibilities of being sexually active, benefits of having the

human papillomavirus (HPV) vaccine, effects of pornography, importance of positive relationships, and consent. Consider Schalet's ABCD model and focus on **A**utonomy, **B**uilding healthy relationships, keeping **C**onnected, and understanding **D**iversity and differences.

- **Ages 14 to 16**
  Teens may begin to start experimenting or thinking about a relationship. It is an important time to review the basics of contraception, preventing sexually transmitted infections (STIs) and pregnancy. Also discuss the effects of alcohol and drugs on consent. Finally, reiterate the core values and beliefs you may have and the importance of developing intimacy gradually and maintaining self-worth in relationships.

- **Ages 16 to 18**
  Understand what peers might be engaging in and keep the conversations open. Encourage them to think about what a positive and healthy relationship means and to develop the skills that will help them to make good decisions. Continue to educate your teens about the effects of drugs and alcohol on consent. Discuss the importance of using protection and getting screened for STIs. Remind them that you will be there if they have any issues or concerns.

- **Age 18+**
  As teens become independent or leave home, empower them to seek care on their own, particularly for STI and HIV screening, pregnancy prevention, and so on.

HOT TOPICS IN SEXUAL HEALTH

Once you feel comfortable starting a discussion and know at what ages to discuss which issues, it is important to be aware of the basics of current hot topics such as having a healthy relationship or protecting against pregnancy and sexually transmitted infections. Here is what you need to know about some of the top issues among global teens, plus strategies to start discussions at home.

Healthy relationships

Teens often ask me questions about how to get into and maintain a romantic relationship, how to get out of a relationship when it is proving not to be a positive one, how to get over a breakup, how not to appear too clingy, and what to do if someone cheats on them. I've also been asked questions like, "Do girls really like sex, or do they do it for their boyfriends?" Adults need to encourage young people to be open about their feelings, stick to their values, create boundaries, and build intimacy gradually. Also, encourage adolescents to ask questions like, "Am I comfortable with this?" or "How do I feel about this?"

Research confirms that when teens have healthy relationships, their first ever sexual experience tends to be more positive.[38] I tell teens that being in a healthy relationship increases their self-esteem and helps them live fuller lives. Warning signs of an unhealthy relationship include being scared, pressured, or controlled. When discussing this, I remind teens that healthy relationships should be based on trust and love and that they need to maintain their self-worth. I reinforce that no one should have sex without their consent and that no means no.

 Some of us have pre-formed notions about the type of partner our teens should have, including their ethnic and cultural background as well as their gender and sexual orientation. Be open to the possibility that your teen will have their own preferences and views. According to the Center for Parent and Teen Communication, shame or embarrassment affects a child or teen's ability to create a healthy and positive sense of their own budding sexuality.[39]

SEXUAL IDENTITY AND GENDER ORIENTATION

Sean is a 17-year-old teen who was born in Brazil and lives in Japan. He knows he is attracted to other men but doesn't feel comfortable disclosing to his parents who have strong views against homosexuality. He has been struggling with his feelings and pretending to be interested in girls so as not to alarm his parents. He does have an uncle who is gay and knows older classmates at university who are in a lesbian, gay, bisexual, or transgender support group. He wants to join the group for some of their events but is afraid of how his parents will respond.

As teens mature, they become aware of their own sexual orientation and gender identity. Many of my teen patients disclose that they knew who they were attracted to by ages 10-11 years. In the USA, nearly 4.5% of high school students self-identify as gay, lesbian, or bisexual.[40] I have some parents who have told me that they think their teen's identity is just a phase and that they will change as they become adults. I tell parents that teens struggle with understanding and being open about their sexual identity during adolescence. However, in many cases, they continue to maintain this identity into adulthood.

In my clinical practice in the US, I ask teens whether they like boys, girls, both, or neither. Increasingly, I have teens who tell me that they are lesbian, gay, bisexual, asexual, or transgender. Many also prefer not to be limited by a category and use broader terms such as queer, asexual, pansexual, gender fluid, or non-binary (those who identify as neither men nor women). Here is a summary of some of the more common terms:[41]

L - Lesbian is a term used to refer to a homosexual female.

G - Gay is a term commonly used to refer to a homosexual male.

B - Bisexual is when a person is attracted to both sexes or genders.

T - Trans is an umbrella term for a transgender (or transsexual) person.

Q - Queer/Questioning: Queer is an umbrella term for those who are not heterosexual or not cisgender (people whose gender identity matches the sex they were assigned at birth). Questioning is when someone is not sure of their identity.

I - Intersex is when a person has a mix of primary and secondary sexual characteristics.

A+ - Asexual is when a person is not sexually attracted to any gender. The plus refers to the fact that this list is always expanding as new identities and orientations are recognized.

I appreciate that this topic can be extremely sensitive in many communities based on religious and cultural values. In fact, I have worked in communities where this topic is taboo. However, it is important to create an environment of respect and understanding. Many of the teens I work with have a classmate or friend or know an adult who identifies as LGBTQIA+. Unfortunately, studies show that those who are not able to disclose are at higher risk of suicide attempts, depression, and anxiety. As such, it is important to ensure that teens have strong connections at home and in the community and are not being bullied or at risk for depression, self-injury, substance use, or sexually transmitted infections. For parents, creating an atmosphere of support and open communication is key, as difficult as that may be.

I encourage teens who are struggling with their gender or sexual identity to find someone they can discuss their concerns and feelings with. Having support from a peer, adult/parent, or support group can be very important. Also, being able to get support via a health provider or counselor if issues or questions continue, particularly if they are contemplating transitioning from one gender to another.

Sexual activity

Factors such as curiosity and peer pressure often drive young people to have sex, including oral sex and intercourse. The age at which teens become sexually active ranges widely according to country and community. I have worked in communities where teens begin sexual exploration by 13-16 years old, and teen pregnancy and STIs are prevalent. I have also worked in places where sexual activity doesn't begin till much later in adolescence, and teen pregnancy outside of marriage (and sexual activity in early or mid-adolescence) is considered highly unacceptable.

Some of the questions I get from young people are: "When is everyone else doing it? Am I behind?" and "When is the right time to become sexually active?" Teens often overestimate what percentage of their peers are sexually active. It is important for them to know there are others that have not been sexually active. The answer as to 'when is the right time?' lies in a teen's (and parents') moral values and beliefs. Also, a clear understanding of what responsibilities come with being sexually active. By having young people consider the responsibilities as part of their process of decision-making (as opposed to simply telling them not to be sexually active), they *are more likely* to make healthy choices. Here are a few of the questions I ask young people for you to consider:

- Are you fully protected against STIs, HIV, and pregnancy?
- Do you know your partner's sexual history?
- Is this a healthy, positive, and mutually consensual relationship?
- Will you feel ashamed, guilty, or uncomfortable later?

In my clinical practice and work in schools, I use role play and scenarios as a way for teens to think about these issues beforehand. One role play involves having a teen girl at a party where she meets a guy she has been interested in. He wants to go further with her sexually. We talk about ways she can comfortably establish boundaries before she is in a real-life scenario. I tell teens they never need to feel pressured. It's always OK to say no and wait. I also encourage them to think about having relationships in incremental stages.

Sexually Transmitted Infections (STIs) and HIV

When I worked at an inner-city school health clinic in Washington, DC, we regularly had teens come in for urine-based testing for sexually transmitted infections (STIs). Over the course of a few days in the late fall, several of the boys for the school football team came in for screening and their test results came back positive for chlamydia, a bacterial sexually transmitted infection. Our school nurse knew all the teens and more importantly who they were dating. She invited the partners of the boys to come in for testing. We had more positive results. Our nurse then mapped out who else may have had contact with them and contacted them as well. Everyone received antibiotic treatment in the clinic as well as information on using protection and safe sex. We also set up a time to repeat test all the students in a few months to ensure the STI had been cleared up.

Although this situation is unusual and you may not always know who is having a relationship with whom, I use this story to illustrate the importance of discussing STIs with teens. Teens should know that it is healthy to ask about their partner's sexual history including STIs, to take steps to protect themselves from infections, and to get screened. Also, that more common STIs include chlamydia, gonorrhea (both of which are bacterial infections), human papillomavirus or HPV (which causes genital warts and cervical cancer), herpes and HIV/AIDS.

 Does oral sex count as sex? I have had several teens ask me this. I have others tell me that they feel oral sex is safer than other forms of sexual activity. I tell adolescents that although they can't get pregnant from oral sex or lose their virginity in the traditional sense, they can get infections such as gonorrhea and herpes. I highly recommend talking to kids about the pressures to give and receive oral sex and the risks that may come with it.

I recommend that teens receive the HPV vaccine before they become sexually active. Also, I tell teens that if they suspect an infection (because they have symptoms such as having pain, burning, or discharge), their partner is diagnosed with one, or they have begun a relationship with a new partner, it is important to be screened. In most cases, teens won't be able to 'see' the STI by just looking at theirs or the partner's genitals. Also, the 'word' of their partner that they have no infection may not be a good enough reason to stop using condoms as their partner may not know their status. Finally, in many cases, boys may not have symptoms at all, even though they are infected.

To be tested for chlamydia or gonorrhea, male teens can give a urine sample. Female teens can also give a urine sample, but if they have any vaginal discharge or pelvic pain, they may need to have more specific tests. There are blood and saliva tests for HIV. Also, blood tests for syphilis, herpes, and hepatitis B.

If a teen is positive for a bacterial infection such as gonorrhea or chlamydia, there are many quick and effective antibiotic treatments available to clear the infection. However, some infections such as HIV and HPV are lifelong, and treatment will only decrease symptoms rather than eliminate the infection. Also, teens need to ensure that their partners are treated at the same time as otherwise they can get the same infection back (which unfortunately occurs quite often).

Of course, the best way to avoid STIs is to use condoms or other barrier methods, have a long-term monogamous relationship, or abstain altogether. Encourage teens to have conversations with their partners about their sexual history, getting tested, and using protection. Young people often want to know where they go for screening and testing and at what age they can go without a parent. In fact, one of the biggest barriers to care for teens, and a reason for delay in treatment, is their concern about discussing these issues with an adult or parent and finding appropriate, teen-friendly health services. I encourage parents, caregivers, and educators to find out about the resources and rules in their community and to talk to teens about where they can go. Also, to ensure that they can come to a parent or an adult if they have a question or concerns about an STI.

Contraception

It is important for teens to have a basic understanding of contraceptive options even though they may not be contemplating sexual activity. Some of the contraceptive methods may also have other benefits such as regulating heavy periods, acne, or pain with periods. In most cases, a teen will need to see a health provider to discuss the ideal method, risk factors, and possible side effects and to start taking contraception. Below is a quick list of options, but be aware that these options do not offer protection against STIs and should be used alongside a condom to prevent infections. Depending on the community, parents will need to go with an adolescent to start contraception.

- **Combined oral contraceptive pills (birth control)**
  Are highly effective at preventing pregnancy if taken daily Other benefits include less acne and menstrual pain. Also, are less expensive compared to other methods. However, there may be estrogen related side-effects such as nausea and in rare cases blood clots. When using, it is best not to miss more than 1-2 days in a row.

- **Birth control patch**
  Sticks to the skin and releases estrogen and progestin into the bloodstream. A new patch is applied once a week for three weeks, followed by one week off. The patch is like a pill in terms of side effects and benefits but needs to be remembered less often.

- **Vaginal ring**
  Is like a patch in terms of hormonal effects. The ring is placed in the vagina for three weeks continuously followed by one week with no ring.

- **Implant**
  Is a thin rod with progestin that can be placed in the arm by a provider and gives pregnancy prevention for up to three years.

- **Depo-Provera**
  Involves the injection of progestin every three months. It is highly effective at preventing pregnancy but can be associated with menstrual irregularities. It requires an office visit every three months.

- **Intrauterine device (IUD)**
  Is a small t-shaped piece of plastic that goes into the uterus. It lasts for 3 to 12 years depending on the type and is increasingly popular among adolescent females because of ease of use. IUDs need to be inserted and removed by a provider but are a very effective form of protection with a low failure rate.

- **Condoms**
  Are effective at preventing pregnancy and STIs although the failure rate can be high compared to other methods, especially if not used properly. It is accessible and low cost. It encourages male involvement which can be useful, but also a challenge in some contexts. Especially with new partners, women should take control themselves and insist that a condom is used.

- **Emergency contraception**
  Is a safe and effective backup method to prevent pregnancies following unprotected sex. It is also used in the event of a sexual assault. Can be used up to five days after unprotected sex although it is best to use within 72 hours of unprotected sexual activity. The main side effect is nausea.

Sexual Assault

Sexual assault is defined by the US Department of Justice as "any type of sexual contact or behavior that occurs without the explicit consent of the recipient."[42] According to US data, the majority of people who are sexually assaulted are first assaulted before the age of 25.[43] In discussing this topic, it is important for parents to talk to their teens about healthy relationships, boundaries, and consent. Remind teens that they have the power to stop at any time and say no. Also that sex without consent is assault. It is never appropriate to approach someone for sex when they are in a vulnerable position or otherwise unable to consent.

One of the questions I get from teens is, "What if both boy and girl are drunk and have sex – is that rape?" Alcohol and drugs can distort perceptions, lower inhibitions, and affect decision-making. The following are some key messages regarding substance use and sexual health that you can discuss:

- If your teen, their partner, or a friend is incapacitated by alcohol or drugs, they *cannot* give consent.
- Not only do teens have the power to say no, but they also have the responsibility to intervene as a bystander if they see someone else in a situation that makes them vulnerable or is even facing assault.
- Most sexual assaults occur among acquaintances, not strangers.
- It is important for teens to trust their instincts and to avoid relationships with those who drink heavily, use drugs, act aggressively, or treat them disrespectfully.

In my clinical work, I regularly ask my teen patients if they have ever been touched or forced to do something in a sexual way without their consent. Sadly, I have young people disclose a variety of situations when asked. For example, I had an 18-year-old male teen in Hong Kong who told me that when he was six years old, he was touched inappropriately by an uncle. A 14-year-old teen in DC told me she was at a school party when an older classmate forced her to have oral sex.

I tell teens that it is important to know it is not their fault and to talk to someone about what happened instead of keeping it a secret. Ideally, they should meet with a counselor or therapist to ensure it doesn't affect their future relationships or self-esteem. Obviously, if an assault has occurred more recently, it is important to get medical screening to rule out infections as well as start counseling as soon as possible. Often teens are afraid to disclose to parents or are in denial about what has happened.

Strategies for discussing hot topics in sexual health

Reassure teens

Kids often worry whether they're normal. Some teens will become interested in the opposite sex while others may wonder whether they are gay or bisexual. Reassure your child or teen that kids at the same age mature at different rates. Explain what happens during puberty such as changes in body shape and size and sexual attraction. Remind them that above all you love them and that they are special.

Teach the importance of respecting choices

"The answer to a partner can change at any point of an intimate interaction and needs to be respected," says Dr. Saxena. "What started as 'yes' can change into 'no' and there should be no confusion. Teens should know that even though they felt a certain way at the start of an interaction, it is perfectly within their right to change their mind." The popular 'Consent: It's Simple as Tea' YouTube video (see *Resources*) is a great way to explain consent.

Get outside support

"Using an open-heart approach and some creativity, parents can initiate a series of conversations in a non-threatening way that allows time for the adolescent to ask questions and share concerns," says Dr. Trent. She also recommends ensuring teens have the chance to meet with providers who are skilled in caring for adolescents and can serve as a key source of support.

THE BOTTOM LINE: SEXUAL HEALTH

- Discussing sexual health can be tough. It is important for parents to have open conversations with teens, build knowledge among their children gradually, and be aware of the hot topics and how to discuss them. To start conversations, consider using everyday moments.

- For young children talk about the proper names of their anatomical parts, good versus bad touch, and the safe use of the Internet or mobile phones.

- With teens, it is important to be aware of peer group behavior and to help them avoid feeling pressured. Enable them to navigate issues like healthy relationships, consent, and sexting. Understand that they can struggle with gender identity and orientation.

- For teens, your discussions should be about the importance of having positive sexual relationships, prevention of sexually transmitted infections and HIV, and a basic understanding of contraception and condom use. Also, what to do if there is a sexual assault and the effects of alcohol and drugs on consent and decision-making.

- Finally, consider the ABCD model, which stands for a teen's **A**utonomy to make individual choices, **B**uilding healthy relationships, creating **C**onnections, and understanding **D**iversity.

- It is never too early to start talking about sexual health!

BIG ANSWERS

Common parent questions on sexual health

1. **At what age should I start talking about sexual health with my child?**
   The 'sex ed' discussion should not be just one 'big talk,' but more of a layered approach with key concepts sprinkled into everyday conversations. It should start early in life (by 2-4 years of age) with using the correct names of body parts and the importance of good touch versus bad touch. The discussion should be built over time and be based on the developmental level, maturity, peer group, and the prevalent culture experienced by your child.

2. **I fear that my kid will learn about sex from their peers or through social media. How can I avoid this and if it does happen, how can I address it?**
   First, don't wait for your teen to learn from his peers or social media. Use daily experiences such as viewing an advertisement or watching

a movie to start a discussion. Also discuss it directly with your teen without appearing embarrassed or judgmental. If an issue does occur, for example, he or she sees porn at a friend's house and later tells you, ask about it and use it as a teachable moment. Let your teen know that he or she can come to you with questions about anything. Finally, if you don't feel comfortable having this discussion then enlist a trusted adult to help you.

3. **How should we educate our kids about the importance of consent in relationships?**

You should explain that it is important to establish boundaries early on in a relationship and that consent is very important. Remind teens that no means no and it is better to ask than to assume. Also, alcohol and drugs can affect decision-making. Finally, when someone is drunk or otherwise incapacitated, they simply cannot give consent.

4. **When it comes to safe sex, what should we discuss with our college/university-bound teen?**

Your teen will meet peers with a wide range of beliefs and experiences regarding sex and relationships in college and university. Encourage your teen to think about what a positive and healthy relationship means and use this as an opportunity to reiterate your views and morals. Also discuss the importance of handling pressure in a relationship and being *clear about boundaries. Review the effects of drugs and alcohol on consent. Ensure they know where they can seek care, especially in the case of sexual assault. Empower them to get services and screening on their own, particularly for STIs and HIV, and pregnancy prevention. Finally, let them know they can come to you (or another trusted adult) if they ever have questions or concerns.*

Common teen questions on sexual health

1. **When is the right time to have sex?**
   This is a very common question that kids ask. The right time is based on your cultural, religious, and moral values. Also, when you feel you are ready to take on the responsibilities that come with having sex, including using protection, knowing your partner's history, and ensuring you are in a positive, consensual relationship. Bottom line, you should never feel pressured to be sexually active, and it is always OK to wait (and to say no).

2. **It seems everybody is in a relationship except me. Am I normal?**
   It may seem that everyone else is in a relationship or has become sexually active. However, there are more kids just like you than you realize. Be aware that part of being a teen is developing and maturing at your own pace. As is answering questions like who

am I attracted to (if at all) and what is my gender identity? Don't feel pressured to make decisions or be in a relationship before you are ready. Finally, speak to a good friend, counselor, or adult if you are really struggling with these issues to give you some additional perspective and support.

3. **How do I tell my parents that I think I am gay or questioning my sexuality?**
Coming out to your parents can be hard and scary. Of course, this depends on the cultural context and your parents' values. Prepare a time to speak to them honestly. Tell them the key points, remind them that you love them, and answer questions they might have. Know it will take time for them to accept the news. Also, be aware that your parents may have a hard time understanding your feelings or supporting your views, especially if they have very strong religious/moral views on the matter. If so, you may want to seek additional help from a friend, school counselor, physician, or a trusted adult in your life.

4. **Can you get a sexually transmitted infection if you only have one partner?**
Yes you can, since you inherit your partner's history of STIs. That is why it is important to have an open conversation about their sexual history, particularly about infections, and to consider getting routine screening with each new partner.

5. **What is the best way to prevent getting pregnant?**
Not having sex is, of course, the surest way to

prevent pregnancies. However, if you are sexually active, you should consider the right form of birth control for you and your partner to prevent pregnancy. Condoms are great for preventing STIs but are not 100% effective against pregnancies. There are many other kinds of contraception available including pills, shots, and patches. In general, a long-acting method such as an intrauterine device or an implant is most effective (particularly if you have a hard time remembering to take something on a regular basis). As a final note, all these methods protect against pregnancy alone. It is very important to use a condom to prevent STIs at the same time.

RESOURCES

Books

Boys & Sex: Young Men on Hookups, Love, Porn, Consent, and Navigating the New Masculinity, Peggy Orenstein, HarperCollins, 2020.

Not Under My Roof: Parents, Teens, and the Culture of Sex, Amy Schalet, University of Chicago Press, 2009

Sex is a Funny Word: A Book about Bodies, Feelings, and YOU, Cory Silverberg, Seven Stories Press, 2015

Would I Have Sexted Back in the 80s? Allison Ochs, University of Amsterdam Press, 2019

Websites and articles

'Start Sex Education Early, Definitely Before Puberty', Robie H Harris, *The New York Times*, 2013: https://www.nytimes.com/roomfordebate/2013/05/07/at-what-age-should-sex-education-begin/start-sex-education-early-definitely-before-puberty

'Teens' Developing Sexuality', Center for Parent and Teen Communication, 2018: https://parentandteen.com/healthy-approach-developing-sexuality/

'Sex Education in the Netherlands', Anisha Abraham, Amsterdam Mamas: https://amsterdam-mamas.nl/articles/sex-education-netherlands

'Tienerwijs', IFMSA-NL: https://ifmsa.nl/projecten/tienerwijs

'Outspoken Sex Ed': https://www.outspokeneducation.com/

'Consent: It's simple as tea': https://www.youtube.com/watch?v=pZwvrxVavnQ

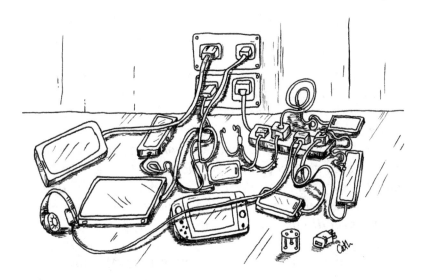

"The creation continues incessantly through the
media of man."
Antoni Gaudí

IN THIS CHAPTER:
- Addressing problematic interactive media use and social media.
- Managing smartphone usage, sexting, and gaming.

Growing up in the US in the early 70s, my childhood memories of media use are of watching a black and white TV with three working channels, located in our dark, slightly dank basement. There was a weekly Friday evening show with Donny and Marie Osmond that my sister and I looked forward to along with the occasional Saturday morning cartoons. Aside from that, we didn't often venture down to the basement to watch TV. I talked to friends on a landline rotary phone. The kind that you had to wait for each number to spin back to the start before you could dial the next one. My parents wrote regular letters to keep my grandparents in India informed of our lives and used telegrams if there was an emergency. My exposure to computers as a teen was at school via enormous desktop machines housed in an air-conditioned room. Social media, smartphones, and remote controls were non-existent. What's more, I don't recall my parents ever discussing media use with us.

So much has evolved since we were kids. My boys now use iPads for school homework, watching YouTube, and listening to music. They read books on their Kindles and use smartphones to check the news, game scores, weather, and social media. They know how to find the newest release on Netflix, and our cable channel provides a steady stream of shows, games, and news in 10 different languages. At school, my boys get classes on digital citizenship and create Google documents and stop motion animation films in the blink of an eye. Our landline is obsolete and most of our conversations occur via WhatsApp, text messaging, and email. We get news, both good and bad, in seconds.

As adults, we are also constantly negotiating the use of electronics with our kids. Given our own limited adolescent experiences with digital media – and the constant changes – many of us don't feel fully equipped to provide guidance to teens on the subject. As a result, screen time, video games, and social media have all become hot topics. In fact, it is one of the teen issues that I am asked about the most as a physician. It is important to know what's out there and how to strike the right balance.

BIG QUESTIONS

Common parent questions on addressing media use

1. What is the right amount of screen time?

2. How should we discuss sexting with our teen?

3. What effect does constant use of social media have on girls' body image and self-esteem?

4. How do we get our son to stop playing video games all the time?

Common teen questions on addressing media use

1. My friend is constantly on his computer. How do you know when someone is addicted?

2. Why is sexting an issue if it is a personal choice between two people?

3. Is it bad to watch porn?

4. Is it OK to listen to music when I am doing my homework? My parents think I get too distracted. I think it helps me to focus. What should I do?

DIGITAL NATIVES

Our new generation of teens are digital natives. And as such, Cross-Cultural Kids often become brokers of media and language. They help to bridge the gap for their less digitally and language savvy parents/family members in a new country or community. According to a United Nations Children's Fund (UNICEF) global survey, children and adolescents under 18 years represent 1 out of 3 Internet users worldwide.[44] In fact, young people are the most connected of all age groups. Not only are teens connected but they also use screens more than ever. According to a study done by Common Sense Media, American preteens spent 4 hours and 40 mins while teens spent 7 hours and 22 mins on screen time each day. In addition, 7 out of 10 kids have a smartphone by the age of 12, and 2 out of 3 are on social media every day.[45] In another study by the US-based Pew Research Center, nearly 45% of teens surveyed say they use the Internet 'almost constantly' while 90% go online multiple times per day.[46]

Jonathan is a 14-year-old teen who moved from Melbourne, Australia, to Hong Kong. He spends several hours a day on his iPad and smartphone. During the week, he does Internet searches for school projects, plays music on Spotify, and watches YouTube videos of other kids playing video games. He also stays connected with his new classmates via WhatsApp and Instagram. On weekends and holidays, he is allowed more time to game and Skype, and he plays on his devices with his old friends in Sydney for 3-4 hours per day. His younger sibling thinks he spends way too much time in his room. His parents want him to stay connected with his friends but are also worried about the amount of time he spends behind screens. They want to know what the benefits and challenges of media use may be, and how to create better guidelines at home.

My firm recommendation to Jonathan's parents is that they need to take an informed and nuanced approach to his media use. As his parents, they have the important role of creating boundaries, relaying expectations, and modeling healthy behaviors. More importantly, they need to start having regular discussions with Jonathan about what he is using and what's out there. I will explain this more in this chapter.

The benefits of media use

There are many benefits to being online and using digital technology. As we learned during the COVID-19 pandemic, being connected allows access to online learning and educational opportunities. Teens say that media use such as gaming can be a form of relaxation and entertainment. It is also an important way for young people to stay connected with peers and family members especially if they are unable to see them because of school closures or travel restrictions.

Digital tools such as apps and text messaging can be used to promote healthy behaviors. For example, in a research study I helped conduct in Hong Kong, we used an online weekly curriculum along with regular cell phone text messaging to connect with obese and overweight teens and help them to maintain their weight management goals. In my experience, being online can also connect young people with disabilities or who are otherwise marginalized with others who have similar needs. Being online (and using a reputable site) can be useful for teens who are trying to seek medical or health information but aren't able to get information readily at school or at home or are embarrassed to ask. Sites that give information on puberty or sexually transmitted infections can offer useful advice to kids that have concerns. Finally, cell phones can be an important way for parents to communicate with kids and ensure they travel safely from school, activities, or work.

 There are many young people who don't have access to a screen at all. In fact, around one-third of the world's youth (around 346 million) are not online, many of whom reside in developing countries. According to UNICEF, lack of access can hinder kids' ability to participate in an increasingly digital economy.[47]

The challenges of media use

University College London researchers Dr. Russell Viner and Neza Stiglic examined the harm of screen time versus its benefits by systematically reviewing studies on teens and screen time. They found that higher levels of screen time were strongly associated with obesity, an unhealthy diet, depressive symptoms, and poor quality of life.[48] Digital technology also impacts vision, physical activity levels, and mental health negatively. For example, the rate of near-sightedness in children has increased dramatically in the past 40 years as media use has gone up.

Screen time can affect physical activity levels too. In my work with obese and overweight patients, I often advise them to cut back on the amount of sedentary time spent on TVs, gaming consoles, and screens to increase their exercise time. Finally, social media may also be associated with an increase in symptoms of anxiety and depression.

The 3 Cs

While researching the handling of media use, I met Dr. Jessica Piotrowski, Director of the Center for Research on Children, Adolescents and the Media at the University of Amsterdam and co-author of *Plugged In: How Media Attract and Affect Youth*. Dr. Piotrowski is a passionate researcher and knowledgeable media expert. During our meeting, she set out to debunk the need to quantify screen time.

"Time is less relevant compared to content and actions," she said. "In fact, you can cyberbully someone online in just three minutes flat but learn from an in-depth educational show lasting over two hours." Her suggestion correlates with the work of American researcher Lisa Guernsey. Lisa discusses the 3 Cs: Content, Context, and Child in her TEDx talk.[49] She recommends we focus on the *content* of what kids are seeing, the *context* of their interactions with the media and understand our *child* enough to know which forms of media enrich them.

In reviewing your teen's screen time, here are some issues to explore:

- What are your teens viewing?
- What is the context for their use?
- What is your teen like?
- Is he or she still connecting with others?
- Is your teen still maintaining friendships and grades, and sleeping well?

Knowing the answers to these questions can help you to decide the right balance for media use.

Problematic interactive media use (PIMU)

Dr. Michael Rich, a pediatrician, media expert and Professor at Harvard University, who is known as "The Mediatrician," recommends that we consider the term Problematic Interactive Media Use or PIMU instead of Internet addiction. According to Dr. Rich, addiction is a medically inaccurate description and its stereotype is stigmatizing, discouraging parents and youth from seeking clinical care. PIMU most commonly manifests as excessive use of video games, social media, pornography, and online information-seeking. The most reliable sign of PIMU is a fixation with screen media. However, symptoms include sleep deprivation, irritability when not online, a decrease in school performance, relationship conflicts, and social withdrawal. Children and teens suffering from PIMU may also suffer from other conditions, such as attention deficit hyperactivity disorder (ADHD), social anxiety, depression, or substance use.

Dr. Rich recommends that parents look for warning signs, such as spending time with screens for long periods, lying about or hiding the amount of time spent, or using media to escape from other issues such as anxiety. He suggests that adults create expectations of healthy media use for specific purposes (such as homework), balanced with time for offline activities.

Says Dr. Piotrowski: "One of the biggest reasons for media use challenges is inconsistent parenting and delivery of consequences." In many cases, the responsibility is on parents and adults to establish and maintain boundaries. Bottom line, we need to look at content and quality and serve as media coaches. Here are some additional recommendations to consider:

Strategies for handling media use

Model tech-free behavior
This can be difficult, but adults need to model behaviors and spend time playing or being involved in non-digital pursuits with kids. Children and teens often demonstrate the same behaviors they see their parents or other adults engaged in around them. In fact, according to recent research, more and more kids are sleeping next to their mobile devices – just like their parents. I tell families to keep meals and social gatherings tech free. Also, to charge devices outside of the bedroom overnight and make devices less accessible in general.

Autonomy-supportive conversations
Dr. Piotrowski suggests that when we discuss media use with kids we need to work on 'autonomy-supportive' conversations. She says, "We need to help kids to develop the tools to be independent users but have conversations to give them skills to do so. In discussing this we need to go over expectations for use and issues to be aware of. Just

like kids have rules and contracts for other issues such as driving or when to come home at night, we need to do the same with media use."

Social media contracts

One way to enforce rules is for parents and caregivers to act as 'coaches' and create a media contract to outline the specifics of what is and is not acceptable. Rules may include no smartphone use after a certain time at night or turning off the phone while sleeping. You can find some good examples from the American Academy of Pediatrics and Common Sense Media (see *Resources*). In our home, my husband and I have drawn up individual contracts with each of our boys regarding the use of electronics, locations, and so on. Although not foolproof, contracts can be a good starting point for rules and boundaries.

Get buy-in

For regulations to be effective, parents must keep in mind that teenagers want to be treated like adults. Creating a joint agreement improves the likelihood that teens will feel a personal commitment to the contract. A 'joint agreement' should also include things the adult will do to keep the agreement effective. Adolescents are more likely to keep an agreement and start to regulate their own behavior if they have some independence in the decision-making.

SOCIAL MEDIA

According to the National Center for Health Research, social media allows teens to make new friends, exchange pictures, develop interests, and try out new forms of self-expression. When youth use social media, they can learn basic skills that are important for day to day functioning.[50] Teens are hard-wired for socializing, and social media makes it easy to do. Teens who struggle with social skills, or who don't have direct contact with others, can benefit from connecting through this medium.

Teens around the world tell me their favorite social media sites include YouTube, Instagram, Snapchat, Twitter, and TikTok. They also tell me that fewer kids are using Facebook than before (although many adults continue to do so). A 2018 Pew Study confirms that nearly 85% of US teens use YouTube, 72% Instagram, 69% Snapchat, and 51% Facebook, followed by Twitter, Tumblr, and Reddit.[51]

As a quick refresher, YouTube allows users to share original videos. Snapchat allows users to share photos and events that disappear after 24 hours. This is often used by teens who don't want their messages around for a long time (although in the era of screenshots, teens need to be reminded that images and posts can still be saved and forwarded). Instagram lets users share their experiences via photos or videos while Facebook lets users share photos, videos, and articles. TikTok is a social media platform that allows users to share short videos and live events. Finally, Twitter has the shortest messaging capability; it allows users to share their thoughts and personal updates in 280 characters or less.

Despite the constant presence of social media in their lives, there is no clear consensus among teens about what they think regarding its impact. According to the Pew Study, nearly 45% of all teens surveyed believe social media has neither a positive nor negative effect on people their age. Meanwhile, 31% say social media has had a mostly positive impact, while 24% describe its effect as mostly negative.[52]

Social media and body image

According to the National Center for Health Research, the number of social media platforms used and how often can contribute to social isolation, even if teens aren't physically isolated. Researchers at the University of Pittsburgh found a correlation between time spent scrolling through social media apps and negative body image. Those who had spent more time on social media had 2.2 times the risk of reporting eating and body image concerns, compared to their peers. Finally, a small study of teens aged 13-18 by the UCLA Brain Mapping Center found that receiving a high number of Likes on posted photos showed increased activity in the reward center of a teen's brain. Teens are influenced to like photos, regardless of content, based on high numbers of Likes. It goes without saying that for many teens it feels good to be 'liked.'[53]

A teen's perspective on social media

To learn more about teens and social media, I spoke to 11th grade high school student Aspen van der Hoeven from the International School of Amsterdam in the Netherlands. Aspen chose to do a school project on how social media affects people, especially teenagers. Says Aspen, "The inspiration for the topic came from years of experience on social media and what I have heard from peers." She adds, "The real question is, how much can parents realistically control social media use – and will regulations and restrictions be effective in driving teens' behavior? Parental restrictions can make social media even more attractive for the child and in some cases could even add to the addiction. However, I also believe that parents should be involved in their kids' online activity. My parents have their own social media profiles that give them access to see whatever I post, and it has motivated me to only post PG rated content..."

Parents and social media

Many parents don't fully comprehend social networking sites. A Swiss father disclosed that his 17-year-old daughter living in Zurich was taking a renewed interest in family holidays with them. She asked if they could choose hip locations and played a big role in organizing them. She also spent quite a lot of time taking selfies in picturesque spots. All of this was chalked up to teen behavior until they traveled to a country where they had limited Internet access. Suddenly she was texting friends to post on her behalf. The parents became concerned when she started receiving multiple packages a week at home. After repeated queries, they learned that she had become an Instagram influencer and amassed a regular following. As a teen influencer, she was posting on a regular basis, often with simple products that sponsors sent her. The father decided to Google "my daughter is an Instagram influencer" and found posts from other concerned parents. He ended up creating his own account and following her. He discovered that her site was open to the public and she had posted a few images in bikinis from their family holidays. He was concerned about quite a few older male followers and decided to have a long discussion with his daughter about maintaining a public site, older strangers as followers, and the need to be constantly posting. Eventually, she agreed to make her site private, allow her parents to check in regularly, not post any identifying information, and to stop endorsing products or being an influencer.

Teens are not always good at self-regulation and are susceptible to peer pressure. Unfortunately, many teens will also be unsupervised in the online world and are at risk of issues like cyberbullying. As Aspen and the Instagram case outlined, balanced parental involvement both online and offline is key.

My own experience

For full disclosure, I was the only mom on my son Nick's class WhatsApp group for a while. I was the only parent because most of his classmates at the time had phones by 11 or 12, except him.

Nick could read his messages on my phone and respond to his classmates but through me. Most posts I happened to see were innocuous. However, there were a few from a classmate that were more concerning in nature. Overall, I would not recommend reading all your teen's posts given the sheer volume they create in a single day. (One holiday I counted over 150 daily.) However, our 'joint' account led to some healthy discussions about what was appropriate to post and what was not.

My take home from this experience? Our role as parents is to provide a clear sense of values and implement safeguards for our kids. We need to teach them to be responsible and use good judgment when it comes to creating online posts in social messaging environments. Also, that a person's relationships and reputation can be affected by comments made online.

 **Sharenting** is the practice of sharing photos and other personal information about our kids. According to author and researcher Dr. Jessica Piotrowski, many parents post pictures of their kids on Facebook, WhatsApp, and other sites without checking if that's OK with their children first. To build trust and foster independence, she suggests that parents check in with their teens. It helps to model the practice of asking for permission when sharing pictures of others in the future.

Strategies for addressing social media use

Be aware of legal minimum ages
The minimum age to access many social media sites is 13. However, age is based on self-reporting, so children younger than 13 can simply lie about their age and open accounts.

Discuss focus
Help teens to avoid focusing on Likes, making comparisons, and having fake friends. The need to gain Likes can cause teens to make choices they would not otherwise make. While it is difficult to avoid engaging in comparisons on social media, have teens consider their level of privacy among armies of online 'friends' when in fact they don't know many of them well or at all.

Be alert
Stay alert when using social networking sites. Encourage your teens to tell you if they feel uncomfortable, upset,

or threatened by anything they see online. I have had patients who met adults posing as teens on the Internet and were put in very vulnerable positions. This is known as 'catfishing.' Children and teens should be taught to notify a parent immediately if they receive any threatening or uncomfortable messages regarding obscene content, cyberbullying, or other objectionable content.

Avoid over-monitoring

Despite being on my son's WhatsApp chat, I think there is a fine balance between checking our preteen and teens' accounts and backing off. Although it is tempting to frequently monitor sites, this can backfire and result in conflict. Also, many teens tell me they have ways to create special passwords and screen names to avoid parental scrutiny. Parents should talk about appropriate media use early and build a relationship of trust surrounding social media. My suggestion is to monitor conversations intermittently at the beginning and if going well, allow more independence. Obviously, if there is a clear break in contract regarding online behavior, this may flag the need to monitor again.

Ensure face-to-face connections

Social interaction skills require daily practice, even for teens. It's difficult to build empathy and compassion when teens spend more time 'engaging' online than they do in person. Ensure teens have time for in-person conversations and relationships. Not just online.

SMARTPHONES

Dirk is a 12-year-old male living in Dusseldorf, Germany. He would like to get a phone to stay connected with his classmates, communicate with his parents after sports practices, as well as play the occasional online game. His parents are concerned that he will spend most of his time playing games or communicating on social media and not be focused on his homework. They are also concerned that he may lose his phone as he tends to lose items regularly.

Clearly, there's no perfect time to allow your teen to have their own phone. It is OK to delay giving your preteen or teen a phone, especially with what we know about brain development and impulse control. The exact timing depends on where you live, your community and school, as well as your child's peer group, need for travel, and their level of maturity and responsibility. In our case, we finally relented when Nick, at 12 years of age, wrote a 5-page typed memo to my husband and I outlining in detail (including data from the Pew Research) why he thought he should have a phone and how he would be responsible using it.

Although kids hate this, when you do choose to let them have a phone, I suggest starting off with a relatively basic phone, before moving on to one with all the latest tools. Also, if you are concerned that your child may lose the phone, consider investing in a slightly cheaper model. However, if you do have a sophisticated phone, have clear rules regarding use of social media, monitoring, sexting, and pornography.

Strategies for addressing smartphone use

Turn off notifications and use a real alarm clock

Consider turning off notifications for a few hours each day or putting the phone into sleep or airplane mode during night-time hours. Insist your teen uses a real alarm clock instead of relying on their phone and keep the phone out of the bedroom. Also, encourage teens to program their phones to switch to grayscale, which makes it less enticing to look at.

Use 'healthy' apps

Encourage teens to use apps that help them to stay calm or encourage healthy behaviors, such as Headspace or a meditation app. Also, use apps that monitor their phone/ social media usage and help them focus on other activities.

Set aside the device at mealtime

Encourage kids to put their phone near the door or put it away during meals or family events, instead of carrying it with them or putting it on the table. Encourage them to spend more time face-to-face with people having conversations and not just via their phones.

SEXTING

Jenny is a 16-year-old born in South Africa who has lived in Washington, DC, for most of her life. She has a 17-year-old boyfriend she met through her cousin at a party last summer, though her parents are not aware of this. They have been having a long-distance relationship for the last year. He recently asked her to send a nude photo of herself so that he could have something to remember. Jenny is inclined to send him a picture but is a little worried her parents may find out.

Sexting is the sharing of sexually explicit images through the Internet or electronic devices. Many cross-cultural teens from Hong Kong to London to Washington, DC, say they have sent or received a sext. According to a 2018 study of over 110,000 teens globally, one in four reported receiving sexts and one in seven reported sending them.[54] There is good evidence that teen sexting, particularly among teens older than 15, is increasing. For some adolescents, it may be a way to explore their attraction to someone. They may sext to flirt, be romantically involved, or to show intimacy. From my work with teens, both boys and girls are equally involved in this trend although girls may be more vulnerable to pressure from a partner or peer.

According to a recent survey, nearly 80% of US adults have sent or received a sext.[55] Many teens believe it is fine to sext too. This is another thorny topic that parents need to broach with their teenagers. Is it enough for them to simply tell their teens to just not do it? I recommend that you take a stepwise approach to sexting as discussed below.

Levels of sexting

There are different levels of sexting according to Amsterdam-based author and social worker Allison Ochs. In her recent book *Would I Have Sexted Back in the 80s?* she outlines the different forms of sexting, ranging from:

1. Written messages or emojis
2. Sexy pictures while fully clothed
3. Partially nude photographs
4. Completely nude photographs
5. Sexually explicit videos

Obviously, any level can be problematic although sending nude videos may have more severe repercussions compared to messages or emojis.

The issue with teen sexting

Since the teen brain is a work in progress, trying things out and testing new experiences is an important part of teen development. As such, it is normal for teens to want to explore, especially with sexual behaviors and technology. However, because of brain maturation, some teens may lack the ability to put the 'brake' on impulses or consider consequences. As such, engaging in sexting may lead to risky situations for adolescents.

The risks of sexting

I tell teens that social media was created to make sharing easy. Therefore, sending a nude post on social media can be shared easily – from what was initially between two people only, to a much larger audience. Once a teenager hits *send*, the picture is out of their control and creates a digital footprint. Sending images or videos may lead to embarrassment, humiliation, and loss of self-esteem. Sexting may set teens up for being bullied, objectified, or worse, becoming depressed and suicidal. In addition, there can be school and legal consequences, as nude images of minors are considered pornography in many countries.

Managing sexting

After counseling teens in various settings to 'just say no' to sexting, I realize that preaching abstinence is not working. Many older teens like Jenny feel that if sexting is consensual, it is their decision and right. As with safe sex, I now discuss the responsibilities and consequences of sexting, the importance of deflecting pressure, and tell them it is OK to say no. I also use role play to get kids to think real time about handling tough situations when sexting.

It is important for adults to take a proactive approach in communicating with teenagers about this issue, especially if the child or teen has their own computer or phone. Again, as with safe sex, conversations about sexting should not be a one-time event, but an ongoing discussion. I suggest starting by asking teens what they know about sending sexy or naked emojis, pictures, or videos. Also, ask whether they know a friend or peer that has sent or received one.

Strategies for addressing sexting

Hit pause
Ask teens to hit pause and consider the following before sending or receiving a sext:
- Would you or a friend get in trouble with this image?
- Would you be OK with the whole school or a family member possibly seeing this?
- Would you feel the same about this decision in six months or a year?

Manage peer pressure
Discuss the pressures that kids often experience from a partner or peer to send photos or videos. Tell teens it is not OK to be pressured to sext, nor is it a way to prove their love or attraction. Have them weigh the pressure to sext with the consequences, which can include embarrassment, bullying, and legal issues. Remind them they are worthy of respect.

Discuss with an adult

Encourage teens to tell a trusted adult and delete rather than forward any inappropriate photos or messages.

If all fails, stay calm

Finally, if a teen tells you that he or she (or a friend) has been sexting, be calm. Ask what led to sending or receiving the photo or message. You may discover he or she is being bullied or doesn't realize the consequences. Discuss what should be done next, what the responsibilities may be, how to resist pressure, and how to make safe choices going forward.

GAMING

Simon is a 13-year-old Chinese Malaysian teen in Singapore. His parents have told him that he is not allowed to spend any time playing his favorite game, Overwatch – a shooter video game – so he can focus on his studies. He stayed up late one night and secretly gamed with a friend. As a punishment, his parents banned him from using his iPad until the end of term. He was previously caught chatting with a friend and had his phone taken away for a month. Simon is frustrated by what he perceives as very strict punishment and a lack of voice in his computer use. His parents say that they set the rules. They also are concerned about the kind of video games he is playing.

Overall, 84% of teens say they own or have access to a game console at home, and 90% say they play video games of any kind (whether on a computer, game console, or cell phone). While a substantial majority of girls report having access to a game console at home (75%) or to playing video games in general (83%), those numbers remain higher among boys. Roughly 9 in 10 boys (92%) have or have access to a game console at home, and 97% say they play video games in some form or fashion.

According to a study by authors Jessica Piotrowski and Patti Valkenburg, when parents take an authoritarian approach to media use, such as threatening punishment, or are inconsistent in their enforcement of media guidelines, family conflict and teen antisocial behavior increase. However, if parents restrict media use in an inclusive way by taking the teen's perspective seriously and developing guidelines together, then family conflict and antisocial behavior decrease. Therefore, trying to make teens feel guilty or simply threatening them with punishment without acknowledging their deeper needs can backfire.[56] As such, Simon's parents may want to consider a more supportive relationship over one that is authoritarian.

Strategies for addressing gaming

Never assume
Don't assume that a website or online game is appropriate just because its name sounds OK. Periodically review the software your teen uses. While many high-quality products are available, some software is not appropriate because it is difficult to use, highlights violent themes, or does not foster language or learning.

Consider location
Consider placing the gaming system in a 'family' area. Teens might play with headsets but the possibility of being watched is modulating for them.

Ensure privacy and think about filters

Tell children not to give out their personal details. If they want to subscribe to any services online, make up a family email address to receive the mail and check out what child protection services your Internet Service Provider (ISP) offers. Consider using Internet filtering software, walled gardens, and child-friendly search engines.

THE BOTTOM LINE: MEDIA USE

- Although our teens are digital natives, many adults don't feel fully equipped to provide guidance on media use. Instead of screen time, focus on the 3 Cs (Content, Context, and Child) and having supportive conversations.

- Creating media contracts can be useful for setting rules and responsibilities.

- Warning signs of Problematic Interactive Media Use (PIMU) include spending time with screens for long periods, lying about or hiding the amount of time spent, or using media to escape from other issues such as anxiety.

- If your teen is having difficulties it is important to seek professional support especially if it affects their relationships, grades, or sleep.

- Sexting is becoming more common. It is important to talk openly about the responsibilities and consequences related to it and why it puts teens in a vulnerable place.

- When using smartphones, make your teen aware of the issues related to privacy, social media use, and pornography.

- Finally, when it comes to gaming, parental filters and behavioral contracts can be helpful.

BIG ANSWERS

Common parent questions on addressing media use

1. **What is the right amount of screen time?**
   There is no perfect answer to this question. However, experts suggest we consider the 3 Cs: Content, Context, and Child. More specifically, focus on the content of what kids are seeing, the context of their interactions with the media, and understand your child enough to know which forms of media enrich them. Here are some additional questions:
   What are your teens viewing? What is the context for their use? Is he or she still connecting with others? Maintaining friendships and grades, sleeping well? Knowing the answers to these questions can help adults to decide the right amount of screen time. Using a media use contract and serving as a media coach are good strategies to put limits and boundaries in place. Modeling behavior and ensuring phones

and devices are charged outside of the bedroom at night are also important.

2. **How should we discuss sexting with our teen?**

Sexting is becoming more common among teens globally. With teens, we should discuss the responsibilities and consequences of sexting and the importance of not being pressured. Also, tell them that it is OK to say no and at the very least hit pause and wait before responding. Again, as with safe sex, conversations about sexting should not be a one-time event, but an ongoing discussion. Start by asking teens what they know about sending sexy or naked emojis, pictures, or videos. Also, ask whether they know a friend or peer that has sent or received one.

3. **What effect does constant use of social media have on girls' body image and self-esteem?**

Researchers at the University of Pittsburgh found a strong association between time spent scrolling through social media apps and having a negative body image. Those who had spent more time on social media had 2.2 times the risk of reporting eating and body image concerns, compared to their peers. If a teen develops signs of a body image issue or an eating disorder, it may also be a good time to limit the use of social media.

4. **How do we get our son to stop playing video games all the time?**

   Kids need clear guidelines about use but also need help developing the tools to self-regulate and make good decisions. Create a media use contract with your son over expectations for use and issues to be aware of if he violates the rules. Commend him when he sticks to the rules. Also, ensure he has other activities to do, strong friendships, and good connections at school and in the community. If you find that he is having a hard time stopping when he is supposed to, is waking up late to play, or is lying about his use, he may have some difficulties with regulation. Some kids with ADHD, for example, may have more difficulty with this than others and may need professional support.

Common teen questions on addressing media use

1. **My friend is constantly on his computer. How do you know when someone is addicted?**

   Your friend may be struggling with Problematic Interactive Media Use (PIMU). Warning signs are spending time with screens for long periods, lying about or hiding the amount of time spent, or using media to escape daily life or challenges. If he is having sleep issues, worsening grades, not talking to his friends, or difficulty getting off a screen, it may be time for you to intervene. Tell him that you are worried about him and that he needs help from an adult or a professional.

2. Why is sexting an issue if it is a personal choice between two people?

Here are a few reasons why I think sexting is concerning:

- *Sending a nude post on social media can be shared easily from two people to a much larger audience. Once you hit send, the picture is out of your control and creates a digital footprint.*
- *Sending images or videos could be embarrassing if others share it. Can you imagine your parent or teacher seeing it?*
- *It could set you up for being bullied.*
- *Nude images of minors are considered pornography in many countries around the world. As such, there could be school and legal consequences.*

Bottom line, you could still decide to sext, but there is quite a lot you may want to consider. May be best to hit pause before responding to a sext request or asking for one.

3. Is it bad to watch porn?

The main reasons young people mention they watch it are curiosity, it's safer than having sex, and it's something they can do in private. As for negatives, it may not be balanced with respect to gender roles, could be violent, and is not a realistic view of what sex should be or how one should look. Also, you could be caught watching porn by an adult or teacher. Although watching porn is common, especially among boys, there are much better ways to learn about healthy relationships.

4. **Is it OK to listen to music when I am doing my homework? My parents think I get too distracted. I think it helps me to focus. What should I do?**
Some kids really benefit from listening to music, while others can get distracted by lyrics, videos, or loud beats. Try background or study music without videos or images that allows you to focus and doesn't tempt you to keep singing along. For example, I heard of a Dutch teen who listened to rock music in Russian because he liked the sound but didn't get distracted by the lyrics since he couldn't understand them. If it really helps you get through your tasks, it may be worth explaining that to your parents and using music to study.

RESOURCES

Books

Growing Up Shared: How Parents Can Share Smarter on Social Media – and What You Can Do to Keep Your Family Safe in a No-Privacy World, Stacey Steinberg, Sourcebooks, 2020

Screenwise: Helping Kids Thrive and Survive in the Digital World, Devorah Heitner, Bibliomotion, 2016

Plugged In: How Media Attract and Affect Youth, Patti M Valkenburg and Jessica Taylor Piotrowski, Yale University Press, 2017: https://yalebooks.yale.edu/book/9780300218879/plugged

Would I Have Sexted Back in the 80s?, Allison Ochs, Amsterdam University Press, 2019

Websites and articles

'1 in 7 Teens Are "Sexting," Says New Research', Sheri Madigan and Jeff Temple, *Scientific American*, 2018: https://www.scientificamerican.com/article/1-in-7-teens-are-ldquo-sexting-rdquo-says-new-research/

'What you need to know about problems with media and children/teens', Center on Media and Child Health, 2019: http://cmch.tv/clinicians/pimu-tips/

Common Sense Media: https://www.commonsensemedia.org/

Center for Research on Children, Adolescents and the Media: https://www.ccam-ascor.nl/

Screenagers: Growing up in a Digital Age movie, 2016: https://www.screenagersmovie.com/

'Their Own Devices' – podcast series on media use and teens: https://thepodglomerate.com/shows/theirowndevices/

STRESS 8

"There is more to life than increasing its speed."
Mahatma Gandhi

IN THIS CHAPTER:
- Understanding the causes and effects of stress on global teens.
- Creating an anti-stress toolkit.
- Preventing overscheduling and creating balance.

Tina is a 16-year-old Latina girl with braces, a few pimples, dark curly hair, and a penchant for acting in school plays. She has a busy daily schedule at a competitive high school in Washington, DC. Most nights she's not asleep until 12.30 or 1am. She wants to go to an elite university and is taking several advanced placement classes. She comes in to see me in clinic on a fall afternoon because of headaches and feeling tired for the last few weeks.

"How are you doing?" I ask when she strolls into the clinic room.

"Not so good," she responds. "I am having constant headaches and am completely freaked out."

"Why?" I ask.

"Well," she says, "I looked it up on the Internet and I know EXACTLY what I have."

"What is it?" I respond curiously.

"Doctor Abraham, I have… I have… a BRAIN TUMOR!" she exclaims and sits down abruptly in a flood of tears.

"Oh," I say, reflecting on how best to respond to her concern. "I am sure this feels very scary."

Tina nods emphatically.

"However, there are many reasons why you can have headaches, more than just a brain tumor. Perhaps we can chat about how you are feeling and what else is happening in your life?"

Tina lets out a big sigh and looks relieved.

BIG QUESTIONS

Common parent questions on tackling stress and creating balance

1. Any tips on getting teens to eat better and sleep more when they are feeling stressed?

2. My son struggles with managing his time and feels very frustrated and stressed when he can't finish his assignments as they are due. How can we support him?

3. How do we help our teens to address the anxiety related to the political and economic challenges and uncertainties we are experiencing in our community?

4. How do we prepare our kids for frequent moves and transitions?

5. We think it's important for our daughter to unwind, but how can we make sure that downtime isn't only screen time?

Common teen questions on tackling stress and creating balance

1. How do you deal with stress when you don't have time to relax?

2. How do you handle pressure from parents or others to excel in everything?

3. If I am not working, I feel that I must be wasting time. How can I change this feeling?

4. I am committed to an extracurricular activity and I am struggling to find a balance between schoolwork and the activity. What should I do?

5. How do you know when you need counseling for handling stress?

TACKLING STRESS

I am amazed how often preteens and teens tell me they feel stressed out. Many will mention that they feel that way at least two to three days during any given week. A few even confide that they are stressed every single day. Some say because their peers are stressed, they are obliged to feel the same. What's concerning is that kids as young as 10-11 years old tell me they are regularly stressed. In fact, only a minority of teens tell me they are never anxious or worried. Global issues like the coronavirus pandemic have also affected the levels of stress among adolescents around the world.

Says Tanya Lau, a school counselor at the German Swiss School in Hong Kong: "Students are under stress in every element of their life nowadays. Their appearance, their academics, their social relations, their status... and that's just online. In schools, stress from different aspects of their life affects how they manage, cope, and navigate their day."

According to the informal survey I conducted among global teens in 2019, maintaining balance and handling stress were top concerns among respondents. Other top concerns, in order of priority from most to least, were:

- Planning for the future
- Handling friendships and relationships
- Getting sleep
- Managing expectations
- Staying organized
- Body image
- Self-esteem
- Addressing depression/mental health
- Peer pressure
- Social media

In addition to issues listed, teens also mentioned concerns about global issues like climate change, the refugee crisis, and political unrest. Of course, having fears and concerns or feeling stressed is OK sometimes – for example, before a performance or big test. But how much is too much?

Chronic stress

Stress – the feeling of emotional or physical tension – is the body's response to demand or pressure. Some stress can be useful for finishing a paper, performing well in a competition, or acing that all-important presentation. From an evolutionary standpoint, experiencing stress has been lifesaving. I tell teens that when we were cavemen and cavewomen, the stress response was to run away from a lion – a very useful reaction if you don't want to be eaten! When stressed, the body releases hormones that prepare us for the fight or flight modes.

But how many of us have run away from a lion recently? Today, while real lions are mostly confined to zoos, we have many virtual 'lions' in our lives that are not contained in a cage. They are caused by academic or job-related stress, round the clock social media, peer pressure, moves, losing friends, or challenging relationships.[57] The presence of these ubiquitous lions puts us in a state of chronic stress. And chronic stress, studies have shown, can cause subtle changes in developing brains and affect cognition. Many teens I work with tell me that too much stress makes them forgetful, feel anxious, and sick to their stomach. Others say they are grumpy, get into fights with family and friends, or even harm themselves.

In Tina's case, we spent a good deal of time discussing school, home, her extracurricular schedule, sleep, and diet in addition to her symptoms. Although a brain tumor can cause headaches and should be ruled out, it is a relatively rare cause of headaches in teens. Headaches in young people can more commonly be related to sinus infections, dehydration, caffeine use, head injury, skipping meals, stress, and lack of sleep. Tina had a normal physical exam. She did complain of feeling stressed regularly, having a packed school schedule, and not enough sleep. After implementing a headache log to track triggers, combined with increased exercise, relaxation, and sleep time, Tina's headaches improved significantly. As with Tina, high levels of stress can contribute to headaches or other complaints in teens. Therefore, simply treating a headache with medications without asking more questions about stress or other mental health issues may risk missing an underlying issue.

 Signs that kids may be stressed can vary by age. For example, grade-school kids may develop sleep problems or eating issues. Teens may show changes in sleeping or eating, avoidance of regular activities, a change in grades, or even experimentation with drugs or alcohol. Kids like Tina can also have physical ailments such as headaches, fatigue, stomach aches, and joint pains.

Cross-cultural teens face additional challenges which can contribute to overall stress such as:

- Moving and experiencing new people and communities
- Questioning their personal identity
- Not having a sense of belonging
- Experiencing grief and loss
- Navigating long-distance relationships
- Handling uncertainty about living situations

"Cross-cultural teens get to experience two or more cultures. Dependent on the culture and parenting, this can allow for extraordinary resilience, adaptability, and curiosity," says Lau. "All teenagers experience stress and this affects teenagers in the same way, universally. Parents can put their children at risk by not responding appropriately to their stressed-out teenagers. How they respond can be based on their cultures, but parents need to challenge their own beliefs with their partners first to ensure they agree on the right intervention for their teen."

Discussing stress is important in relation to global events. For some Millennials and Generation X members, there is less of a sense that they can exert any control over their environment. As such, they may feel fear, apathy, and disconnection.

If we don't have conversations with teens and educate young people to handle stress effectively, it can affect them in other ways. I have met teens who use marijuana regularly, binge drink, overeat, vape, and use other less healthy ways to counter their feelings of anxiety, frustration, and stress.

Adverse Childhood Events (ACEs) and Toxic Stress

Global teens may also be at risk for adverse childhood events (ACEs), which are early traumatic events that can lead to toxic stress and impact adult health. "Toxic stress is not about failing a test or losing at a sports match. It is related to talking about threats that are severe or prolonged – things like abuse or neglect or growing up with a parent who is mentally ill or substance-dependent," says Dr. Nadine Burke Harris in a *New York Times* interview. Dr. Burke Harris is a pediatrician, the author of *The Deepest Well: Healing the Long-Term Effects of Childhood Adversity*, and Surgeon General of California. She suggests that when the stress response is activated repeatedly it can become overactive, which affects brain development, the immune system, and even how DNA is read and transcribed.

More specifically, high doses of stress hormones can affect the brain's executive functioning and appear on imaging studies known as MRIs as a shrinking of the hippocampus, the brain area important for memory and emotional regulation, as well as an increase in the size of the amygdala, which is the brain's fear center. For those who are exposed to high doses of adversity in childhood, the pleasure and reward center of the brain – which is stimulated by drugs, sex and high-sugar foods – can be significantly affected. As a result, individuals feel less pleasure and need higher and higher doses, which can in turn lead to risky behaviors and substance dependence. In addition to affecting brain development, ACEs can impact the immune system and put teens at risk for chronic inflammation and autoimmune diseases like asthma. Says Dr. Burke Harris: "A child with four or more ACEs has double the risk for asthma as one with no ACEs." Finally, ACEs can affect the way DNA is read and created. More specifically, exposure to ACEs can shorten telomeres (which protect DNA from wear and tear) and cause premature cellular aging.

According to Dr. Burke Harris, risk is related to the total exposure to adversity and whether there was a caregiver who could decrease the effect of that chronic stress. She states that two-thirds of Americans have been exposed to one adverse childhood experience, while between 13% and 17% percent have been exposed to four or more. Also, that being exposed to high doses of childhood adversity increases the risk for seven of the ten leading causes of death in the United States. Of course, ACEs are relevant to all global teens because they cross ethnic, socioeconomic, gender, and geographic lines.

Dr. Burke Harris says that while many of her teen patients were told that they were screw-ups, explaining the effects of ACEs on behavior can be very helpful. She tells patients, "Because of what you've experienced, your body makes more stress hormones than the average person, and that can look and feel like being quick to anger, or having difficulty controlling your impulses, or getting sick easily when you feel overwhelmed."

Addressing Toxic Stress

So how do we address toxic stress? The presence of a positive caregiver or parent is critical. Says Dr. Burke Harris: "One of the key ingredients for keeping the body's stress response out of the toxic stress zone is the presence of a healthy buffering caregiver. So, we need to educate parents and caregivers about the impact a child's environment and exposures may be having on their health. We also know that if a caregiver can self-regulate, their kids have much better outcomes."

She emphasizes the importance of six core concepts for addressing the biology of toxic stress: sleep, exercise, nutrition, mindfulness, mental health, and healthy relationships. "Certain diets support a healthy immune system and neuroplasticity. And when you exercise, it helps to metabolize stress hormones and release other hormones that counteract effects of stress and also support cardiovascular health and reduce chronic inflammation." Dr. Burke Harris also strongly recommends universal screening by health providers for ACEs, getting mental health counseling, and creating public health campaigns against toxic stress.[58]

Creating an anti-stress toolbox

As illustrated by Dr. Burke Harris, there are quite a few things that parents and caregivers can do to help teens with stress. Start by asking your teen if they experience stress and if so, how often. Then explore what may be triggering the stress and whether there have been significant life events that may be contributing to it. Also, ask what strategies they are using to prevent feeling too anxious or frustrated. Some of these strategies may be positive such as exercising, while others may be less healthy like binge eating. In tackling stress, I tell teens to visualize a toolbox. I recommend that they fill their 'anti-stress toolbox' with tools that work for them such as:

- Having downtime
- Talking to friends or a family member
- Watching a funny show or listening to music
- Exercising
- Sleeping

I remind teens (those who are open to it) that yoga, mindfulness, and meditation are great alternative methods of addressing stress. For example, the breathing and stretching techniques taught in yoga help relax muscles and release tension. Meditation and mindfulness can help kids to be in the present moment and bring awareness to their mood and reactions. In addition, I also encourage teens who enjoy writing (and don't see it as another stressful activity) to keep a journal to express their mood and reduce stress.

Some teens tell me they prefer getting help on finding the root causes of their stress and changing it rather than being told to meditate. Therefore, finding triggers and taking control by brainstorming specific strategies to combat them are key. Here are some additional ideas.

Strategies for tackling stress

Prepare kids to handle mistakes

For many teens, stress may come from the fear of making mistakes. According to Lynn Lyons, a psychotherapist and co-author of the book *Anxious Kids, Anxious Parents: 7 Ways to Stop the Worry Cycle and Raise Courageous and Independent Children*, we need to remind teens that it is

OK if they don't know how to do everything right and they mess up. While making a good choice is an important skill, what may be even more valuable is learning how to recover when things go wrong. We need to help teens to correct their mistakes, learn from their experiences, and move on.

Stop comparing

Stress can occur if teens (like adults) are constantly comparing themselves to each other. Of course, this can be magnified by social media. Remind teens that it is not about being the most athletic, prettiest, smartest, or popular, but about being the best version of their authentic selves. Everyone is 'uneven,' meaning they may excel in some areas, but not others. Figuring out how to cut out the constant comparing can go a long way to decreasing the stress that teens place on themselves.

Introduce the concept of time management

Many teens get stressed because they find it hard to stay organized and balance their needs. Encourage teens to set goals, prioritize tasks, break large assignments into smaller steps, work for designated periods of time followed by a short break, and use reminder systems like homework journals and Google Keep. Also, to turn off screens or set times and places where they are forced to take a break from phones or social media. Finally, to seek professional help if they are having persistent difficulty with concentration and organization and finishing tasks in time. In some cases, they may have difficulty with executive functioning skills and could benefit from educational support.

Maximize sleep

Lack of sleep can lead to irritability and moodiness, as well as decreased focus and memory. The term 'social jet lag' describes the phenomenon of teens surviving on inadequate sleep because of late nights doing homework or checking social media. On top of that, young people experience a change in melatonin secretion during teenage years and don't feel sleepier till later (see more on this in *Chapter 2*). Make sleep a priority and create a home environment that allows for it. I tell teens to start slowly by making their bedtime even 5-10 mins earlier each night until they get closer to the recommended 7-8 hours of sleep. Using an old-fashioned clock instead of a cell phone as an alarm and charging devices outside of the room may cut back on disruptions at night. Adequate sleep goes a long way to helping kids to recharge and reduce stress.

Eat well
There is a strong link between mental and physical health. Since the brain is a highly active organ, it needs a lot of blood, oxygen, and nutrients. Encourage teens to optimize their health and immunity by eating lots of healthy fats, fruits, veggies, and protein. Also, avoid highly processed or sugary foods, which may cause rapid changes in energy level and mood. Finally, drink lots of water to stay hydrated and to maximize focus.

Exercise
Exercise produces chemicals called endorphins that provide a feeling of well-being and help counteract stress. For me, running alone or with a group has been an important way to handle stress ever since university. I tell teens to choose whatever exercise works for them and do it regularly, even if it is only for 20-30 minutes. Exercise can be walking, jumping rope, dancing, soccer, swimming, biking, and many other physical activities.

Know the warning signs and get additional help

Teach kids to be aware of warning signs, such as stomach aches or headaches, and encourage them to be proactive about using their anti-stress tools. As is the case for Tina, stress can manifest itself in a variety of ways – one of my teen patients bites her fingernails, another pulls out her hair. A few sessions with a psychologist or counselor may be enough to work towards improving patterns or behaviors. Persistent stress can lead in extreme cases to irritability, mood swings, or even depression and self-injury. If these occur, it is very important to get professional help. Also, be aware that underlying adverse childhood events such as divorce and abuse can affect teen behaviors and contribute to toxic stress.

CREATING BALANCE

Lillian is a 16-year-old Korean-American teenager in Los Angeles. Like many teenagers she has a very busy schedule. At 6am, she heads to swimming practice, followed by school, and after school it's piano lessons before arriving home for a rushed meal and homework that often keeps her up past midnight. Her typical week is filled with attending weekday sports practices and weekend competitions, playing piano, and studying for exams. She is finding it increasingly difficult to juggle schoolwork with swim team and spending time with her family and friends. She has thought of quitting the swim team so she can have some downtime but is afraid that this will affect her applications to top universities and perhaps getting a swim scholarship. She also enjoys the camaraderie of the team and the discipline of swimming. When asked, she says she feels stressed a lot of the time, particularly about keeping up her grades and getting into a good college.

Handling overscheduling

According to the Cross-Cultural Kids I work with, the most common reasons for stress are pressure from parents and peers, preparing for tests, and completing homework. However, many also mention going from one activity to another without downtime and trying to stay organized as contributory factors. It is not uncommon for cross-cultural teens to juggle extracurricular activities like language classes and sports with extra-tutoring sessions or after-school jobs and homework. There are clear benefits to having kids participate in extracurricular activities. They provide academic and social opportunities, help develop confidence and discipline, and in some cases, help keep kids busy and off screens.

At the same time, as in Lillian's case, there can be downsides to scheduling your kids' every waking hour because being involved in too many structured activities can cause huge amounts of stress. Pressure to perform, especially at young ages, may decrease the pleasure children receive from participation over time. Overreliance on tutoring can place the focus on attaining academic achievements. Overscheduling may also lead to chronic sleep deficits, which have serious implications for mood, focus, and health.

Allowing boredom

Parenting, Inc. author, Pamela Paul, writes in a *New York Times* piece entitled 'Let Children Get Bored Again' that all too often we observe parents believing that "every spare moment should be optimized, maximized and driven towards a goal."[59] Paul believes this is a mistake, arguing that boredom should teach kids that life isn't a parade. Boredom can help foster creativity and self-sufficiency. In a 2018 US-based study on social class, gender, and contemporary parenting standards, researcher Patrick Ishizuka found that regardless of class, income or race, parents who felt their kids were bored after school believed they should be enrolled in after-school activities.[60] I often remind parents to recall how they spent their own childhood. I also ask how much non-digital, unstructured free time their kids now have. Often the answer is: we had quite a bit; they have none.

Growing up, my sister and I had very little by way of regular structured activities, particularly over the summer. We roamed the neighborhood and played with whoever was free. We took frequent trips to the local library for armfuls of books, and yes, we were bored often. Of course, this was prior to the advent of iPads, smartphones, and social media. The concept of unstructured, non-digital free time can be tricky, especially as kids get older and discover the lure of electronic devices. I confess I don't have the perfect answer for our home either. However, I marvel at what my teens are capable of when bored. For example, one of my boys spent hours creating the most intricate mystery 'escape room' when he had a few hours of parent-encouraged 'non-digital' free time on a recent weekend. Parents, educators, and adults need to help teens to create balance and think of alternatives that allow them to unwind and that don't just involve media use or screens.

Happiest kids on earth

Dutch children are noted to be some of the happiest kids

in the world according to a UNESCO study and a recent book entitled *The Happiest Kids in the World: How Dutch Parents Help Their Kids (and Themselves) by Doing Less.* As a pediatrician based in the Netherlands at the time of writing, I have learned a lot from the Dutch way of creating balance. When Dutch kids engage in play their parents make sure it is not constantly pressured. Most local schools have half days off on Wednesdays to allow kids to relax or play sports. On Fridays, schools start one hour later, so kids can sleep in. Finally, I love the Dutch word *niksen,* which refers to the concept of letting your mind do nothing and zoning out.

My experience is that kids do better when the school and the community are aware of the importance of balance. I have worked with schools that actively encourage parents to limit younger kids from participating in several activities a week and have discussions with older ones about creating realistic schedules and expectations. There are clearly perils to overscheduling and perks to boredom. Here are a few thoughts to help create and maintain balance:

Strategies for creating balance

Each kid has a different threshold for stress and balance
One child may enjoy taking part in a variety of activities on a regular basis. Another may best enjoy a time of rest and rebooting with a less packed schedule. Be aware of your child's threshold and focus on quality not quantity of activities.

Re-evaluate activities periodically
Does your teen still enjoy the activities they take part in? Some activities may be helpful for kids to develop a hobby or

sense of discipline. Others may become a source of constant frustration and resentment. Let older kids and teens have a say in the choice of their activities. Take time to re-evaluate whether the activity is enjoyable and of importance. Also, if kids have time to recharge or are constantly eating and doing their homework on the run. The key is moderation and realistic expectations.

Be a good role model

When discussing stress, one of my patients confided in me that she was very worried about her mom and wanted to know how to help her to deal with chronic stress. Kids watch parents in all areas of life, including their health habits and ways of handling time. According to counselor Tanya Lau, "We are busy people and we run tight ships, but it is important to be present. When you are present, listening, and open then your child will be present, listen, and open with you. Establish routine but allow your child's input too. Share with your child how *you* take care of yourself when you're stressed and how *you* identify stress in yourself. This will model what stress looks and feels like, and more importantly, what to do about it."

THE BOTTOM LINE: STRESS

- Stress is a constant problem today that affects teens everywhere. Some stress can be beneficial for completing a task. Too much stress can have negative effects both physically and mentally.

- Help teens to build their own anti-stress toolkit and get help early on if there are warning signs of bigger problems, such as depression.

- Be aware of overscheduling and allow downtime to build balance.

- Chat with your teen about whether they feel stressed. Take time to explore ways to relax, recharge, and be creative.

- Without support, stressed global teens may be at risk for depression, substance use, and other issues. Parents and care providers play an important role in helping teens to address stress and should communicate regularly with their teens on the topic.

BIG ANSWERS

Common parent questions on tackling stress and creating balance

1. **Any tips on getting teens to eat better and sleep more when they are feeling stressed?** *There is a strong link between mental and physical health. Encourage teens to optimize their brain health by eating lots of healthy fats, fruits, and vegetables, avoiding highly processed or sugary foods, and drinking lots of water. Start by avoiding unhealthy foods in the grocery store and stocking healthier options at home. Lack of sleep can lead to irritability, moodiness, and poor memory, while adequate sleep is helpful for ensuring kids recharge and reboot. Make sleep a big priority and try*

to create a home environment that allows for optimal resting. Finally, ensure teens are charging all electronic devices outside of their room so they get adequate zzz's at night.

2. **My son struggles with managing his time and feels very frustrated and stressed when he can't finish his assignments as they are due. How can we support him?**
It would be important to understand why he has difficulty organizing his time. Check to ensure that he doesn't have a specific issue with focus and concentration. Also, that he is not overscheduled and that he is getting adequate sleep. Encourage him to set goals, prioritize tasks, and break them into smaller steps. Also, to turn off screens or set times and places to take a break from phones or social media. Finally, if he is still feeling stressed or struggling, it may be time to discuss his concerns with teachers and counselors and get additional support.

3. **How do we help our teens to address the anxiety related to the political and economic challenges and uncertainties we are experiencing in our community?**
When we experience a shake-up, be it a move, political upheaval or a health pandemic, we have the choice to respond in one of two basic ways. We can break down by letting toxic fear and stress overpower the ability to act or we can rise to the challenge by taking stock of what works and opening windows to

a better tomorrow. For teens, having regular family meetings, keeping a journal, creating new rituals, and making an action plan may all be useful. In our home, we try to have our gatherings on Sunday evenings to replay the highlights (and less happy moments) of the week and to discuss what work and personal projects we would like to tackle next. Challenging times are a great opportunity to map out intentions and try some goal setting. Planning also prevents toxic stress by increasing feelings of control and decreasing feelings of vulnerability. Finally, take time to establish rituals like family meals or movie watching.

4. **How do we prepare our kids for frequent moves and transitions?**
Talking about fears and concerns related to moves may be the first step in handling challenges. Next steps may include enlisting the help of others that may be going through similar issues to provide support and advice. Trying to keep in touch with old friends and familiar places is helpful. Finally, be aware that kids may experience grief/loss and ensure they are using healthy ways to combat the related stress such as sleeping and eating well, exercising, and connecting with friends and family members.

5. **We think it's important for our daughter to unwind, but how can we make sure that downtime isn't only screen time?**
Although screen time is one way to unwind, ask your daughter to identify other ways to relax and support her in doing them such as going for a walk or hike, playing a game, or visiting a favorite park or museum. If needed, create and review limits on the use of screen time as well.

Common teen questions on tackling stress and creating balance

1. **How do you deal with stress when you don't have time to relax?**
If you don't have time to relax, it may be time to re-evaluate your schedule. What are you doing after school or work? Are you rushing from one thing to another? Is there a way to prioritize your activities and simplify your schedule? Also, what are the things that help you to relax? Sometimes a short walk, a minute of mindfulness, or a quick chat with a friend may be enough to start relaxing. Over time, try to build several mini-breaks into your day, until you feel like you have balance.

2. **How do you handle pressure from parents or others to excel in everything?**
Having goals or ambition is important. However, feeling constantly pressured is not a good feeling. Try to talk to your parents about what you may be experiencing. Remind them

that all teens are 'uneven' – they may excel in some areas but not others (and some may not excel in anything at all till much later in life and that's fine too). If that doesn't work, see if you can enlist another adult or family member to discuss this with them. The bottom line is that too much pressure and stress is not healthy for you and won't help you do your personal best.

3. **If I am not working, I feel that I must be wasting time. How can I change this feeling?**
Having time to do nothing or chill out is important for your well-being. Constantly working can lead to burn out and less than healthy habits. Try to create a time management plan to organize your time. Enlist your friends, family, or even a mentor to help you make the switch and feel good with having some relaxation time.

4. **I am committed to an extracurricular activity and I am struggling to find a balance between schoolwork and the activity. What should I do?**
Is the activity still enjoyable and doable? Are you constantly eating or doing your homework on the go? Are you getting enough sleep? Do you have time for fun things or just doing nothing at all? The key is feeling balanced. If you don't feel this, it is time to re-evaluate the activity and how much you are doing.

5. How do you know when you need counseling for handling stress?

For many teens, stress may affect their sleeping or eating, cause a drop in grades, or lead to using drugs or alcohol. Also, it can lead to emotional issues such as irritability, anxiety, and depression, or physical problems such as headaches, fatigue, stomach aches, and joint pains. If you are struggling with any of these or are feeling depressed or suicidal, it is time to get counseling and support.

RESOURCES

Books

Anxious Kids, Anxious Parents: 7 Ways to Stop the Worry Cycle and Raise Courageous and Independent Children, Reid Wilson and Lynn Lyons, Health Communications, 2013

Building Resilience in Children and Teens, Kenneth R Ginsburg, American Academy of Pediatrics, 2014

The Deepest Well: Healing the Long-Term Effects of Childhood Adversity, Nadine Burke Harris, Houghton Mifflin Harcourt, 2018

The Happiest Kids in the World: How Dutch Parents Help Their Kids (and Themselves) by Doing Less, Rina Mae Acosta and Michele Hutchison, The Experiment, 2017

Parenting Inc., Pamela Paul, Times Books, 2008

The Mindful Teen, Dzung X Vo, Instant Help, 2015

Why We Sleep: Unlocking the Power of Sleep and Dreams, Mathew Walker, Simon & Schuster, 2017

Under Pressure: Confronting the Epidemic of Stress and Anxiety in Girls, Lisa Damour, Ballantine Books, 2019

Websites and articles

'Adverse Childhood Events Aware', State of California Department of Health, 2020: https://www.acesaware.org

DEPRESSION, ANXIETY, AND SELF-INJURY

9

"You are beautiful because you let yourself feel, and that is a beautiful thing indeed."
Shinji Moon

IN THIS CHAPTER:

- Reviewing risks and protective factors for depression, anxiety, and self-injury.
- Identifying and managing depression and anxiety.
- Recognizing and preventing self-injury and suicide.

Ahmed is a 13-year-old dark-haired Pakistani-American patient of mine. When I first met him for a routine physical exam, he was a shy and thoughtful teen, chatting about his recent volunteer work with an environmental club and his involvement in the school debate team. However, over the last few months he has been increasingly withdrawn. According to his mom, he has been refusing to go to his after-school activities and has instead been spending most of his time in his room alone listening to music. His appetite has dropped, and he doesn't want to spend time with his friends. He also recently made a comment on a group chat about not wanting to be around anymore. One of his friends sees the posting and mentions it to his own mom who in turn tells Ahmed's mother, Gulnaz, at a school event. Gulnaz tries to speak to Ahmed about the posting, but he refuses, saying, "I don't want to talk about it." Ahmed's father, Fazil, who came to the country as an immigrant and works several jobs for the family, tells Ahmed that he should be ashamed of himself after all that he has done to provide for the family. Fazil is strongly opposed to seeking further intervention and wants to close his son's social media accounts and take away his phone. Concerned about her son's behavior, Ahmed's mom calls me to ask what may be happening and what to do.

Ahmed has been more irritable and doesn't want to spend time with his friends. Of course, young people can have mood swings as part of their normal development and want time alone. Mood swings can increase during the teen years when kids experience hormonal fluctuations and pubertal changes. However, Ahmed seems to have also withdrawn from his usual activities and friends. His comment on social media should be taken seriously as a sign of depression and possible suicidal behavior. Given that his father is opposed to seeking further care, it will be important for the family to understand what the signs of major depression may be and why early treatment is so important.

Many adults assume they will know if their teen is depressed or anxious. However, some signs of depression can often appear different for teens than adults and may be mistaken for typical teen behavior. For example, depressed teens may present with irritability or withdrawal. Untreated depression and anxiety can have many negative consequences such as poor school performance. Stress can affect teen mental health and is a big topic among cross-cultural teens. The good news is that there is a lot that parents and caregivers can do to help young people who are struggling.

BIG QUESTIONS

Common parent questions on mental health

1. What puts teens at risk for depression or anxiety?

2. How do we help our daughter to manage depression?

3. Are cross-cultural teens at higher risk for mental health issues?

4. How can we prevent teen suicides in our community?

Common teen questions on mental health

1. How do I know if I am depressed?

2. What do I do if a friend tells me she is suicidal but doesn't want her parents to know?

3. What do I do if I have a panic attack?

4. Any tips for stopping yourself from self-harming?

MENTAL HEALTH IN GLOBAL TEENS

Mental health is one of the top issues that I discuss with teens and their parents in clinic, schools, and communities. According to the World Health Organization, depression is the third leading cause of illness among adolescents globally, and suicide is the third leading cause of death in older teens. Anxiety is also an increasing issue among adolescents. According to the National Institute of Mental Health, nearly a third of adolescents aged 13-18 suffer from anxiety in the US.[61] It is important for parents to know how to identify and prevent mental health issues, particularly depression, anxiety, and self-injury, given how common these are among young people.

Depression

Depression is defined as a constant low mood that affects behaviors and well-being and may also lead to physical problems such as difficulties sleeping, eating, or focusing. In severe cases, teens may feel that life is not worth living and be at risk for suicide. Depression in teens may occur along with other mental disorders, behavioral problems, or substance use. Although there has been a lot of research on the topic, little is known about what causes depression. Research among twins, for example, shows that both the environment and genetics are important. A teen's individual behavior and tendency to be pessimistic about the future can be a factor. The level and activity of chemicals in the brain such as serotonin or dopamine (neurotransmitters) also affect the development and course of depression.

Who is prone to depression?

For teens living in different settings or between cultures, the potentially resulting isolation, difficulties integrating, and frequent moves can precipitate depression. Difficulties with developing a sense of belonging, connectedness, and rootedness may also accentuate the feelings of isolation and possible depression among Cross-Cultural Kids.

To explore this more, I spoke to Kate Berger who is a child and adolescent psychologist and founder of The Expat Kids Club which provides counseling services to Cross-Cultural Kids in the Netherlands. According to Kate, "The inherent mobility means people, places, ideas, culture – all factors that any of us use to help contextualize our identity – are in flux. This means there can be an unstable sense of self, which can make cross-cultural teens insecure. This type of insecurity may impact many facets of their behavior.

For example, how they engage in relationships or take risks." She adds that, because of mobility, "Sometimes struggling teens go under the radar because they don't stay in one place long enough for anyone to realize they are having a hard time and receive adequate support."

Issues to be aware of:

- Ongoing medical issues such as obesity or ADHD
- Early exposure to a traumatic event such as abuse or loss of a loved one
- Uncertainty about sexual orientation
- Family history of depression, especially in a parent or sibling
- Significant conflict or dysfunction among family members
- Negative outlook on life or poor coping skills
- Experience of being bullied or cyberbullied
- Recent change in friendships or breakup of a romantic relationship
- Difficulties with schoolwork[62]

Warning signs of depression

- **Sad or irritable mood**
  Feeling down or sad, not just sometimes but most of the time, is a key marker. I have seen it displayed in teens as brooding about real or future events, a gloomy outlook, or feeling that everything is unfair. They may also have, as Ahmed did, an irritable mood or feel grouchy all the time. They may pick fights, be negative, or respond easily to minor issues with angry outbursts.

- **Decreased pleasure or withdrawal**
  Teens with depression may no longer derive pleasure

from doing the things they used to enjoy such as hobbies. Teens may also withdraw from friends. Those who are sexually active may have a decreased interest in sex.

- **Change in appetite or sleep**
  Appetite and weight can either decrease or increase as part of depression. Teens may sleep too much or too little or have odd patterns of sleep such as waking too early. They may feel unrested and have a hard time getting out of bed in the morning.

- **Restlessness or fatigue**
  Teens with depression can feel restless or very tired. They may also have trouble starting or completing tasks, which may be mistaken for laziness or avoiding responsibilities.

- **Feeling worthless**
  Depressed adolescents often feel inferior or like a failure.

- **Decreased concentration**
  They can have problems with attention and memory, which can affect their performance at school or work. [63]

What you can do

Without adequate help and early treatment, depression can lead to more serious issues. I have seen young people use the Internet to escape their feelings of sadness or frustration. Some young people may also use binge drinking or drugs like marijuana to self-medicate their mood-related issues. The good news is that depression is a very treatable condition. In cases of mild to moderate depression, Cognitive Behavioral

Therapy may help teens improve symptoms. Counseling can be provided through school counselors, social workers, psychologists, or psychiatrists and helps teens understand their feelings and develop strategies for coping. In cases of more severe depression, a trial of medication alongside therapy may be warranted.

Barriers for global teens

The American Academy of Pediatrics recommends routine screening for depression among all young people ages 12 to 21 (regardless of whether they appear depressed or not). However, teens in settings around the world may face significant barriers to getting screened and receiving treatment for depression. Dr. Deborah Christie is a professor of Paediatric and Adolescent Psychology at University College London Hospitals NHS Foundation Trust. She tells me that "young people living in cross-cultural environments often have to overcome barriers to help-seeking which include the lack of health care professionals that speak their or their parents' language and stigma related to seeking help outside the community."

In many communities, including among Asian families, there is stigma attached to depression or a sense that it is better not to discuss mental health issues outside of the home, much less with a psychologist or psychiatrist. Also, there is a perception that it is better not to seek care to avoid being labeled as having an issue. Although these perceptions are not easy to change, discussions with family members and adults, and stressing the danger of suicide and other risk behaviors may help lead to appropriate care. In rural settings and in developing countries, there are often not enough mental health professionals to provide services to teens. In some countries, it may take weeks or even months to find a provider covered by the health system. In some communities, getting a private provider may be quicker than in the public system, but also more expensive. Getting regular appointments and ensuring the provider is a good fit, speaks the same language, and is culturally sensitive are other challenges for global teens.

Protective factors for global teens

As for protective factors, global teens can be more resilient than their less mobile cross-cultural peers. Berger states that for some global teens such as expats, a mobile lifestyle "forces kids to develop a degree of resilience that protects them. They get so good at dealing with change, loss, and unpredictability that this gives them skills – developed through experiential knowledge – that help them face (and overcome) some of life's most difficult circumstances in ways that their non-mobile counterparts cannot."

Strategies for addressing depression

Be aware of signs
The first step in addressing depression is to ask teens if they are feeling down or depressed. Choose a safe place to talk, and let your teen know what you have seen and why you are concerned. Also, ask them to share what they are feeling and get ready to listen without interrupting. Be aware of body language, offhand comments, and other subtle clues to changes in mood and behavior. Concerns voiced by peers or social media posts by your child may also be an important sign of a problem. If you suspect something might be wrong, trust your gut and talk to your teen openly.

Ensure a smooth transition

Transition, changes, and moves can cause grief, loss, and occasionally depression among global teens. Dr. Preethi Galagali is a pediatrician and adolescent medicine specialist based in Bangalore, India. Her recommendation is that parents plan an exploratory trip to the new home before moving to prepare teens for the change and help to head off 'difficult' issues that may arise because of the move. She also points out that "marital harmony and family collaboration" is important and that, if needed, parents should "work out differences and adjustment problems in private... not in front of the kids." Dr. Galagali recommends reviewing the school curriculum in detail and planning for sports and extra academic activities in advance. Finally, she suggests that parents "be open to youth deciding to migrate back if they are unable to adjust and after discussing the pros and cons of pursuing academics or a job."

Validate emotions and acknowledge strengths

Simply acknowledging a teen's sadness is key to making them feel understood and validated. Take time to focus on talking about their strengths and what teens are doing well rather than on areas of weakness. See *Chapter 13* on building strengths and resilience.

Increase personal and family time

Studies have shown that when families spend more time together, such as during meals, kids do better emotionally. Listen and talk to your teen about their school life and activities, how they are handling problems, and making good decisions. Setting aside time every day to talk and connect meaningfully may go a long way to addressing (and preventing) depression.

Get kids connected

As in the case of Ahmed, kids who are depressed may pull back from friends and activities that they used to enjoy. Encourage them to reconnect or help facilitate activities that bring them together with people they enjoy and who are positive.

 Your teen's peers may show signs of depression too. I tell teens that it is important they are aware of the signs and realize it is too big an issue for them to handle alone. I suggest that they encourage their depressed peers to get help from an adult such as a parent, counselor, or health provider, especially if they are suicidal.

Get moving

Exercise such as running, walking, and swimming produces endorphins. These feel-good chemicals are a healthy way to combat depression.

Find the right provider

Often, the biggest challenge is finding a culturally sensitive counselor or support group that a teen feels comfortable with. Being clear about special needs such as gender, office location, or speaking in one's mother tongue can help ensure there is a good relationship with a therapist or provider. Ask through community groups, counselors, chat sites, and providers who is proficient in working with adolescents. Finally, many providers are now using telemedicine to provide counseling and to support teens globally.

SUICIDE

Many teens who attempt or commit suicide have trouble coping with failure, rejection, and family turmoil. They might also be unable to see that they can turn their lives around. Studies show that girls are more likely to attempt suicide than boys. The risk factors for suicide are like the risk factors for depression, such as having a family history of depression, poor coping skills, being bullied or cyberbullied, or experiencing a recent change in friendships or breakup of a romantic relationship. However, it is important to be aware of the warning signs and act immediately.

Warning signs of teen suicide risk

- Withdrawing from social contact
- Talking or writing about suicide
- Increasing use of alcohol or drugs
- Giving away belongings
- Showing mood swings and changes in sleep

What you can do

If you think your teen is in immediate danger, contact your local emergency service or a suicide hotline number. If you suspect that your teen might be thinking about suicide, talk to him or her immediately. Listen to what your child is saying and watch how they are acting. Never shrug off threats of suicide as teen drama. Also, be aware of isolation. Encourage your teen to spend time with supportive friends and family. If your teen is sad, anxious, or appears to be struggling, ask what's wrong and offer your help. Teens who are feeling suicidal usually need to see a psychiatrist or psychologist experienced in diagnosing such issues.

Finally, access to weapons or medications can play a role if a teen is already suicidal. Remember to store guns, sharp objects, or medications safely away.

Strategies for preventing suicide

Model positive coping skills
The best way to help kids to learn how to handle life's stressors is to lead by example and show them that you, as an adult, use positive coping strategies when things get tough.

Don't be afraid to ask
Parents should know that asking about suicide does not increase the likelihood of their teen self-injuring. In fact, it may be a lifesaving opportunity for a teen to get help early on.

Be aware of the warning signs
The causes of suicide can often be multi-factorial. Being able to identify the underlying root causes and getting early intervention are key. The risk of suicide is greater if a warning sign has suddenly developed or seems related to a stressful event or change. Pay attention to signs of other issues such as worsening signs of depression or anxiety which could also put teens at risk for suicide. Don't delay in getting treatment for the underlying issues.

ANXIETY

I am about to speak to a big audience at an evening event in a cavernous auditorium in Washington, DC. They announce my name and my heart starts beating fast, my palms get sweaty, my hands tremble when I touch the podium...

Sound familiar? Public speaking is one of adults' top fears. My teen patients tell me that going to the dentist and taking a test are other situations where they commonly feel anxious. Anxiety is an alarm system that is switched on when a person perceives danger or threats. The rush of adrenaline can cause a hot face, dry mouth, racing heart, sweaty palms.

Not all anxiety is a cause for concern. A little anxiety or stress such as mine before a big event can help us do our best in situations that involve performance. Most people can switch off these responses if the danger is not real. However, in teens with anxiety disorders, the 'fight or flight' response stays switched on even when there is no real danger.

As outlined in the American documentary movie *Angst*, there is evidence that anxiety disorders among teens, particularly on college campuses, is on the rise. Anxiety might also worsen during major life changes, such as starting college, or in unstable social and political times, such as civil unrest, elections, marches, and protests. This anxiety is magnified in situations of marked upheaval and change, for example among young Syrian refugees who are forced to leave their home country and resettle in another.

Tim is a 17-year-old cross-cultural teen who has been refusing to go to school for the last two weeks. His mom contacted me for support. He has been feeling very worried about the future and unsure that he is capable of graduating from high school. He is also having frequent stomach pain. Although Tim has been a decent student, he has been struggling with an additional load and new curriculum plus deciding about university choices and what to pick as his major. Tim is also a basketball player and has a good relationship with his coach. He is not sure of his abilities and is having a hard time staying focused and completing his assignments. Tim moved several years ago from one city to another, around which time his parents went through a divorce. His mother doesn't think that he has been drinking or using drugs but is not sure.

Tim may be struggling with generalized anxiety, which is defined as excessive and persistent worry about everyday life events or activities.

Warning signs of generalized anxiety:[64]

- Feeling overly afraid, worried, or nervous
- Having unexplained chest pain, headaches, stomach pain, or vomiting
- Feeling short of breath or having 'butterflies' in your stomach

In addition to generalized anxiety, there are a few other types of anxiety that young people can have. Incidentally, many educators that I work with tell me they have seen an increase in students having panic attacks at school as expectations and stress levels increase.

Other types of anxiety include:

- **Social anxiety**
  Triggered by social situations or speaking in front of others.

- **Panic attacks**
  Episodes of anxiety that can occur with no apparent reason. Symptoms can include having a pounding heart, shortness of breath, dizziness, numbness, or tingling.

What you can do

It is important for teens to talk about their feelings. Listen, and let them know you understand, love, and accept them. In Tim's case, he and his parents should meet with the school to discuss how he can gradually return to school and make up the workload. Tim should also talk with his coach with whom he has a good rapport and continue to train for basketball. He and his family would also benefit from meeting with a therapist or physician to discuss Tim's fears, insecurities, and organizational issues while also ensuring he isn't using drugs or alcohol to self-treat his anxiety. Although it may not be easy, with multi-level support, Tim can gradually address his anxiety.

Most often, anxiety is treated with Cognitive Behavioral Therapy (CBT). CBT teaches teens that what they think and do affects how they feel. Also, when teens can confront their fears, the fears will get weaker and ultimately resolve. Teens may also benefit from medication for severe anxiety, obsessive-compulsive disorder, or post-traumatic stress disorder.

Strategies for addressing anxiety

Consider mindfulness and alternative methods
According to Berger, mindfulness-based interventions can be very powerful for teens with mental health issues including anxiety. She says, "They help because they help young people develop awareness about how their thoughts and feelings impact their behavior, thereby empowering them to choose how they want to respond to circumstances (rather than react)." She says that this type of approach can increase empathy, which allows "young people to become kinder, more compassionate, and more connected

with those around them in more meaningful ways." Other strategies for reducing anxiety include deep breathing and yoga. Also, keeping a gratitude diary or a daily journal.

Manage panic attacks

Panic attacks can be scary and are often associated with the feeling of terror or doom, sweats or chills, a racing heart, and tingling or numb fingers. During panic attacks, teens may take short, shallow breaths, which prevent enough oxygen from getting to the brain. This can lead to hyperventilation or breathing too fast. Encourage teens to take deep breaths in and out, which can help calm the mind. For example, hold for six counts and slowly exhale for six counts. If panic attacks continue, consider cognitive behavioral therapy with a psychologist or health provider.

SELF-INJURY – CUTTING

Maria is a 14-year-old from Mexico City and has a history of asthma. She enjoys painting, music, and photography. Her parents have noticed scratches on her wrists and arms. When they ask her what happened, she tells them the neighbor's cat scratched her or avoids answering the questions altogether. While she is more on the introverted side, Maria lately has been uncharacteristically moody, spending a lot of time in her room. Her parents have also noticed that she is wearing long-sleeved clothing quite often even when it is warm or when they go to the beach. They are worried that something may be going on, but Maria denies that there is a problem. On a follow-up visit for her asthma, I ask Maria how she is feeling about herself and particularly whether she has thought about hurting herself or tried cutting. Eventually, Maria confides that she has occasionally cut herself with a razor blade on her wrist in the last few months.

Maria is engaging in a form of self-injury and needs additional help. Kids who cut generally use a sharp object such as razor blade, knife, scissors, or even paper clips and pens to make marks, cuts, or scratches or to carve words on the body. Some kids also self-harm by burning their skin with the end of a cigarette or lit match. Approximately 15-20% of adolescents in the US and UK are reported to have tried self-injury.[65] Although rates are not well-documented, cutting is becoming a growing phenomenon in other countries. Teens in nearly every country I have worked in disclose that they are cutting. Most of the teen patients I've seen that cut are girls between the ages of 12 and 24, but boys and children as young as 5-7 have been known to self-harm as well.

Risk factors for cutting

- Dealing with trauma or facing a difficult life experience, such as bullying
- Intense feelings of anger, sadness, or despair that are hard for a teen to control or manage
- Being exposed to an authoritative style of parenting or teaching
- Having a history of depression, substance use, obsessive thinking, or eating disorders

Cutting is a way to control or release feelings. Although cutting may provide some temporary relief from tension, the relief doesn't usually last. One of my patients told me that she kept a razor in her room and when things got tough, she started cutting. It made her feel good for a short time and then the stress and tension occurred all over again. When cutting becomes a compulsive behavior, it can be very difficult to stop. However, cutting is generally not the result of suicidal thoughts. I ask teens directly about cutting, particularly if I am concerned about mood changes and depression. Most of my teen patients tell me that they keep their cutting a secret and are unlikely to discuss it unless they are asked directly and feel comfortable with the person asking. It's important for parents to be that person.

Signs of cutting

- Unexplained cuts on the arms or legs
- Withdrawal from family and friends and changes in communication, eating, or sleeping patterns
- Wearing long sleeves or pants (even when it is quite hot) or wristbands and bracelets to hide marks
- Avoiding the pool or sports practice where cuts may be revealed

What you can do

I tell teens that cutting is often related to painful experiences or intense pressures, but it is not a good way to handle feelings. It is important to help teens find a therapist, counselor, or psychologist that they feel comfortable with. Treatment by mental health professionals usually involves an evaluation of underlying triggers plus individual or group therapy, raising awareness, and developing distraction techniques. In Maria's case, we turned to her art and photography as ways to express her anxiety and fears. In combination with a few counseling sessions, it helped her significantly to stop cutting over time.

Strategies for addressing cutting

Be aware of your own feelings as parents
Parents may feel surprised, repulsed, or even guilty about the self-injury behavior. Acknowledging these feelings and avoiding being overly critical will go a long way towards helping your teen.

Encourage communication
Most teens don't disclose that they are cutting without being asked. Encourage your teen to talk about what they may be feeling, even if it feels awkward or difficult. If they haven't brought it up, discuss it in an objective, non-confrontational way. For example, you could say, "I noticed you have some marks on your wrists and I want to understand what's happening."

Try distraction techniques
Getting teens to engage in alternative activities such as journaling, exercising, or yoga may help teens to avoid actively cutting.

THE BOTTOM LINE: DEPRESSION, ANXIETY, AND SELF-INJURY

- Young people face many pressures these days, particularly cross-cultural teens. It is not unusual for teens to experience occasional sadness or mood swings, particularly as they enter puberty or after a move or transition to a new school or community.

- As a coping mechanism, teens sometimes seek activities and experiences to temporarily lift their mood, such as thrill-seeking and alcohol use.

- Signs of depression and anxiety include withdrawing from friends, acting irritable or sad, and not taking pleasure in usual activities. In the case of self-injury, teens may be afraid to admit their behavior.

- Cross-cultural teens may be more resilient because of their exposure to different cultures and communities but may have more changes to cope with.

- Parents and caregivers are a key source of support and guidance for teens with mental health issues. Take time to talk with your teen, help them to reconnect with friends and family, and seek additional counseling services if needed.

BIG ANSWERS

Common parent questions on mental health

1. **What puts teens at risk for depression or anxiety?**
   There are a number of reasons teens are at risk, including a chronic medical condition, exposure to a traumatic event (such as the loss of a loved one), uncertainty about sexual orientation, a family history of depression especially in a parent or sibling, conflict among family members, poor coping skills, being bullied, a change in friendships, or severe challenges with school or employment.

2. **How do we help our daughter to manage depression?**

   Counseling may help improve symptoms and can be provided through counselors, social workers, psychologists, or psychiatrists. Counseling helps teens to understand their feelings and develop strategies for coping. In some cases, a trial of medication alongside therapy may be warranted if counseling alone doesn't work. Increasing family time, using mindfulness, and encouraging exercise are other helpful techniques. In severe cases, teens may need to be admitted for further care and treatment.

3. **Are cross-cultural teens at higher risk for mental health issues?**

   Global teens may experience the loss of friends, a known culture, and a community, all of which can add to an overriding sense of grief. Young people may also struggle with identity and belonging. However, global teens are also more adaptable and resilient than other teens in handling transition and change. Bottom line, it depends on the individual teen, their family history, the coping strategies they use, and their access to resources and community support.

4. **How can we prevent teen suicides in our community?**

   This is a big public health question that many health providers, researchers, educators, and community leaders struggle with. Overall, education about the warning signs of suicide, finding positive ways to handle stress and building resilience are key. Also, improving communication at home and at school, decreasing stigma to get care for mental health, providing easy access to counseling services, and screening are important ways to prevent teen suicides, particularly among high-risk communities.

Common teen questions on mental health

1. **How do I know if I am depressed?**
   Feeling sad or having an irritable mood, experiencing decreased pleasure or a change in appetite or sleep are important signs, as are feeling restless or worthless and having decreased concentration. If you or a friend is feeling this way, it is important to talk to a parent or another adult.

2. **What do I do if a friend tells me she is suicidal but doesn't want her parents to know?**
   Although you may want to maintain their confidence, keeping this information a secret can hurt your friend (and you). Tell them that you are very worried about them as their friend and get an adult or counselor involved as soon as possible.

3. **What do I do if I have a panic attack?**
   Panic attacks can occur among teens. Stay calm

and breathe slowly from the stomach. Focus on taking deep breaths in and out. Try to push any negative thoughts that you may have out of your mind. Think about moments when you managed situations well and remind yourself that you are fully in control. Since anxiety can cause your body to get very tense, try to relax each muscle starting from your legs all the way up to your head. Finally, if your attacks are recurrent, it may be time to get help from a health professional.

4. **Any tips for stopping yourself from self-harming?**
Teens may cut because they think it relieves pressure or negative feelings, but it is not a good way to handle stress. It can easily lead to severe injuries and a vicious cycle of self-harm. If you feel like hurting yourself, considering distracting yourself by listening to music, exercising or talking to an adult or close friend. Also, do get help from a health professional as soon as possible.

RESOURCES

Books

Depression and Your Child: A Guide for Parents and Caregivers, Deborah Serani, Rowman & Littlefield, 2013

Helping Teens Who Cut, Michael Hollander, Guilford Press, 2017

Navigating Teenage Depression: A Guide for Parents and Professionals, Gordon Parker and Kerrie Eyers, Routledge, 2010

Recovering from Depression: A Workbook for Teens, Mary Ellen Copeland and Stuart Copans, Brookes, 2002

The Journey of the Heroic Parent: Your Child's Struggle & the Road Home, Brad Reedy, Regan Arts, 2016

Websites and articles

Angst: https://angstmovie.com/

'Child and Teen Therapy', The Expat Kids Club: https://www.expatkidsclub.com/

'Depression', Center for Young Women's Health, 2019: https://youngwomenshealth.org/depression

'Signs of Depression and Anxiety in Teens', Nicole Harris, *Parents,* 2019: https://www.parents.com/kids/teens/depression/signs-of-depression-and-anxiety-in-teens/

'Cutting and Self-Harm', Melinda Smith et al., Help Guide, 2019: https://www.helpguide.org/articles/anxiety/cutting-and-self-harm.htm

The Child Mind Institute (mental health information): https://childmind.org/

EATING DISORDERS AND OBESITY   **10**

"It's not the size of your shape or the shape of your size, but what's in your heart that deserves first prize."
Becky Osborn

IN THIS CHAPTER:
- Understanding the importance of building a positive body image.
- Recognizing and supporting teens with eating disorders, including anorexia, bulimia, disordered eating, and binge eating.
- Understanding how to help teens that are overweight or obese.

When I was in high school, I had a summer camp friend called Julie. She was brunette, popular, and extremely smart. She had a tall, lithe build and excelled at sports and music. To my sixteen-year-old self, Julie seemed to have it all. After graduating from high school, she went off to a top US college on the West Coast and majored in business. However, midway through her first year in university, she was diagnosed with anorexia. Julie was subsequently hospitalized and had to take several months off from school to recover. Years later I bumped into her. Julie had retained her mega-watt smile and brunette locks but looked prematurely aged, frail, and rail thin. I learned that despite being married with kids, she continued to struggle with her eating disorder as an adult, battling one hospitalization after another. Although as teens in camp together I had no idea she may have been struggling, I suspect that there were signs even then. I wonder if we had been educated on body image and the importance of getting help before a distorted self-image and disordered eating become embedded, her lifelong struggle could have been averted. Even though Julie seemed at the time to be the poster child of happiness, on the inside she was not doing well, and we didn't know.

This story is a painful reminder for us adults (and teens themselves) to have conversations early on with preteens and teens to help instill a healthy body image and prevent eating-related issues.

BIG QUESTIONS

Common parent questions on eating disorders and obesity

1. My daughter is constantly dieting and worried about her weight. She just became a vegan; what can we do to make sure she stays healthy?

2. Can my feelings about my own body image affect my teen's body image?

3. What can we do if we suspect our teen has anorexia?

4. How can we help our teens to challenge societal norms about body image?

5. Our son is obese and gets teased at school. What can he do to lose weight?

Common teen questions on eating disorders and obesity

1. What can happen if you don't feel good about yourself on a regular basis?

2. Can boys get eating disorders?

3. At what age is it OK to get plastic surgery as a teen?

4. My friend secretly goes to the bathroom and throws up after eating, but denies she has a problem. What should I do?

5. I have ADHD and find it very hard to stick to any kind of weight loss plan. What can I do?

BODY IMAGE

Body image refers to how we see ourselves. Having a positive body image is extremely important for good self-esteem. Poor body image, on the other hand, can start early among both girls and boys and be lifelong. Poor body image can put teens at risk for having low self-esteem as well as eating disorders, substance use, and other behavioral issues. Body image can also be affected by parents, media, peer group pressure, and the changes that occur during puberty.

Body image and global teens

For cross-cultural teens, having a height, weight, physique, hair texture, complexion, or a mix of features that is apart from the community norm, can sometimes add to the complexities of self-esteem and body image. For example, among some of the non-Asian expatriate teens I work with in Hong Kong, having a larger body type or being very tall is considered less desirable since many of their Asian peers are slimmer and more petite.

When asked what defines beauty or what is attractive, many global teen girls tell me about the importance of being thin, having facial symmetry, or long legs. For boys, they describe needing to have a six-pack, chiseled muscles, or being tall. For teens in certain parts of the world, including Asia and Africa, being attractive also includes having lighter skin and straight hair. The popularity of countless skin-lightening creams (such as 'Fair & Lovely' in India) and hair straightening products and treatments helps reinforce this concept.

On a positive note, many global teens will also mention the idea of inner beauty, being confident, or having a good sense of humor. Teens are often also aware of how (social) media presents a distorted concept of what beauty is. Celebrating their own uniqueness is particularly important for global teens in building a positive body image, although not always easy to do.

Signs of poor body image

Often, teens do not tell their parents, friends, or other adults in their life how they feel about themselves. It is important that parents and adults be aware of the signs of low or poor body image and help teens to address it early on. The following are some signs for parents to be aware of:

- Obsessive self-scrutiny in mirrors
- Frequent comments about their body and comparison of their appearance to others
- Excessive envy of a friend's or celebrity's appearance

The mirror test

I often ask teens both in clinical settings and during workshops in schools around the world, "When you look at yourself in the mirror, what do you see and are you happy with it?" In response, I get a range of answers including: "I have a big nose, but so does everyone in my family," or, "I think I am too short and have small biceps," or, "I have a big butt, but I am happy with the rest of my body." Everyone is entitled to having an occasional 'bad hair' day in relation to their body, a feeling that their body is less than perfect. This is particularly so during the teen years when kids feel awkward about physical changes. However, if a teen is consistently unhappy with their appearance, always upset about being too big, too spotty, or too tiny, it is time to get support before things get worse.

 As mentioned in *Chapter 4, Puberty – Physical Development*, puberty and the changes in body fat composition can be big triggers for body image issues and eating disorders. Particularly among girls, it can occur at a time where they feel awkward and unhappy with themselves.

To nip and tuck

Is it OK for teens to have cosmetic surgery? Plastic surgery is becoming increasingly common among young people. In a review piece for *The Journal of Adolescent Health* I co-wrote with Dr. Diana Zimmerman of the National Center for Health Research, we found that breast augmentation (breast implants) and rhinoplasty (nose reshaping) are two of the most common forms of plastic surgery among US teens. The types of surgeries can vary by country.[66] In Asia for example, blepharoplasty (eyelid surgery) is very popular. Often the trends for teens are dictated by pop stars and reality TV actors (think Korea's K-pop, the US's Kardashians, and the UK's *Love Island*).

There are clear medical indications for having plastic surgery as a teen, such as having a cleft lip, very large ears, or macromastia (large breasts which cause back pain). However, I recommend that elective cosmetic surgeries are only done – if at all – after the pubertal development is complete, which is over the ages of 18-21. Teens' bodies are still growing and developing, and they keep changing their concept of self-image and acceptance as they mature. Although young people have told me that having a cosmetic surgery procedure improved their self-esteem, having elective procedures at a young age can increase their preoccupation with appearance and reinforce low self-worth. It is therefore important that teens seeking elective procedures are first screened for body dysmorphism (preoccupation with physical appearance) and other issues. They also need to be counseled about the complications and risks of such procedures and encouraged to wait if possible.

Strategies to improve body image

Focus on the inside
In the era of Snapchat, Instagram, and photoshopping images, the focus is often on one's external appearance. Help teens train the lens on what's on the inside (such as their values, intelligence, or strengths) instead. Encourage them to spend time with friends who feel good about their bodies and are not always criticizing themselves or others. Be aware of their social media use and consider limiting it or having them take digital holidays from popular sites if body image concerns develop.

Think about role models

Help your teen cultivate role models who have unique strengths and looks rather than an idealized appearance or physique.

Avoid making weight related comments

Try not to make remarks about weight or body types, whether you are discussing your own teen or someone else. Also, actively discourage teasing by family or friends based on physical characteristics, including size. If teasing does happen, discuss with friends and family members the importance of helping teens to build a positive self-image and trying to switch the pattern of teasing.

Be aware of your own body image

Teens often model parental behavior. If you are overly preoccupied with your weight or appearance and are constantly making comments about the need to go on a diet, get bigger biceps, a flatter stomach or otherwise change your look, your kids will too.

Challenge the norm

When working with teens in schools, I ask students to look at current magazine advertisements and decide whether the models have attainable physiques and what effect it may have on their own body image. They often remark that they know full well the images have been photoshopped and are not realistic. It is important for teens to be critical of stereotypical images and messages they receive from social media, their peers, and their community. Above all, teens need to create a strong sense of their own strengths and self-image (see *Chapter 14*). Have teens look at organizations that are trying to challenge media norms. The Dove soap company, for example, has created a wonderful series of adverts and videos based on normal looking individuals to promote positive body image among women.

DISORDERED EATING

When teens have irregular meals, restrict the amount or type of foods, or frequently diet, they may be engaging in disordered eating. This may start because teens want to change their weight or believe they feel better by eliminating certain foods like gluten or fat from their diet. However, these behaviors could lead to nutritional deficiencies or even eating disorders. If you have a teen that is skipping meals or restricting the types of foods they eat, ask why they are doing so and if they are concerned about their appearance or weight. Also, work with them to identify more balanced choices and plan meals and schedules ahead of time. If you are still concerned, it may be a good time to see a nutritionist, therapist, or general health provider to help break the cycle early on.

Suddenly becoming vegan or vegetarian during adolescence can be a tip off for restricted eating or an eating disorder. Of course, some kids may be vegetarian for religious or ethical reasons, but others may use it to control the calories they take in. It is important that teens who choose to be vegetarian or vegan learn how to get enough vitamin B12, iron, and protein by including lentils, nuts, tofu, and green leafy vegetables in their diet.

EATING DISORDERS

Eating disorders, which include anorexia or restricted eating, bulimia (which involves purging or vomiting), and binge eating disorder or eating large amounts of food without displaying self-control at one time, often begin during adolescence and are currently some of the most common chronic health conditions among teens. In many cases, teens may initially struggle with poor body image and disordered eating before progressing to anorexia nervosa, bulimia nervosa, or binge eating. Obesity is not defined as a true eating disorder, but also leads to malnutrition and health complications and has become a significant adolescent health issue in many parts of the world. It will be covered later in this chapter.

The media in Western culture may influence the rise in eating disorders globally. There is a famous study, conducted in Fiji, that found the incidence of eating disorders dramatically increased after television was introduced to the Pacific island nation in the 1980s. Prior to that event, disordered eating, anorexia, and bulimia were unheard of in Fiji.[67]

In researching eating disorders, I spoke in Washington, DC, to Dr. Tomas Silber, an international eating disorder expert and adolescent medicine physician at Children's National Hospital. Originally from Argentina, he has taken care of many cross-cultural teens with eating disorders throughout his career. Dr. Silber points out that teens are at risk for eating disorders regardless of their community, ethnicity, or socio-demographics. However, over the years, he has seen more families from African American, Asian, and Latino backgrounds affected. "Unfortunately," he says, "not all families, particularly in less urban areas, are aware of the diagnosis and what they need to do."

Risk factors for eating disorders

- A family history of anorexia, bulimia and/or binge eating disorder (particularly a first degree relative like a mother or sibling).
- Poor communication and conflict resolution at home. Teens learn quickly that controlling their eating habits is a way to exert control.
- Low self-esteem or self-confidence.
- Personality traits such as perfectionism, an extreme desire to succeed, or impulsiveness.
- Family values about a specific body size, appearance, and food.
- Participation in sports that focus on body shape and size such as ballet dancing gymnastics, or wrestling.
- Being obese or overweight, especially those who may have been told to lose weight.
- Early puberty or a history of substance use.
- Having a chronic illness (such as insulin dependent diabetes).
- Abusive relationships that cause feelings of loss of control, such as physical or sexual abuse.
- Specific cultural attitudes and norms about appearance.

Anorexia

Teens with anorexia restrict food intake, have a strong desire to be thin, and as a result, fear putting on pounds and find maintaining a healthy body weight difficult. Anorexia is less common than disordered eating but certainly occurs. Anorexic teens view themselves as overweight even when they are clearly below normal body weight. It more commonly afflicts adolescent girls, although anorexia can also occur among males.

Anorexia can trigger a low heart rate, dizziness, and amenorrhea (loss of periods). It can also lead to more damaging health effects, such as bone loss, electrolyte abnormalities, and heart arrhythmias. Anorexia can start in the early teen years but, as in the case of my summer camp friend Julie, can continue well into adulthood. Sadly, I have known anorexic patients who have died of complications related to their eating disorder in adulthood, underscoring the importance of getting comprehensive care early on.

Tania is a 16-year-old competitive runner who comes into our teen clinic for a routine physical exam. She had experimented in the past with eliminating gluten, skipping meals, and being a vegetarian after having several bouts of stomach pain last year. Her mom, who is Russian, is a competitive tennis player and concerned about maintaining her own weight and diet. Tania mentions that there has been more stress than usual at home as her parents are divorcing and her sister has been recently diagnosed with a chronic illness.

Tania often skips breakfast and has steamed vegetables, salad, or soup for lunch and dinner. Since her mom works, they rarely have time for family meals. Tania denies trying to restrict her intake, although she is not sure she would like to gain more weight. She mentions that she started her periods a few years ago and has not had periods in a few months. Her growth curve shows that over the last year she has lost a substantial amount of weight. Her heart rate and body mass index are low (having a heart rate less than 60 beats per minute and a Body Mass Index of less than 18 are low). Tania sees me because she wants to get clearance to run in the upcoming track season.

Tania has several risk factors for anorexia, including being a competitive runner, having a mother who is concerned about her weight, and having a history of disordered eating. Her significant weight loss, restricted diet, concern about regaining weight, low heart rate, and loss of periods are worrisome. She is at risk for low bone density and possible stress fractures in the future. In this case, I discuss with Tania the importance of increasing calories, ensuring she has enough protein and vitamins as a vegetarian. Also, that we need to make sure she doesn't have any heart irregularities or electrolyte issues before she is cleared for sports. We also discuss that she would benefit from speaking to a nutritionist about her diet and a counselor to address stress and eating habits. I emphasize the importance of her family working with her to help her gain weight and get healthy.

Supporting teens with anorexia

As with Tania, it is important to get help. Outpatient treatment may include seeing a nutritionist to increase calories and review a diet plan, a therapist to help with emotions and the root cause of the eating disorder, and a health provider such a pediatrician to monitor laboratory tests, weight, and heart rate. Psychologists may use

Cognitive Behavioral Therapy, which focuses on identifying problematic beliefs as well as healthy ways to cope with emotions. The Maudsley method, or Family-Based Therapy, is a form of care where the family is highly involved and has been used successfully in many places.[68] Peer support groups may also be useful.

One parent in Amsterdam caring for a teen struggling with anorexia has some advice when it comes to outpatient care: "Once you have been referred for more specialized help, learn as much as you can about the team that will support your teen in the journey back to healthy eating. Get to know the team personally: you want to make sure you establish a good relationship with them. Ask how they intend to support your child. What will the nutritional plan be? What tools of psychological support will they use? How regularly will your child need medical check-ups? How can you communicate with them if you have any questions or doubts?"

If a teen experiences severe weight loss that is not improving with outpatient treatment, a low heart rate, or suicidal thoughts, he or she may need to receive inpatient care. The level of treatment available can vary greatly based on location and country. While rare, I know families who have moved back to their home countries or traveled to get an evaluation outside of their host country due to a lack of appropriate services there.

Bulimia

Teens who suffer from bulimia may fear weight gain and feel severely unhappy with their body size and shape. The condition is marked by cycles of extreme overeating, known as binging, followed by purging (self-induced vomiting) or the use of laxatives and diuretics. Bulimia is also associated with feelings of loss of control about eating and poor body image. Parents often report food disappearance or empty wrappers, frequent trips to the bathroom after meals, the sounds or smells of vomiting, or sighting packages of laxatives or diuretics. Bulimics may skip meals, avoid eating in front of others, or eat small portions. They may wear baggy clothes to hide the body or complain about being 'fat.' In addition, they may also have scarred knuckles from repeated vomiting.

Sandra is a 17-year-old teen who is referred to our clinic for binging and purging daily. When Sandra was 14 years old, her physician told her that she was obese. Over the last 12 months she lost 25 kgs and is now closer to a normal weight. She says that she purges once or twice a day and skips meals but has not been using diuretics or laxatives. Her parents notice that she is spending a lot of time posting on and reading her Instagram and Snapchat accounts. She makes frequent comments about her friends' appearance and the need to be thin. Sandra says she has been feeling depressed occasionally but denies cutting or feeling suicidal. She is planning to leave for a study abroad program in Italy in a few weeks and is eager to attend.

Supporting teens with bulimia

Sandra is showing signs of bulimia with her frequent purging and binging. Although she is now at a normal weight, she may be at risk for nutritional deficiencies and electrolyte imbalances, in addition to dental related issues from her frequent purging and recent weight loss. As with Tania, she would benefit from speaking to a nutritionist to discuss normal portions and healthy eating. It would also be useful for her to see a psychologist about her depressed mood and regaining control of her eating habits. It may be worth cutting back on social media use and incorporating mindfulness, yoga, or exercise into her life. Since she is planning to go abroad for a year, it is important to make sure she gets an appointment with a health provider in Italy who understands teen eating disorders and maintains regular electronic communication with her caregivers at home. Should Sandra start to display signs of worsening or increasing depression, she may benefit from starting medication for her mood. She and her parents may also want to consider deferring her trip.

Teens who have bulimia and purge frequently may benefit from a day treatment program to break the binge-purge cycle followed by intensive outpatient counseling with a therapist and regular follow up with a pediatrician. The use of antidepressants (called selective serotonin reuptake inhibitors – SSRIs) may well be effective. If left untreated, bulimia can result in long-term health problems such as abnormal heart rhythms and dental problems. However, addressing behaviors early on helps to ensure teens do well.

Binge eating disorder

Teens who suffer from binge eating disorder will frequently lose control over their eating and eat large quantities of food at one time despite not being hungry, often when they are alone and to a point that they feel uncomfortable. Unlike bulimia, episodes of binge eating are not followed by purging, fasting, or excessive exercise. Because of this, many people may be obese and at an increased risk of developing other conditions, such as cardiovascular disease. Teens who struggle with this disorder may also feel intensely guilty, distressed, and embarrassed. Screening involves asking about eating habits and body image and getting baseline laboratory tests. Treatment of teens includes Cognitive Behavioral Therapy and weight loss counseling. There is also good evidence to support the use of certain medications such as antidepressants.

 For cross-cultural teens, there may be stigma and shame associated with eating disorders, which may prevent them from getting care because of cultural issues. There can also be significant challenges for families living outside of their passport or home country related to culture, language, and access to resources. According to Dr. Silber, more families are making use of online means of receiving counseling and services that may be useful for global teens.

Strategies for addressing eating disorders

Ask specific questions
- Have you ever tried to diet or cut back on your food intake? Do you eat big quantities of food at one time without control?
- Have you tried to vomit?
- Have you used laxatives or other diet pills?
- Do you exercise constantly? Do you feel the need to exercise all the time?
- Have you felt sad, depressed, suicidal, or anxious?
- Are any of your peers dieting or concerned about their weight?
- Are there certain parts of your body that you are unhappy about?

Be proactive

"Ask for help as soon as you notice that your child is cutting off entire categories of food, such as carbohydrates," says one expat mother whose daughter struggled with anorexia. "It's important to act immediately, as the more time goes by, the easier the disorder may take over. Consider possible mistakes or a slow response from the health system, which may be inevitable," she adds.

Realize you are not alone

If there is a delay in getting referrals and specialists, consider using local organizations that can support your child with coaching and ad-hoc nutritional plans, especially if you are in an international setting. Another parent of a teen adds, "Reach out to your community without shame or sense of guilt. This can happen to anyone. You are not a bad parent if it happened to you. Probably you have a very sensitive child who's looking for his or her place in this world."

Be aware of Pro Ana sites

Pro Ana websites are created by teens and adults to support restricted eating and maintaining anorexia. Knowing a teen is searching these sites may be a tip off that they are experimenting with restricted eating.

Consider mindfulness and yoga

Yoga and mindfulness are therapeutic practices that may help with recovery from an eating disorder. Practicing yoga has been shown to help improve body image and create greater awareness of feelings and emotions. Yoga has also been shown to help kids to eat balanced meals and prevent purging and over-exercising.

OBESITY

Obesity is becoming an epidemic globally, hence the term 'globesity.' My experience from working across the world is that this is increasingly a phenomenon in both developed and developing countries. In fact, more and more global teens in places like Mexico, India, and China are being diagnosed as overweight or obese, as well as in the UK, Canada, and Australia. Most obese teens remain obese in adulthood which is why – again – it is so important to address these issues early on.

Causes of obesity

Obesity can be attributed to several factors, including genetics and hormonal triggers. For example, children who have obese parents are twice as likely to become obese themselves. In some communities (such as among Indian households like my own), there is a tremendous cultural value placed on food and eating. For some families, particularly those in countries with limited access to food, being slightly overweight as an infant is perceived as a sign of well-being, financial success, and health.

In my view, more global teens are becoming obese because of their lifestyle and environment. There is also a growing shift globally towards more sedentary behaviors (less walking and outdoor playtime at school or home and more reliance on using cars and looking at screens). Also, an increase in the consumption of processed foods (such as frozen pizzas and take-out), ready-made foods and snacks, and sweetened beverages (such as juice and soda), is having a big impact. Having less sleep, being depressed, and having poor impulse control (such as kids with ADHD) can also affect eating habits.

 One of my favorite studies on obesity is the pet study. Researchers found that families that are obese are more likely to have pets that are also obese. This highlights the importance of family and lifestyle in addressing the issue.[69]

Overweight

Body mass index (BMI) is a measurement using height and weight that estimates how much body fat a person has. For teens under the age of 18, the body mass index is plotted on a chart by age (separate for boys and girls) to determine whether they fall within a healthy percentage range. Using the body mass index is not a perfect way to determine body fat but it is widely used as a screening tool. Being overweight is defined as having a body mass index at the 85-94% level for their age and gender. Teens may also have issues like high blood pressure, irregular periods, and high cholesterol.

The emotional impact can also be significant. "Teasing and bullying can be big issues for kids that are overweight," says Kelly, a parent I interviewed in a popular seaside resort in Turkey. Kelly is originally from Scotland and has been married to her Turkish husband for over 11 years. Kelly says there is a significant focus on weight and being petite in Turkish culture. She says their cross-cultural daughter is often the target of negative comments by peers in her local school. In addition, other parents often make comments to Kelly like, "What are you doing to her?" and, "You shouldn't feed her so much," which Kelly says compounds her daughter's feelings of guilt and shame.

Obesity

Being obese is defined as having a body mass index of 95% or greater for age and gender. (The body mass index threshold for overweight and obesity is lower for South Asians). Kids that are obese are at risk for diabetes, sleep apnea (difficulty breathing at night), and high blood pressure.

In my work with obese youth, I find they often struggle with low self-esteem and depression. In fact, teens who were obese reported having the same quality of life as kids who had been diagnosed with cancer and were undergoing chemotherapy. In many cases, the accompanying depression needs addressing first before starting a teen on a weight loss program.

Salil is a 15-year-old originally from India, but he has lived with his family in Kuwait for many years. His weight has slowly been increasing over the last few years since starting puberty. His mother says that he has been diagnosed as obese recently with a body mass index over 99% for his age and height. His parents and sister also struggle with obesity. In reviewing his diet, he has regular meals and occasionally several servings of rice, but snacks on cookies and candy with friends. He also has two to three glasses of juice per day. He is frequently on his computer playing video games and goes to sleep close to 11:30pm every night. He doesn't enjoy sports activities but does take part in gym at school twice per week. He denies being teased at school but is worried about his appearance, especially his chest area and stretch marks, and doesn't like taking off his shirt in front of classmates before gym. His blood pressure has been elevated and he has been snoring at night.

Salil's case is concerning as his weight has steadily been increasing. He also has had high blood pressure readings, snoring, and pseudo-gynecomastia (excessive fatty tissue that gives the appearance of breasts). In Salil's case, he needs to be evaluated by a provider for abnormal changes in his cholesterol, blood sugar, and other blood levels, as well as for sleep apnea and hypertension. The focus should be on whether he is motivated to change his behavior and what his main motivations are. Teen boys are often relieved to learn that their fatty breast tissue may resolve completely when their weight decreases. I encourage teens to work on gradually changing their eating habits and activity levels. For Salil this may include cutting back on cookies and juice, getting to bed earlier and – yes – minimizing screen time.

Supporting teens who are overweight or obese

When counseling teens about weight management, I ask my patients to come up with two or three personal goals related to diet and exercise and we create an action plan together. I try to see them back in 3-4 weeks for follow up. Typical goals may start with not gaining any additional weight, and over time we move towards bringing the weight to a healthier level. Depending on the severity of their issues, teens may also benefit from seeing a nutritionist and therapist to help co-manage diet and mood. Medications may have limited benefit in helping with weight loss, although they are not generally used for younger teens. Finally, in cases of severe obesity with significant complications such as diabetes and high blood pressure, teens may be candidates for bariatric surgery (reducing the size of the stomach with a band), which helps them to lose weight by feeling full earlier.

Strategies for addressing obesity

No quick fix
Unfortunately, there are no quick fixes when it comes to long-term weight loss. It can be challenging to change weight. Therefore, finding good teen-friendly providers that can motivate and educate will really help. In severe cases, a multidisciplinary obesity clinic or even residential treatment may be helpful.

Be a role model
Parents who eat healthy foods and participate in physical activities set an example for their teens to do the same. Parents, caregivers, extended family, and the teen's peer group are important in providing positive cues and motivation.

Getting buy-in is key
It is crucial to ensure that teens are motivated to make a change and are committed to the process. I often ask teens to brainstorm why they want to make a change (to be healthier, wear more figure-hugging clothes, avoid being teased, have more regular periods, decrease blood pressure or the appearance of having breasts – pseudo-gynecomastia in boys – for example). I tell teens that their providers and family are part of their extended support team, but that making real change is up to them.

Be aware of depression and ADHD
In addressing obesity, it is crucial to screen for depression and other mental health issues. Studies, for example, have shown that teens with ADHD may have a harder time with impulse control and therefore sticking with meal plans and exercise regimens. Treating the underlying issue first such as depression, anxiety, or ADHD, may help significantly with managing and maintaining weight loss.

Get digital support

Many institutions and providers are using online tools to supplement provider visits. For example, in Hong Kong, our team piloted an online curriculum and used weekly text messaging to help teens meet weight loss goals. There are also online tools that can help with tracking daily diet, being aware of nutritional choices, and sending reminders regarding exercise and sleep.

THE BOTTOM LINE: EATING DISORDERS AND OBESITY

- Having a healthy body image is important for global teens. However, media, peers, family, and pubertal changes can all negatively affect it.

- Disordered eating and eating disorders such as binge eating, anorexia, and bulimia can occur among teens. Warning signs may include skipping meals, becoming vegetarian, eating in secret, intense fear of gaining weight, purging or laxative use, a constant need to exercise, poor self-esteem, and moodiness.

- Treatment includes behavioral/nutritional counseling and in some cases hospitalization.

- Alongside eating disorders, global teens may be at risk for being overweight or obese. Teens dealing with increased weight may benefit from exercise, changing diet, and/or getting family and community support.

- For both eating disorders and obesity, be aware of warning signs and get help as soon as possible.

BIG ANSWERS

Common parent questions on eating disorders and obesity

1. **My daughter is constantly dieting and worried about her weight. She just became a vegan; what can we do to make sure she stays healthy?**

   Constantly dieting, being preoccupied about weight, and suddenly becoming vegan or vegetarian during adolescence can be a tip off for disordered eating and possibly anorexia, bulimia, and binge eating. Teens that are vegan or vegetarian need to learn how to get enough vitamin B12, iron, and protein by including lentils, nuts, tofu, and green leafy vegetables in their diet. It is also an important time to ask about body image, peer group, and social media use and to ensure your daughter is feeling positive about her weight and appearance.

2. **Can my feelings about my own body image affect my teen's body image?**

   Parents' feelings, concerns, and attitudes towards diet, exercise, and their own bodies can certainly affect teens. If you are constantly preoccupied with or making comments about your appearance, your kids may too.

3. **What can we do if we suspect our teen has anorexia?**

   The first step is to talk openly to your teen about your concerns. The focus is on making sure they stay healthy. The next step is to consider seeing a health provider to ensure there are no additional issues such as a low heart rate or nutritional deficiencies. Treatment may include seeing a nutritionist to increase calories, a therapist to help with emotions and behaviors, and a physician to monitor laboratory heart rate and other issues. The Maudsley method of family-centered care can be very useful (see Resources). The level of treatment available can vary greatly based on location and country. However, it is important to find providers that can connect and communicate well with your teen, especially if you are not in their home country. The good news is that teens do better when eating disorders are addressed early on.

4. **How can we help our teens to challenge societal norms about body image?**
It is important for teens to be critical of images and messages they are receiving from social media, their peers, and their community about having a certain appearance. Also, teens need to create a strong sense of their own strengths and self-image. Have discussions at home. Encourage them to have unique role models. Have teens look at organizations in the community or online that are challenging norms about body image.

5. **Our son is obese and gets teased a lot at school. What can he do to lose weight?**
A few questions to consider include:

a. *Is he motivated to make a change?*
b. *What are his eating and exercise habits like?*
c. *How many hours does he sleep, and how much screen time is he having?*
d. *Is he skipping meals, eating outside of the house, or consuming sugar-sweetened beverages regularly?*
e. *How is he handling the teasing?*
f. *Is he feeling depressed?*
g. *Are there other family members that are also obese?*

Teens do best when they are motivated to make a change and take steps towards improving their diet and increasing their activity level. Family involvement is key, particularly in relation to eating habits and exercise. Having a family mealtime is an excellent way to check on eating habits and ensure teens get a balanced meal. Your son may also benefit from speaking with a provider about self-esteem and bullying.

Common teen questions on eating disorders and obesity

1. **What can happen if you don't feel good about yourself on a regular basis?**
Not feeling good about yourself can affect your self-esteem and over time put you at higher risk for other issues such as depression. It is important to switch the focus from the outside (and your appearance) to your strengths and

other abilities. Try chatting with your parent, an adult, or friend about how you feel. If you don't feel comfortable or your feelings are persistent, it may be time to talk to a counselor or health provider.

2. **Can boys get eating disorders?**
    Although eating disorders like anorexia are more common in girls, they can happen among boys too, especially those struggling with gender identity issues, who have a history of abuse, are in certain sports, or work where maintaining a certain weight or appearance is important.

3. **At what age is it OK to get plastic surgery as a teen?**
    Your body (and how you feel about it) is constantly changing during the teen years. In general, it is better to wait till you are over 18 so your body is fully developed before you have a surgical procedure like breast enhancement or nose reshaping.

4. **My friend secretly goes to the bathroom and throws up after eating, but denies she has a problem. What should I do?**
    It is important to tell your friend that you suspect she has bulimia and that you want to make sure she gets the right help early on before it affects her more and leads to serious health issues. You may want to also enlist the help of an adult or parent.

5. **I have ADHD and find it very hard to stick to any kind of weight loss plan. What can I do?**
   Studies have shown that teens with ADHD may have more issues with impulse control and sticking to a weight loss program. Getting help for your ADHD with behavioral support and/ or medication will be useful in addressing your weight issues.

RESOURCES

Books

Eating Disorder: Recover From Your Eating Disorder and Fall in Love with Life, John Locke, CreateSpace Independent Publishing Platform, 2017

Overcoming Obesity in Teens and Pre-Teens: A Parent's Guide, Richard Travis, RLT publishing, 2012

Reviving Ophelia: Saving the Selves of Adolescent Girls, Mary Pipher, Riverhead Trade, 2005

Websites and articles

'Maudsley Method Family Therapy', Eating Disorder Hope, 2012: https://www.eatingdisorderhope.com/treatment-for-eating-disorders/types-of-treatments/maudsley-method-family-therapy

'Parent Toolkit', The National Eating Disorders Association, 2018: https://www.nationaleatingdisorders.org/parent-toolkit

'Tips for Parents – Ideas to Help Children Maintain a Healthy Weight'. Centers for Disease Control and Prevention, 2018: https://www.cdc.gov/healthyweight/children/index.html

"Drugs are a bet with the mind."
Jim Morrison

IN THIS CHAPTER:
- Risk factors for using alcohol and drugs.
- Recent teen trends including binge drinking and vaping.
- Common signs and side effects of alcohol and drugs.
- Ways to prevent and manage global teen substance use.

Tommy is a 16-year-old teen in The Hague, the Netherlands. He attends an international school and is tall and lanky with cropped brown hair. I notice an air of sadness when he asks if he can speak to me after a talk I give at his school. He confides in me that he smokes marijuana several times a week. He has a history of ADHD, and marijuana use seems to work much better than any other drug he's been prescribed over the years. In addition to using marijuana he has started drinking on the weekends with friends, about 5-6 beers at a time. He has recently started drinking alone. He says alcohol helps him with his anxiety about schoolwork and friends and allows him to feel calm.

Although there are many reasons why teens use substances, I have seen more and more teens who try it to 'self-medicate' and cope with depression and anxiety. Studies show that children whose parents talk to them about the risks of alcohol and other drugs are much less likely to use them. However, as teens may experiment or even use addictive substances on a more regular basis, it is important to know what may be triggering it (as in the case of Tommy), and when to get additional help. This chapter outlines key concepts related to alcohol and drug use and what we need to be aware of while speaking to Cross-Cultural Kids.

BIG QUESTIONS

Common parent questions on substance use

1. How do you help underage teens to stop drinking?

2. How can we help our teen to handle peer pressure to vape?

3. I smoked and drank when I was much younger. Do I lie or tell the truth to my teen about this if it comes up?

4. I've heard of home drug-testing kits. Can I use these to test my kids if I suspect they are using alcohol or drugs?

Common teen questions on substance use

1. How should I tell my friends I don't want to drink?

2. Is it OK to mix caffeine and alcohol?

3. How do you know if someone has alcohol poisoning?

4. In many places, recreational marijuana use is legal. So, what's the big deal if I use marijuana?

5. How come the legal drinking age is lower in some countries?

SUBSTANCE USE

I regularly ask teens whether they have friends who drink and if they feel pressure to do the same. Many underage teens confide that they know someone who has drunk alcohol, often to the point of being 'smashed' or 'out cold' on the ground. Boredom, curiosity, and the need to fit in are big drivers among young people. If teens have friends using alcohol or drugs, they are more likely to start engaging at the same level.

The term 'substance use' refers to the use of drugs or alcohol, and includes substances such as cigarettes, prescription drugs, inhalants, and illegal drugs. A substance use problem occurs when using alcohol or other drugs causes harm to teens. Substance use problems can lead to addiction.[70]

Risk factors among global teens

In general, having a significant transition or change, such as the loss of a relationship, onset of puberty, or a parent's divorce can be triggers for substance use (and abuse). Kids without a sense of connectedness in their families or school or who feel different in some way because of their appearance or background might also be at risk. As cross-cultural teens often struggle with their inherent sense of identity and belonging, as well as issues related to grief, loss, and moving, they may be particularly vulnerable. Poor self-esteem and impulse control are other risk factors. As Tommy's case illustrates, teens with a history of ADHD, depression, or low self-confidence are at a higher risk of substance abuse. They may find that using alcohol or drugs is their way of numbing their pain and managing challenges, which can be a form of self-medication. Having a family history of substance use can also put some teens at higher risk.

Culture and substance use

Adolescent substance use can also be affected by norms and attitudes in the community. Navigating norms can be particularly challenging for cross-cultural teens who need to address a mixture of beliefs and values in their own families, peer group, and community. For example, my German husband has a very different attitude towards alcohol in adolescence than I do. He grew up with wine being served with family meals and teens drinking beer (in fact, in many parts of Germany you can still get beer from a vending machine).

My own more conservative South Asian parents were closer to being teetotalers when I was a teen and rarely drank wine or beer with family meals. Using alcohol as an adolescent in our South Asian culture was strongly frowned upon. In addition, in the US where I grew up, there were strict rules about underage drinking on university campuses. As a result, my spouse and I have somewhat different attitudes regarding alcohol use among teens and young adults and need to be very clear about our own joint views and expectations for our cross-cultural boys.

Protective factors

When it comes to substance use, communication and connections count for cross-cultural teens. In a study conducted among Hispanic immigrants in the US, parent-teen communication on substance use was shown to have a very positive effect on decreasing the likelihood of binge drinking, cigarette smoking, and other markers of substance use.[71] The research also suggested that helping recent immigrant youth with connections to community, peers, and resources may be very useful in the prevention of substance use. Other protective factors include a peer group that doesn't engage in substance/alcohol use, parents knowing about the peer groups and families of peers, frank discussions with teens, and keeping an open dialogue. Given that cross-cultural youth often struggle with issues related to identity and belonging, it is vital that young people are encouraged to develop roots in their community and feel valued.

What do you as a parent need to know? It is important to have a clear understanding of what teens are experimenting with these days. Also, to develop a thoughtful and informed response to preventing and addressing alcohol and drug use.

ALCOHOL USE

Alcohol slows the body down, causes changes in vision and judgment, which then affects decision-making skills. Poor judgment can lead to motor vehicle accidents, drownings, and risky behaviors such as unsafe sex. In addition to affecting decision-making, teens who start drinking regularly before the age of 17 are also more likely to become alcohol dependent for life than teens that wait till they are older.[72]

How does alcohol work? Gamma-aminobutyric acid, or GABA, is a major neurotransmitter found throughout the brain. Its activation is associated with sleep and relaxation. Alcohol mimics the effects of GABA by binding to these receptors in the brain. Small amounts of alcohol also increase serotonin and dopamine in the brain, which creates a feeling of pleasure. Drinking too much can overstimulate GABA pathways, causing sedation and, in severe cases, toxicity. Regular alcohol use desensitizes the GABA receptors causing teens to feel more stressed or anxious, which may make them want to drink more often.[73]

Many of the teens I work with report binge drinking at parties and other events. Binge drinking is defined as having five or more servings of alcohol as a male, or four or more as a female, on a single occasion within the past two weeks. A serving is a shot of hard alcohol or 8ozs (30ccs) of beer or wine. Research in the US has shown that nearly 80% of high school kids have tried alcohol, and approximately 5.1 million people aged 12-20 reported binge drinking in the past month.[74]

Many teens don't think that a few episodes of binge drinking can affect them. However, imaging studies (MRIs) of binging teen brains tell a different story. Even after one episode of binge drinking, changes were documented in the structure and function of teen brains.[75] In an informal systematic review we conducted at the Vrije Universiteit Amsterdam Medical Center, we also found that binge drinking had a negative effect on executive functioning and memory among young people aged 12-24 years.

What does this all mean? Drinking alcohol, particularly binge drinking during adolescence, can damage the parts of the brain responsible for decision-making, self-control, memory, and learning. Although alcohol use is common, the significant effect on the developing brain is one of the issues to discuss with teens.

Identifying alcohol use

Jamie is a 16-year-old cross-cultural teen born in New Zealand and living in London. I meet his parents at a talk that I am conducting on communicating with teens. They mention that his grades have recently dropped, and he is having problems focusing at school. Also, that he is an accomplished guitarist. Lately, Jamie is less interested in playing guitar or doing any extracurricular activities. His parents have noticed that some of the liquor in their home cabinet has gone missing and they know some of Jamie's older friends have been going out to parties where there is alcohol.

In my discussion with Jamie's parents, I discuss some of the signs of a teen or preteen using alcohol. Also, that it is important to have an honest discussion with him about drinking, the physical and psychological effects of alcohol on teens, and ways to handle peer pressure.

Warning signs of alcohol use

- Changes in mood, grades, or interest in daily activities
- Eating or sleeping more or less than usual
- Keeping to themselves, always in their bedroom
- Showing difficulty focusing, skipping school or work
- Acting defiant, getting in trouble with authority figures
- Spending time with peers who are using drugs
- Attending parties where drugs and alcohol are consistently being used
- Taking or borrowing money or alcohol from home
- Red eyes, slurred speech, difficulty with coordination

Sarah, 15 years old, was one of my teen patients from Bethesda, Maryland. She attended a local private school and was struggling with alcohol use and depression. On one occasion she went to a party and remembers drinking one beer after another. She can't recall the rest of the night, except that at one point she was naked in a hot tub with five other boys at 1am. She didn't think anything happened to her, but after reluctantly telling part of this story to her parents a week later, her mom brought her in to see me. When I speak to Sarah alone, she confides that she was embarrassed and upset and revealed that she had been drinking for a couple of years, mainly at parties and with friends. She also tells me she started drinking to fit in with her friends. Later, she began drinking to 'numb' the pain from a breakup with a boyfriend and release the stress she was experiencing about getting good grades, handling expectations, juggling her extracurriculars, and schoolwork.

Sarah and I ended up having a long discussion about the risks of her alcohol use, including increasing her risk for pregnancy and infections. We also did some screening for sexually transmitted diseases and pregnancy. In follow-up visits, we continued to discuss her drinking and how to address stress in other ways. She finally agreed to involve her parents in cutting back on alcohol and getting outside counseling to address her stress and anxiety.

I use this story in part to emphasize the importance of the developing teen brain and the fact that teens may be more likely to experiment with alcohol and drug use during the adolescent years. Unfortunately, I have had to counsel and support too many teens who have been the victims of sexual assault. Every year, young people die because of acute alcohol intoxication or accidents and related injuries. It illustrates the need for parents to engage young people in making good health decisions and provide support when decision-making is poor.

Strategies for addressing alcohol use

Talk about peer group
For example, "Have you heard about other kids using alcohol or drugs in your school? What do you think about it?" Their interests may be affected by what their friends believe, so work with your child to say no to peer pressure and discuss the importance of thinking and acting on their own. Role playing scenarios can also be helpful to anticipate situations in which teens might find themselves.

It's OK to say no
If a drink of any kind is offered, remind teens it is OK to say no and not to give in to the pressure. Alternatively, they can state that they are the designated driver or the sober member of a group.

Have a backup plan
Encourage teens to leave a situation in which they feel uncomfortable. Make sure they have a way to get home or a phone number where an adult can be reached. In communities where teens may be driving, encourage young people never to accept a ride from someone who has been drinking. Some parents or adults find that offering to pick up a teen from an uncomfortable situation (with no questions asked) helps encourage adolescents to be honest and to call when they really need help. Parents can work with teens to develop a coded message that teens can send via text to get them out of otherwise uncomfortable situations.

Model behavior
Be a good role model and consider how your own use of alcohol may influence your kids. Avoid excessive preaching that kids tend to ignore anyway and focus instead on providing love and support. Remember to model

responsible drinking behaviors. Teach young people that even when life is difficult or stressful, using alcohol as an escape can make a tough situation even worse as it doesn't address the underlying stressor.

Be aware of date rape drugs
Remind teens to always ask what's in the drink. Also, to never take a drink that has been unattended as it is hard to know what may have been put into it (such as Rohypnol – 'date rape' drug – or other substances).

Have a wingman (or woman)
Encourage teens to have a clear buddy or 'wingman' at an event or party. If they have an emergency or feel uncomfortable, they have someone who can check on them and make sure they are OK.

Think about consequences
Discuss legal consequences such as school suspensions for possession of alcohol, court trials, or fines. Also, serious consequences such as car accidents or death. Consider making a written contract between you and your child about the rules and boundaries when going out, but also how you will support your son or daughter. By discussing your expectations about behaviors, you can help minimize surprises.[76]

Discuss sexual assault
Remind teens that binge-drinking young people are at higher risk of becoming the victim – or perpetrator – of sexual assault. Although, it is NOT their fault if they were assaulted, alcohol can blur boundaries. Both girls and boys need to understand that they are impaired in these situations and that impairment translates into an *inability to consent.*

Know the signs of acute alcohol poisoning

Teens need to be aware of the warning signs of acute alcohol intoxication. If they notice that someone is unconscious or not responding to basic stimulation, very pale, breathing fast, or has dilated pupils, they may have high blood levels of alcohol and are at risk for choking or death. It is always best to get help rather than assume someone is going to sleep it off or be OK.

Know the laws

Many families travel all over the world and it is important to always know the laws of the jurisdiction in which you reside. What is legal in one country could be illegal in another country and land a teen in jail.

 Mixing caffeine and alcohol, such as Red Bull and vodka, is a popular combination among young people that concerns me. Drinking caffeine allows you to stay awake longer (in order to drink more alcohol). This combination can increase the likelihood of reaching dangerously high blood alcohol levels quickly while significantly affecting decision-making, consent, and vulnerability to sexual assault. This is a combination to discuss with kids and to encourage them to avoid!

What you can do

Signs of abuse include drinking more alcohol than originally planned, failing to control consumption, spending a large amount of time using drugs/alcohol, having withdrawal symptoms when not drinking, and craving alcohol. If there is alcohol abuse, get help from a professional service. If your teen is 18, he or she is legally an adult in most countries, but you can still request help. Take your teen to a medical provider to discuss addiction treatment centers and rehabilitation centers. Try for providers that are culturally sensitive and can communicate well with your teen.

DRUG USE

Globally, nicotine and marijuana are the top drugs used among teens. In recent years, e-cigarettes and vaping have gained popularity. Tobacco products can be smoked, chewed, sniffed, and vaped.[77] Smoking tobacco via cigarettes is common among teens globally. The use of flavored tobacco smoked via a hookah pipe is also popular and gives a high dose of nicotine. The drugs favored by teens can vary tremendously based on location and age. For example, in Hong Kong, ketamine is the drug of choice for local teens. In Brazil, the use of crack cocaine is increasing. In Turkey, adolescents report using marijuana, heroin, and ecstasy (MDMA). In the US, younger teens cite use of inhalants while older teens report using stimulants, opioid pain medications, and synthetic marijuana. How do you know that your teen is using drugs? The following are some of the signs to be aware of and what you need to know about nicotine, marijuana, inhalants, stimulants, and pain medications.

Warning signs of drug use

- Change in friends or peer group (hanging out with kids who use drugs)

- Change in mood – such as being more cranky, anxious, or isolated
- Change in grades, ability to focus, and school absences
- Red or puffy eyes, persistent cough, or runny nose
- Rapid weight loss or gain
- Smell of smoke on clothes
- Poor hygiene or personal appearance
- Unexplained disappearance of money

Nicotine

Nicotine is contained in tobacco products and affects brain development in young people, which can make it harder to learn and concentrate. Some brain changes are permanent and can affect mood and impulse control later in life, which is why addressing and preventing use is so critical. Smoking cigarettes and tobacco use can increase heart rate and raise blood pressure, irritate the throat, cause bad breath, and damage the airways. Studies also confirm that young cigarette smokers are more likely to use marijuana.[78]

Vaping

According to a recent study in the *Journal of the American Medical Association*, nearly 28% of American high schoolers and 10% of middle schoolers report vaping.[79] Vaping is the inhaling of a vapor created by an electronic cigarette (e-cigarette) or other devices. E-cigarettes are battery-powered smoking devices containing cartridges sometimes called 'pods.' These cartridges are filled with a liquid that contains nicotine (sometimes as much as a whole pack of cigarettes) and come in a variety of flavors that are appealing to teens such as bubble gum and cotton candy. The liquid is heated into a vapor, which the user inhales. The e-cigarettes or 'vapes' come in many different shapes and sizes but most are small – some even look like USB flash drives.

Vaping is not yet a worldwide phenomenon, but its popularity is increasing. It is particularly common among 12-15-year-old students in countries such as the US and the UK since it is discrete, relatively odorless, and easy to hide and use in a bathroom. The nicotine in vaping can be very addictive, which in time can affect brain development, memory, concentration, self-control, and mood. The substances found in e-cigarettes have been linked to serious respiratory problems, hospitalizations, and even deaths among teens.

Teens sometimes feel that e-cigarettes are not as harmful as regular cigarettes since e-cigarettes were developed to help addicts cut back. Also, even though not designated as such by the industry, most of the marketing is geared towards teens, advertising e-cigarettes with attractive packaging and flavors. However, it is important to know that e-cigarettes are very addictive to children and teens (with developing brains) compared to adults. Young people's brains build synapses or connections faster than adult brains. Nicotine changes the way these synapses are formed.[80]

Warning signs of vaping

- Increased thirst and/or energy levels
- Nosebleeds, acne
- Unexplained charges on bills
- Vape-related accessories like USB drives, battery chargers, or music devices

What you can do

It is important to have an open and honest discussion about your concerns, why they are vaping, if they feel pressure from peers to do so, the complications that can arise from continuing, and best steps to stop.

One of the best ways to address vaping is to increase their desire for respect and awareness of injustice. According to the Center for the Developing Adolescent, "If we can find ways to convey health information in ways that authentically honor teens' natural motivation to feel admired and respected instead of just lecturing, we're more likely to have a positive impact on the rapidly emerging vaping epidemic."[81]

I tell teens that the design and flavors are aimed at a young audience. Also, that if they are vaping by age 14-15, they are more likely to continue smoking through adulthood. As a result, teens are being 'targeted' to become lifelong users. This strategy may allow teens to realize they are being unjustly manipulated by e-cigarette companies. Finally, if a teen is having a hard time stopping, I recommend they see a health provider to discuss ways to quit safely.

Marijuana

Teens use marijuana to feel relaxed and high. Popular ways to use it include smoking it in joints or blunts (cigars stuffed with marijuana), inhaling it via a water pipe (bong), or eating foods cooked with it. Although some teens report that they feel marijuana use is safer than smoking cigarettes, there can still be significant effects. In the short-term, it can affect coordination and attention, while long-term it can cause permanent changes in working memory. One study showed that even 25 years after stopping marijuana use, users had a six to eight-point reduction in IQ.[82] There has been renewed concern about the effects of marijuana on developing teen brains as legislation about its use has relaxed in many parts of the world.

Warning signs of marijuana use

- A distinct smell or red eyes
- Delayed reaction times
- Increased appetite
- Abrupt anxiety and panic

Legalization of recreational marijuana in many communities across the world can give both teens and parents a false notion of safety. What's more, the marijuana that adults may have used in the 70s/80s is not the same product teens use today. Remind teens that marijuana may be adulterated and in a much stronger form than in the past, which can put them at greater risk for abuse and other complications. Treatment of marijuana use includes counseling to address underlying issues such as depression.

Prescription Drugs

More teens than ever are taking prescription medications inappropriately. Common types of drugs abused include stimulants used for ADHD, opioids used for pain control, and depressants used for anxiety. According to the US National Institute on Drug Abuse, a common misperception is that prescription drugs are less harmful to one's body than other kinds of drugs. Signs and consequences of the prescription drug used can vary.

- **Stimulants** such as methamphetamines may cause paranoia, an irregular heartbeat, and sleeplessness

- **Opioids** such as oxycodone can cause drowsiness, nausea, and constipation

- **Depressants** such as sleeping pills and sedatives can cause slurred speech, shallow breathing, fatigue, disorientation, lack of coordination, and seizures upon withdrawal from chronic use.[83]

The misuse of stimulants is particularly high among college and university students in many countries. Many of my teen patients report that they can buy stimulants from peers to use before exams and tests. According to the Substance Abuse and Mental Health Services Administration, one in four US teens think that prescription drugs can be used as a study aid and nearly one-third of parents say they believe that attention deficit hyperactivity disorder (ADHD) medication can improve their teen's academic performance (even if they don't have a diagnosis of ADHD). Also, nearly two-thirds of US teens surveyed who misused pain relievers obtained them from family and friends, making it important to store medications safely in the home, throw away medications that are no longer being used, and educate teens and adults about the dangers of sharing prescribed medications.[84] Also, pharmacies and providers of prescribed medications have made efforts to strengthen monitoring in an attempt to reduce misuse and abuse. If you suspect your teen is misusing or abusing prescription medications, it is important to educate them about the potential dangers and seek further medical support.

Inhalants

Inhalants include gases, solvents, and products in an aerosol can like markers, glue, spray paint, and gasoline. Kids get a temporary high from these drugs but breathing these gases can cause brain, kidney, and liver damage and in rare cases, death. Inhalants are found everywhere – in homes, schools, and stores. They are inexpensive compared to other drugs and are easy to obtain. Since they are common and legal, their use may go unnoticed. Younger children may just use inhalants while older youths are more likely to use inhalants with alcohol and other drugs.

Warning signs of inhalant use

- Empty aerosol containers or paint cans
- A glue or gasoline odor
- An unusual, harsh breath odor

As with marijuana use, treatment for inhalant abuse is via behavioral counseling.

What you can do

Jamal is a 17-year-old boy who recently started high school in New York City. His parents have noticed that he has become more aloof. He is often with older classmates at a nearby park on the weekends. His eyes at times appear very red and he has frequent bouts of colds and bronchitis. His parents are concerned that he may be depressed.

It is very possible that Jamal is using drugs to handle depression. His recent move and loss of friends and support could be potential triggers. I suggest that his parents ask him directly about his peer group and if they are doing drugs before moving on to ask their son about drug use of his own. Next, it would be helpful to discuss the importance of using positive coping skills such as sports and considering getting additional counseling support for transition and grief. In addition, his parents should try to ensure Jamal feels connected to his new community by joining extracurriculars such as a club or engaging in sports.

Addressing teen drug use is not easy but there is a lot you as a parent can do to help. The first step is having an open conversation about drug use, peer group, and where the need to use comes from. Also, about their motivation to quit and their level of commitment to change the behavior. Teens may benefit from establishing a quit date and engaging peers and family members to support them. Speaking to a health professional, coach, or mentor can help.

Set clear rules about drug use and your expectations. Teens' increasing need for independence may make them want to defy your instructions. Remember, if you make your teen feel accepted and respected, you increase the chances that your teen will be open with you.

Strategies for addressing drug use

Encourage them to be angry for being targeted
Some brands market to teens by making special flavors, advertisements, or packaging. Remind adolescents they are being targeted to start using drugs at a young age.

Think about friends
Have them consider hanging out with friends that are less likely to use drugs and alcohol on a regular basis as their main way to relax.

Be aware of family history
If you or a family member smokes cigarettes regularly, your teen may be more likely to do so. Remind them there is a strong genetic association to substance use. If they start as

a teen, they may have a harder time stopping than others.

Remind them it affects their body and brain

Vaping and inhalants may lead to lung inflammation (irritation) and affect athletic performance and asthma. For younger teens who are focused on concrete details as opposed to more abstract consequences, I tell them that their teeth will turn yellow and they will have bad breath. Discuss how nicotine is very addictive and can significantly affect their developing brains. Show them the data related to vaping risks. For example, calculators. org has excellent graphics and visuals explaining the latest research on vaping that can be used to explain risks to teens (see *Resources*).

Understand withdrawal

The signs of withdrawal are highest in the first few days after stopping and improve over time. They include very strong cravings for nicotine, headaches, crankiness, angry or depressed mood, and trouble sleeping.

Get a health provider involved

Have your physician talk to your kid about the dangers of using drugs. Some teens may benefit from medications to help them stop their addictive behavior. Teens may also be self-medicating for other medical conditions (such as ADHD, depression, anxiety, and so on) and a health provider can screen for such conditions and provide appropriate care (therapy and/or medications).

Quitting substance use

- Ask your teen why they want to quit and write it down on paper or on their phone. They can look back at the reasons each time they feel the urge to vape or smoke cigarettes or marijuana.

- Get them to pick a date to stop. They can put it on the calendar and tell supportive friends and family that they're quitting on that day.
- Get rid of all supplies.

If a teen has already tried quitting or reducing use and failed, then it's important they receive treatment as soon as possible. If a teen continues denying using drugs but the parent still suspects he or she is not honest, then you may need a professional. Therapists, pediatricians, and addiction specialists can help diagnose a teen drug problem. Treatment may include day or inpatient treatment, support groups, and ongoing therapy. The level of support, language of care providers, and degree of cultural sensitivity can vary tremendously from place to place, so it is important to start early.

A report by the Substance Abuse and Mental Health Services Administration (SAMHSA) shows that one in ten parents said they did not talk to their teens about the dangers of drugs. However, surveys of teens aged 12-17 show that teens who believe their parents would strongly disapprove of their substance use are less likely to do it.[85] As with alcohol use, having conversations about drug use is very important. Parents who are educated about the effects of drug use can give their kids correct information and clear up any misconceptions.

THE BOTTOM LINE: SUBSTANCE USE

- Teen brains are more vulnerable to the effects of even small doses of drugs and alcohol, and your teen needs to be made aware that regular drinking can have severe consequences.

- Initiate age-appropriate conversations about these issues with your teen at all stages of their development. No parent, teen, or family is immune to the effects of drugs or alcohol.

- Any kid can end up in trouble, even those who have made efforts to avoid it and even when they have been given proper guidance from their parents. However, certain groups of kids may be more likely to use drugs than others.

- Teens who have friends who use drugs are likely to try drugs themselves. Also, those feeling socially isolated or who have underlying medical conditions such as anxiety, depression, or ADHD, may be more likely to use drugs or alcohol.

- Pay attention to how your kids are feeling and let them know that you're available and willing to listen in a non-judgmental way. Also, be aware of signs of potential drug or alcohol use so that you can seek additional care if needed.

Big Answers

Common parent questions on substance use

1. **How do you help underage teens to stop drinking?**
   Talk to your teen about the concrete effects of alcohol on their body. For example, alcohol can damage your brain and body, including

your looks, and puts you at a much higher risk of becoming an alcoholic when you are older. Ask your teen about what his peers are doing and look out for underlying triggers, including mood issues. Also, consider getting outside help.

2. **How can we help our teen to handle peer pressure to vape?**
   Vaping is becoming increasingly popular, particularly as some teens view it as safer than regular cigarettes. Discuss the addictive quality of nicotine and the increased likelihood of continuing to use e-cigarettes or other tobacco products if there is a family history of smoking. Also, talk about how many companies are targeting teens in their marketing. Role play saying, "No thanks" or, "I don't like how this makes me feel," to peers who suggest they vape and explain the consequences of vaping at school or home. Remind teens that vaping has been linked to respiratory illness and even death among teens. Have teens consider hanging out with peers that don't pressure them to vape or use other drugs and that can respect their personal decisions. Brainstorm how to create a community or group where it is not cool to vape. For more strategies, see vaping articles in the Resources section of this chapter.

3. **I smoked and drank when I was much younger. Do I lie or tell the truth to my teen about this if it comes up?**
   This is not an easy question, but the short

answer is that you never want to lie to your child or teen as you lose credibility and trust. On the other hand, you don't want to overshare risky behaviors that you took part in and normalize them. One approach may be to say, "I did drink and smoke a bit in school. I turned out OK, but some of my friends weren't so lucky. In fact, their drinking and smoking led to bigger issues. We now know a lot more about the challenges related to drugs and alcohol. Bottom line, I don't want you to do them because they are illegal and not healthy for your brain or body."

4. **I've heard of home drug-testing kits. Can I use these to test my kids if I suspect they are using alcohol or drugs?**

   Drug-testing kits are easily available through the Internet and pharmacies. Although some argue for the benefits of testing, the American Academy of Pediatrics states that "drug testing poses substantial risks – in particular, the risk of harming the parent-child and school-child relationships by creating an environment of resentment, distrust, and suspicion."[86] Also, drug testing does not test for all drugs available, and results can be falsified. Bottom line, better not to do routine drug testing unless you have discussed with your health provider and have very specific indications for doing so.

Common teen questions on substance use

1. **How should I tell my friends I don't want to drink?**
   You can say that you don't feel your best when you are drinking or that you want to be the designated driver. Alternatively, you can say that you don't feel you need to drink to have fun. Understand that true friends should not force you to do something against your will and will respect your decision not to drink.

2. **Is it OK to mix caffeine and alcohol?**
   Using alcohol with caffeine lets you drink more for longer and therefore puts you at higher risk for getting drunk quicker. High caffeine drinks such as Monster and Red Bull can also lead to fatal heart conditions (arrhythmias).

3. **How do I know if someone has alcohol poisoning?**
   Looking pale or blue, having shallow breaths, and not reacting to others may all be signs. It is better to err on the side of caution and call for help if in doubt.

4. **In many places, recreational marijuana use is legal. So, what's the big deal if I use marijuana?**
   Even though marijuana is legal in many places, the effect on teens is very different than with adults. Marijuana can have long-term effects on your developing brain and affect memory, concentration, and even your IQ.

5. How come the legal drinking age is lower in some countries?
Alcohol is more accessible and part of local and family traditions and culture in some countries, less so in others. For example, 16-year-olds in Germany can consume beer and wine. Some countries do not have drinking age laws, while others completely ban alcohol use for teens. Many countries have rules about drinking below 21 years of age. This can lead to a wide range of practices around alcohol use. It is important to be familiar with the rules and culture of the community that you are visiting or living in.

RESOURCES

Books

Raising Drug-Free Kids: 100 Tips for Parents, Aletha Solter, Da Capo Lifelong Books, 2006

Websites and articles

'Prevention Tips for your High-School Aged Adolescent', Mass.gov, 2019: https://www.mass.gov/service-details/prevention-tips-for-your-high-school-aged-adolescent

'Principles of Adolescent Substance Use Disorder Treatment: A Research-Based Guide', National Institute on Drug Abuse, 2014: https://www.drugabuse.gov/publications/principles-adolescent-substance-use-disorder-treatment-research-based-guide/frequently-asked-questions/what-drugs-are-most-frequently-used-by-adolescents

'Evidence-Based Treatment Improves Overall Adolescent Health Outcomes', Abigail Nover, *Psychiatry Advisor*, 2019: https://www.psychiatryadvisor.com/home/topics/child-adolescent-psychiatry/evidence-based-treatment-improves-overall-adolescent-health-outcomes

'Tobacco, Nicotine, & Vaping (E-Cigarettes)', National Institute on Drug Abuse for Teens, 2019: https://teens.drugabuse.gov/drug-facts/tobacco-nicotine-e-cigarettes

'Analyzing the Health Risks of Vaping', Calculators.org, 2020: https://www.calculators.org/health/vaping-risks.php

'How to Tell if Your Kid is Vaping', Natasha Burgert, *U.S. News,* 2018: https://health.usnews.com/wellness/for-parents/articles/2018-07-27/how-to-tell-if-your-kid-is-vaping

'Teenage Cannabis Use Linked to Memory Problems', Kashmira Gander, *Newsweek*, 2019: https://www.newsweek.com/teenage-cannabis-use-linked-memory-problems-1433884

'Prescription Drugs', National Institute on Drug Abuse for Teens, 2020: https://teens.drugabuse.gov/drug-facts/prescription-drugs

SPECIAL EDUCATIONAL NEEDS AND GIFTED TEENS 12

"Every student can learn, not just on the same day, or in the same way."

George Evans

IN THIS CHAPTER:

- Identifying and supporting global teens with special educational needs including Attention Deficit Hyperactivity Disorder (ADHD), autism, and learning disabilities.
- Identifying and supporting gifted and twice exceptional teens.

Abasi is a 14-year-old teenager from Cameroon. His parents work in a large multinational organization and he has moved several times in his life. He comes into our clinic for a sports injury but while he is being evaluated his father mentions that there have been significant conflicts at home regarding his schoolwork since starting high school this year. He mentions that Abasi has had more and more difficulty focusing on homework and finishing his assignments.

BIG QUESTIONS

Common parent questions on special educational needs and giftedness

1. How can we access services for a teen that has special educational needs when we live abroad?

2. What exactly is high functioning autism syndrome and how do we help our teen that may have it?

3. Our teen daughter struggles with focus and concentration, has been recently diagnosed with attention deficit hyperactivity disorder (ADHD), and could benefit from medication. My spouse doesn't believe in the condition or using medications for it. Any tips?

4. Our son gets bored easily in school and is often reading a book instead of listening to the teacher during class. He is also more

advanced than his classmates in most of his subjects. What resources should we look for to make sure he stays engaged at school?

Common teen questions on special educational needs and giftedness

1. I recently started high school in a new town. I have a hard time staying organized and getting my homework done. Is this normal?

2. I get easily distracted and often lose things. My parents are always yelling at me for being lazy and absent-minded and not putting enough effort into my schoolwork. What should I do?

3. I can get extra time to take tests because I have ADHD, but I don't want any of my classmates to know I have a diagnosis. How do I handle this?

4. I tried my friend's ADHD medication and I thought it really helped me to get more work done. Do I have ADHD?

SPECIAL EDUCATIONAL NEEDS

In the informal survey I conducted among cross-cultural teens, nearly half of the respondents mentioned staying organized as a significant concern along with handling academic stress. Of course, for many this is simply a matter of juggling priorities and sleep. However, for some teens, this could point to a more significant issue requiring educational and psychological support from school or a health provider. For example, adolescents with special educational needs such as ADHD (a condition associated with inattention and/or hyperactivity and impulsiveness), learning disabilities, or autism may have difficulties that make it harder for them to learn. Being aware of these issues and getting support early on can help teens to stay confident and successfully navigate both their academic and personal lives.

Living in a community outside your host country or navigating cross-cultural issues can make it much harder to spot and deal with special educational needs issues. It can also be tough to source the right sort of support available locally. In many of the places I've worked, there is stigma and shame attached to having a special educational needs diagnosis or getting additional help.

In researching the topic, I met with Dr. Roby Marcou, an accomplished developmental pediatrician and educator. Dr. Marcou has worked with young people in Asia for over 26 years and currently leads a popular practice in Singapore. "In general, children become less dependent on their parents in their teen years," she told me. "However, in the case of teens with special needs, the adolescent may continue to be more dependent on their parents and caregivers for support and for navigating the educational and health system." In these situations, she adds, "Cultural differences at home such as language and expectations can be magnified and can potentially add to the challenges of getting care."

Attention Deficit Hyperactivity Disorder (ADHD)

ADHD can show up by early childhood and continue into adulthood, although many times it is not till the teen years that it is formally identified. ADHD can affect thinking, school performance, feelings, and relationships. Also, it can present differently in boys (primarily as hyperactivity) rather than girls (more inattentiveness). Teens tend to outgrow hyperactivity (around age 13), but don't tend to outgrow inattentiveness (in either sex). The causes of ADHD are not exactly known. Studies do show in individuals with ADHD that special chemicals known as neurotransmitters don't work in the same way as in people without ADHD. Also, there are differences in the activity levels of the brain part that controls attention.[87]

 There is a strong genetic component in ADHD. In fact, many parents I have worked with realize that they have the condition themselves after their child or teen is diagnosed and have sought treatment as adults. Of course, knowing a sibling or parent has ADHD can certainly help global teens to understand they may also struggle with similar issues.

ADHD can occur with mainly inattentive or hyperactive or combined inattentive-hyperactive types. What should you look out for? Symptoms usually start before the age of 12 and may include the following:

Symptoms of ADHD

ADHD – inattentive

- Difficulty focusing on the most important elements of a task
- Failure to provide close attention to detail, careless mistakes
- Difficulty maintaining attention in play, school, or home activities
- Difficulty organizing tasks, activities, and belongings or completing assignments

ADHD – hyperactivity-impulsivity

- Has difficulty awaiting turn
- Interrupts or intrudes on others (butts into conversations or games, blurts out responses)
- Fidgets with hands or feet or squirms in seat
- Feelings of restlessness
- Difficulty playing or engaging in leisure activities quietly
- Appears 'on the go' or acts as if 'driven by a motor'
- Talks excessively

ADHD – combined

Teens with ADHD may have difficulty disengaging from screens/computers and may need clear boundaries. They may also struggle with falling asleep at night. If they are obese or overweight, they may have difficulty regulating impulsive eating. The good news is that with clear understanding and support, global teens with ADHD can do well in any setting.[88]

Diagnosing ADHD

Returning to the case of Abasi, according to his parents, he often procrastinates on big projects and needs to get an extension or stays up late before a paper is due to complete it. According to his mom, he did better in middle school when he had one homeroom teacher and a more structured schedule but has always struggled with finishing on time, staying focused, and sitting still. Abasi's primary mother tongue is French, but he started learning English three years ago and is relatively fluent. He stays up late at night and has a hard time sleeping. Abasi says he is not depressed or anxious. He does say he feels his parents constantly nag him about getting his work done and tell him that he is lazy. They have also threatened to take away his computer and video games unless his grades improve and he gets his assignments done on time.

In order to decide if a teen has ADHD, it is important they have a complete medical, developmental, psychosocial, and educational assessment done by a health provider such as a pediatrician and/or a psychologist who does educational testing. Providers will often ask parents and teachers to fill out behavioral scales and questionnaires to make the diagnosis. They will also screen for conditions like depression, anxiety, substance use, and sleep issues, which can mimic and occur alongside ADHD. Teens with ADHD have real challenges with impulsiveness, organization, focus, or concentration. The issues rarely begin in adolescence; however, difficulties may be magnified when teens transition to high school and university.

In Abasi's case, his problems may be a combination of normal development coupled with transition, language, sleep cycle changes, cultural differences, and possibly

ADHD. Many 14-year-olds are still developing executive skills related to time management and awareness of consequences. They often start to gather speed as they transition to the independent schedules of high school or university. Learning to prioritize needs and balance activities are important life skills that teens learn in adolescence, often with the guidance (but not nagging) of parents and adults.

Abasi may be experiencing a normal delay in his sleep onset as he goes through adolescence, as explained in *Chapter 3* on the teen brain. Some children who are learning in a secondary language – one that is not their mother tongue – may have difficulty focusing at school when their issue is really related to language proficiency. However, Abasi may also have ADHD given his history of difficulty with focus and organization since childhood and his worsening symptoms after leaving a more structured setting and moving to high school. He would benefit from seeing a health provider such as a pediatrician or child psychologist for a more thorough evaluation.

Supporting teens with ADHD

Most experts agree that untreated ADHD can have numerous consequences including low esteem, school failure, and depression. It can also affect a teen's ability to control behaviors and affect everyday needs such as listening to someone in a conversation, being on time, managing schedules, or turning in assignments, which ultimately affects relationships with peers, family members, and work colleagues. Teens with ADHD may be at higher risk for substance and alcohol use. Finally, untreated ADHD can lead to distractibility and increased motor vehicle accidents, particularly for boys.

The many symptoms of ADHD can be managed with a combination of behavior modification, therapy, and medication. Useful behavior modification strategies include sitting at the front of the classroom to avoid being distracted. Counseling can help teens with ADHD learn how to handle their emotions and frustration. It can also help family members understand how to support a teen with ADHD. Finally, there are a range of medications such as the long-acting forms of methylphenidate and amphetamine/dextroamphetamine that help control hyperactive and impulsive behavior and increase attention span. Dietary supplements with omega-3 fatty acids have also shown some benefit. Parents also need to be aware that medications prescribed in one country are often not available in another. Some teens with ADHD have additional challenges with anxiety, learning disorders, or sleeping. The treatment of these associated problems may help improve a teen's overall functioning with ADHD.

When I see teens with ADHD, I talk to them about school performance, organizational habits, and focus. I discuss how getting extra time, having a structured environment and schedule, and/or taking medications may help them to perform better and feel confident about their abilities. I also encourage them to work with their school counselors and teachers to ensure they can get extra test time or services. Being aware and proactive about needs can go a long way in helping teens with ADHD to thrive.

Strategies for teens with ADHD

Find out how and where to get evaluated

Getting an assessment for ADHD can be challenging depending on the health care system, location, cost, and culture. In the US, for example, students in public schools can ask for assessments by a school psychologist, even though there may be long wait times. Students in private schools can go to private providers, which may or may not be covered by insurance. In some countries, as was the case for one teen patient in Bosnia, there may not be many, if any, providers doing assessments in the teen's native language. Parents should start with their local health care providers for initial screening and management. They may have to look at getting help outside their usual network if the management is insufficient or they live in a location with limited services. Speaking to other parents that have had teens in similar situations can be very useful in these difficult cases.

Think about pomodoros

Most kids (and adults) with ADHD are not able to sustain focus unless the work is broken down into smaller segments. According to the pomodoro time management method, the ideal amount of time for adults (known as a pomodoro) is about 25 minutes followed by a 3-4 minute break. Teens with ADHD do best with two to three pomodoros in a row followed by a longer break (15 minutes). Marking homework due dates in a digital or physical calendar, using special clocks and apps that show how much time is left to complete a task, sitting in a special chair that allows kids to move or wiggle, and getting extra time to take tests are all other ideas that have been shown to help. Finally, it is also important to work with the school to create an educational plan and ensure teachers understand your needs.

Maximize sleep and exercise

Having structure and a routine can help teens with ADHD tremendously. Also, most of the teens I have worked with do better when they get daily cardiovascular exercise such as swimming, biking, martial arts, or running. Although teens with ADHD may struggle with falling asleep, having a regular sleep regimen, avoiding excess caffeine, and using melatonin can all be effective. Finally, yoga and mindfulness are proven ways to help with focus and concentration.

Be aware of cultural differences
There can be differences in cultural views between parents as to whether the diagnosis exists and whether medical treatment is needed. This was the case for one cross-cultural couple I interviewed regarding their 12-year-old son in Washington, DC, who had moderate ADHD. The father was raised in a country where ADHD is not widely viewed as a real diagnosis and felt that starting any medication would be damaging for his son. The mother, on the other hand, felt very strongly that her son would benefit from stimulant treatment for his inattention and hyperactivity. This led to some significant family conflict and disagreements at home, until the father agreed to meet for a family session to discuss options and to read a book on helping teens with ADHD (see the *Resources* list at the end of the chapter).

Learn about local resources
Teens may refuse to take medication or take extra test time because they don't want to be perceived as different or feel that they can't be themselves. Some families are also concerned about their teen being identified as different or taking stimulants. In general, working to educate schools and family members about the diagnosis and needs is useful. Support groups for people with similar issues and needs such as Children and Adults with Attention-Deficit/Hyperactivity Disorder (CHADD) can help parents and teens with ADHD get acceptance and receive support.

AUTISM

Autism Spectrum Disorder (ASD) is a developmental disorder that causes difficulties with socializing, communicating, and behavior. The term 'spectrum' refers to the fact that some kids have a few mild symptoms while others have severe symptoms that can affect daily life. Teens who used to be diagnosed with a specific type of autism such as high functioning autism (Asperger syndrome) are now given the diagnosis of Autism Spectrum Disorder.[89] The disorder is classified according to the levels of severity and support needed for problems with social communication and with restricted or repetitive behaviors. It is not clear how Autism Spectrum Disorder develops. It is widely thought that it is a neurodevelopmental disorder that affects brain development and social and communication skills. Symptoms of Autism Spectrum Disorder are usually present by early childhood and can include the following:

Symptoms of Autism Spectrum Disorder

Communication
Kids are generally evaluated in childhood because of their challenges with communication. Undiagnosed adolescents may have more subtle difficulties with language and expression.

Social interaction
Ongoing difficulty communicating with or otherwise interacting with family and friends is a red flag for Autism Spectrum Disorder in teens. A teen that does not make eye contact, prefers to sit alone, and has very limited or awkward conversations with peers may be a sufferer. These behaviors would generally be present from childhood and not just develop in adolescence.

Nonverbal behaviors
Teens with Autism Spectrum Disorder have difficulty using and interpreting facial expressions, gestures, and body postures.

Restricted and repetitive behaviors or activities
Changes in routine can be upsetting for an Autism Spectrum Disorder teen. They may perceive sounds (such as a loud party), tastes (some refuse to eat certain foods), or touch (such as wool or other scratchy materials) differently too. Autism Spectrum Disorder teens may have hand or finger flapping, repetitive rocking, or walking on tiptoe from childhood.

Cognitive skills
An ASD teen may perform tasks that require memorization but may have difficulty or be uneven with higher-level skills such as reasoning and processing information. Some have special skills in memory or mathematics despite significant difficulties in other areas. One of my teen Autism Spectrum Disorder patients had an uncanny ability to recall addresses and license plates.

Language skills
There is a wide variability in the severity and quality of language problems for teens with Autism Spectrum Disorder. Some may have difficulty starting or sustaining a conversation with others. In languages different than their mother tongue, this is a challenge.

Diagnosing Autism Spectrum Disorder

Shaun is a tall, shy cross-cultural 16-year-old who is struggling to make friends at his middle school. He also doesn't make eye contact easily and will occasionally chew his sweater or shirt sleeve when he is anxious or worried. In fact, he has quite a few holes in his shirts. He prefers to be with adults and talk to teachers rather than the kids in his class and has difficulty with certain classes at school. However, according to his parents he can remember dates of events years ago. His parents would like to know how to help him. They feel that these behaviors have been present since childhood but have become more apparent in middle school.

Parents or educators who notice that a child or teen has one or more symptoms of Autism Spectrum Disorder should talk to a health care provider as soon as possible. The evaluation for autism usually includes a complete medical history, physical and neurological exam, and assessment of a child or teen's social, language, and cognitive skills. It is very possible that Shaun has high functioning autism. He would benefit from a management plan at school.

Supporting Teens with Autism Spectrum Disorder

Early diagnosis and treatment of Autism Spectrum Disorder can improve some behaviors and is very important in establishing self-confidence and social skills during the teen years. As with other special needs, there can be challenges to finding specialists and overcoming cultural and familial stigma about having a diagnosis.

For cross-cultural teens, there is the additional challenge of getting diagnosed early enough and having access to adequate resources within the community. The lack of proficiency in a local language and the stigma of having the Autism Spectrum Disorder label can be problematic for teens and families. These difficulties can be compounded by cultural barriers and integration into the broader community. For example, a cross-cultural teen with Autism Spectrum Disorder may be unable to understand the facial expressions associated with annoyance, which can be a challenge when trying to understand norms or fit into peer groups. In summary, while Autism Spectrum Disorder is a lifelong issue, a good provider and school support team can develop a treatment plan to help a teen to reach his or her full potential and ensure they do well.

Strategies for teens with autism

Prepare for changes
Teens with Autism Spectrum Disorder may not be able to handle transitions as well as others. Prepare them for changes or disruptions in schedule or routine far ahead of time if possible.

Give explicit instruction in social thinking
Since reading facial expressions or understanding body language is more challenging for teens with Autism Spectrum Disorder, help them to recognize social cues by doing role play or giving clear instructions as situations are occurring on how to interpret them.

Support educational challenges
Mild Autism Spectrum Disorder may be harder to detect in teens who change schools often and are in multicultural schools. Also, with school changes or moves between divisions in school, there is a loss of 'institutional memory,' and often teachers are unaware of the previous diagnosis. Parents have to advocate through high school. Be prepared to get additional help on group learning, abstract reasoning, and higher-level language challenges.

Strengthen strengths
Building on a teen's unique strengths is an important way to maintain self-confidence, particularly for teens with Autism Spectrum Disorder.

LEARNING DISABILITIES AND DIFFICULTIES

Learning disabilities generally affect teens with average to above average intelligence and are related to difficulty with reading, writing, or math skills. Although memory problems, attention problems, and difficulty managing social interactions are not considered typical learning disabilities, they can co-exist with them. The disorder shows up as a gap between expected skills and true academic performance.

Some teens struggle long before being diagnosed, which can significantly affect their self-esteem and motivation. Others can experience severe anxiety before tests or act out to distract attention from their challenges at school. It is very important for parents, educators, and providers to be aware of the signs of a teen with learning disabilities.

Symptoms of Learning Disabilities

- Difficulty with reading, spelling, writing, or math at/ near age and grade levels
- Difficulty understanding and following instruction
- Lack of coordination in walking, doing sports, or using skills such as holding a pencil

- Resistance to doing homework or activities that involve reading, writing or math, or inability to complete homework assignments without significant help

Diagnosing Learning Disabilities

Early intervention is very important. A good evaluation should include a check for vision or hearing problems or any underlying medical conditions. There should also be a series of examinations conducted by a team of professionals, including a psychologist, special education teacher, social worker, or nurse.

Supporting Teens with Learning Disabilities

Treatment is based on the actual type of learning disability and providing focused, evidenced-based remedial education/services. For example, consider enlisting a reading specialist, math tutor, or other trained professional who can help teach techniques to improve academic, organizational, and study skills. Look for school services that might include more time to complete assignments or tests, being seated near the teacher to promote attention, the use of computer applications that support writing, or providing audiobooks to supplement reading. Some children with writing problems can benefit from occupational therapy to improve motor skills. A speech-language therapist can help address language skills. As with the other special educational needs, ensuring teens get support and resources and that parents and providers act as their advocates goes a long way in building self-esteem and helping them to do well. According to Dr. Marcou, "Kids with a learning disability have their struggles amplified if they are changing from one curricular approach to another.

Parents need to be very aware that services will vary considerably among school locations and international schools."

Strategies for teens with Learning Disabilities

Keep things in perspective
Remember that everyone faces challenges. It's up to you as a parent to teach your teen how to deal with these challenges without becoming frustrated. Don't let the barriers distract you from giving your teen plenty of emotional and moral support.

Be your own expert
Do your own research and keep on top of new developments in programs and techniques.

Become an advocate for your teen
You may have to speak up for your teen repeatedly to get the help and services they need. Realize the school system is dealing with many students. Before school meetings, write down what you want to accomplish. Decide what is most important, and what you are willing to negotiate.[90]

GIFTED AND TWICE EXCEPTIONAL TEENS

Gifted teens have exceptional abilities in a specific academic area or areas. They also generally have high degrees of curiosity, independence, perseverance, and enjoyment in developing and expressing their talents. Twice exceptional teens are considered exceptional both because of their giftedness (their intellectual, creative, or motor skills) and their special needs (such as a learning disability).

Symptoms of Gifted Teens

Katherina is a 14-year-old expat teenager in an international school in Amsterdam. When I meet her, she tells me she is taking online math and English courses at university level. She says she often gets bored in class and reads a book instead. At lunchtime, she typically sits alone and reads. She finds it hard to engage with her peers and feels it is easier to have conversations with older classmates and adults. Her parents are concerned that she is not getting the stimulation she needs in school and is socially isolated.

Diagnosing Gifted and Twice Exceptional Teens

Identification is usually through screening tests done by an educational psychologist. According to the US-based National Association for Gifted Children (NAGC) website, intelligence quotient or IQ tests such as Stanford-Binet or the Wechsler Intelligence Scale for Children (WISC) may be used for testing intellectual areas. In general, teens with an IQ of 120-130 are considered high achievers and those with an IQ of 130 or greater (which accounts for perhaps 2% of all children and teens) are classified as gifted.

Supporting Gifted and Twice Exceptional Teens

Katherina was tested and found to have an IQ of 145. Her math and verbal abilities were three grade levels above her classmates. After much discussion, Katherina's parents decided to relocate to their home country and place her in a local school with a well-known gifted and talented program. Katherina relays that she is much happier in her new setting with other teens that have similar abilities and interests.

Gifted youths need academic challenges to prevent boredom and lack of stimulation. They also need to feel valued by the educational system and encouraged to reach their potential and develop their natural curiosity. Finally, they need to find a peer group of teens who also learn at the same rate. Some gifted teens may have challenges socializing with others or being involved in activities with their peers.

Some gifted students from a culturally different background may curb their curiosity because they've been trained to refrain from questioning authority and could be perceived as hostile or belligerent. They are also trained to work cooperatively rather than pursue independent tasks. Gifted students with learning disabilities have the same strong questioning attitude but are not always independent. As such, being aware of their unique abilities and recognizing their social-emotional needs are key.

Strategies for gifted and twice exceptional teens

Ensure academic stimulation in areas of strength
For gifted teens, focus on getting them additional training and stimulation in the areas they do well in. This may be through higher-level courses at school or in college or by online classes or additional coaching. Talk with a counselor or educational specialist to help assist you with resources in your community.

Manage the patterns of perfectionism often associated with giftedness

Gifted teens may be very independent and put pressure on themselves to do well, for example in the arts or music. Helping them to manage expectations and stress can be very important.

Choose the right curriculum for a gifted teen

Gifted teens may have unique curricular needs. In some cases, these may not be met by your current school or setting. Although, in general, putting teens in a higher-level grade may put them at risk for not being as emotionally mature as their peers, it may be an option to ensure gifted teens get the educational stimulation they need.

THE BOTTOM LINE: SPECIAL EDUCATIONAL NEEDS AND GIFTED TEENS

- All teens will encounter learning challenges at some point in adolescence. For most global teens, these challenges are temporary and can be overcome with support and encouragement both at home and in school.

- However, teens with special educational needs such as ADHD, autism, or learning disabilities may struggle and may benefit from a thorough evaluation by a health provider such as a pediatrician or psychologist.

- Treatment is based on the issue and level of severity. In ADHD it may include behavioral modification, counseling, and medication.

- For autism, support at home and at school is required. For learning disabilities, treatment may include extra support in certain areas, such as math or reading, both in and outside of school.

- Gifted youths, on the other hand, need academic challenges to prevent boredom and lack of stimulation. They also need to feel valued by the educational system and encouraged to reach their potential and develop their natural curiosity.

- As with other special educational needs, being aware, communicating with teachers, and getting appropriate resources are key. Challenges in certain communities may include getting testing done, which can be costly and not covered by insurance, and finding the right schools and peer group for gifted teens.

BIG ANSWERS

Common parent questions on special educational needs and giftedness

1. **How can we access services for a teen that has special educational needs when we live abroad?**
   It is not always easy to get services, depending on where you live in the world. Reaching out to local health providers and school counselors may be the first step. In the case of expat families, they may need to use summer holidays to access specialized services when they are

abroad. There are expat, multicultural, and other online community forums that may be very helpful in providing tips and strategies for assessments and other needs (see Resources *section). In some cases, families have considered relocation to a home country if they are not able to get resources.*

2. **What exactly is high functioning autism syndrome and how do we help our teen that may have it?**

   Autism Spectrum Disorder is a developmental disorder that causes difficulties with socializing, communicating, and behavior. The term 'spectrum' refers to the fact that some kids have a few mild symptoms while others have severe symptoms that can affect daily life. Teens with high functioning autism (Asperger syndrome) may have an ability to remember numbers or dates but still struggle with aspects of socialization. If you suspect your teen has Autism Spectrum Disorder, it is important to find a knowledgeable health care provider to do a more comprehensive assessment and help your teen feel confident and supported in school and at home.

3. **Our teen daughter struggles with focus and concentration, has been recently diagnosed with attention deficit hyperactivity disorder (ADHD) and could benefit from medication. My spouse doesn't believe in the condition or in using medications for it. Any tips?**

There can be significant differences in cultural views between parents as to whether the condition exists and whether medical treatment is needed. In some cases, when a teen is diagnosed with ADHD, a parent may also realize he or she has similar behaviors and challenges too. See if your partner would be willing to meet with your health provider or other individuals with similar issues or read more on the diagnosis and benefits of treatment (see Resources*). Explain that there are a wide array of treatments and that medication is one part of management that can be very important for helping teens to stay focused, confident, and at lower risk for issues like accidents and alcohol use.*

4. **Our son gets bored easily in school and is often reading a book instead of listening to the teacher during class. He is also more advanced than his classmates in most of his subjects. What resources should we look for to make sure he stays engaged at school?**
   Your teen may benefit from being tested to see whether he meets the criteria for being Gifted and Talented. Talk to the teachers about providing advance level work for him. He may also benefit from being in a setting with other teens like him. Finally, there are great online and in-person programs available (see Resources *section).*

Common teen questions on special educational needs and giftedness

1. **I recently started high school in a new town. I have a hard time staying organized and getting my homework done. Is this normal?**

   All teens may struggle with getting things done on time, especially if you have gone through a major change in your routine or environment. Reach out to friends, parents, and mentors for support. Look at what you can do, possibly using productivity apps, to create a system that works for you.

2. **I get easily distracted and often lose things. My parents are always yelling at me for being lazy and absent-minded and not putting enough effort into my schoolwork. What should I do?**

   There are many reasons why this may occur. Do you enjoy school and feel engaged in your classes? Are you tired and getting less than 7-8 hours of sleep at night? Are you feeling overscheduled? Sad or depressed? Has this been an issue since you were young or has it come up more recently? Do you smoke marijuana or use any other drugs on a regular basis? These are just a few questions to consider but it may be time to talk to a health provider or school counselor so you can get more formal help.

3. **I can get extra time to take tests because I have ADHD, but I don't want any of my classmates to know I have a diagnosis. How do I handle this?**

   This is tough but working with the school to ensure your extra test time is done in a sensitive way is the first step. Also, realize the importance of having extra time even if your peers know you have a diagnosis.

4. **I tried my friend's ADHD medication and I thought it really helped me to get more work done. Do I have ADHD?**

   Just responding positively to medications doesn't mean you have ADHD. Signs of ADHD include having challenges with focus, concentration, and/or restlessness, impulsiveness, and fidgeting. All of this usually starts in childhood. There are online screening questionnaires that you could do to see if you have some of these issues. If you have not had any of these signs, chances are you may not have ADHD. When a doctor prescribes a medicine, he or she takes a thorough history to know if it is safe for you to take that drug. Using medications such as stimulants that are not prescribed for you puts you at risk for serious (and sometimes fatal) side effects such as nervousness, dizziness, difficulty sleeping, or a heart arrhythmia. Avoid taking someone else's medications and talk to a parent or doctor if you are worried you may have ADHD.

RESOURCES

Books

Taking Charge of ADHD: The Complete, Authoritative Guide for Parents, Russell Barkley, Guilford Press, 2013

The Misunderstood Child: Understanding and Coping with Your Child's Learning Disabilities, Larry Silver, Three Rivers Press, 2006

Twice-Exceptional Gifted Children: Understanding, Teaching, and Counseling Gifted Students, Beverly Trail, Prufrock Press, 2010

Websites and articles

Children and Adults with Attention Deficit/Hyperactivity Disorder: https://chadd.org

Monthly newsletter with tips for living as adults and kids with ADHD: https://www.additudemag.com/

ADHD screening tools: https://addfreesources.net/adhd-screening-tests/

Understood (Learning Disabilities and ADHD): https://www.understood.org/en

'What are Special Educational Needs', Family Lives: https://www.familylives.org.uk/advice/your-family/special-educational-needs/what-are-special-educational-needs/

National Association for Gifted Children: http://www.nagc.org/

John Hopkins Center for Youth Development: https://cty.jhu.edu/

Khan Academy: https://www.khanacademy.org/

BUILDING SELF-ESTEEM AND RESILIENCE

13

"The oak fought the wind and was broken, the willow
bent when it must and survived."
Robert Jordan

IN THIS CHAPTER:
- Helping teens identify their unique strengths
  and develop positive self-esteem.
- Developing strategies to support teens when
  they become self-critical.
- Allowing teens to problem solve and handle
  their own challenges to build resilience.

Queenie is a 16-year-old patient of mine in Hong Kong who is referred to me for weight management. She lives in a high-rise apartment in public housing with her mom. Queenie's parents separated when she was a child. Her mom is originally from mainland China, works long hours and is rarely home. Queenie struggles with obesity, being bullied, having a poor self-image, and learning disabilities. When we first meet, she can barely look me in the eyes, has severe facial acne, a small overbite, and is wearing dark, baggy clothes.

When I talk to my teen patients, I routinely ask about home, school, and extracurricular activities and I always start the conversation by asking what their strengths are. When I ask Queenie what she thinks she is good at and what she wants to do in life, she brightens up.

"I like drawing and I want to be a fashion designer," she says.

"Really?" I ask. "Do you have any sketches?"

"Yes!" says Queenie animatedly.

We proceeded through the interview and at the end of our session, I ask Queenie to help me create some goals for managing her weight. I also ask her to bring in her sketches for the next visit.

At our next meeting a few weeks later, her weight has not changed much, but she does bring in her sketchbook. It's clear she is excited when she describes her elaborate illustrations of dresses and gowns. We even joke that one day she can design a gown for me. I tell her she has a real talent and that she should focus on her passion for fashion design. I also encourage her mom to get her an old sewing machine to make some outfits and to enroll her in some local art classes.

A few months later when I see Queenie, she is wearing bright, tight-fitting clothing and her hair is well groomed. She is smiling and a quick check of her weight confirms she has lost a few kilograms. She brings me a picture of a cocktail party outfit that she has designed for me. Queenie also shows me a few dolls' dresses she has created and sewn from scraps of material. She has started taking an after-school drawing class and is excited to report that she has made a few friends. She is also getting some extra support in her math and writing classes and her grades have improved.

During the teen years, adolescents may struggle with self-esteem and self-worth. They may also have difficulty moving past mistakes and failures. Asking about their strengths, supporting them to develop their unique abilities, and allowing them to problem solve and handle their own challenges are key to building self-esteem and ultimately, resilience.

BIG QUESTIONS

Common parent questions on developing self-esteem and building resilience

1. I have noticed my previously self-assured 13-year-old daughter becoming more worried about what others think of her and how she dresses and behaves. She is always second-guessing her abilities. How can I help her feel more confident and secure about herself?

2. When is self-confidence developed – in childhood or adolescence?

3. Can you build resilience? Are some people more inherently resilient than others?

4. What is the right balance between supporting our kids when they ask for help or are having difficulties, and allowing them to face uncertainty and challenge alone?

Common teen questions on developing self-esteem and building resilience

1. How do you manage expectations from parents, teachers, and friends without putting too much pressure on yourself to be perfect?

2. How do you help a friend that thinks she's a complete failure?

3. You make one mistake. You handle it, then comes another. How do you stop the downward spiral?

4. How do you stay positive and in control when so many things are happening around you that you can't control such as family members losing their jobs, being unable to travel, a major recession, or a global public health crisis?

DEVELOPING POSITIVE SELF-ESTEEM

Knowing your own strengths and unique abilities is critical to building and maintaining self-esteem. By focusing on strengths when counseling adolescents, you also build their resilience. And developing resilience helps kids handle failure, which is an important predictor of success in adult life.

 According to renowned author and teen health specialist Dr. Ken Ginsburg, "Recognizing strengths does more than just help teens feel good about themselves. It positions them to understand that they possess the capacity to do the right thing, to move beyond temporary setbacks, and to correct mistaken decisions."[91]

Building unique abilities

When I ask teens about their strengths, they mention a broad range of characteristics and skills. "My friends think I have a great sense of humor and make them laugh," says one 12-year-old teen from Madrid. A 12-year-old from Bombay tells me, "I am really good at listening to my friend's problems." A 17-year-old from São Paulo mentions that he has taught himself to play the guitar and feels his strength is composing music. Another 13-year-old London teen relays that she creates animated videos that she posts on YouTube. Sometimes teens aren't sure about their abilities. Says one 16-year-old from Portland, "I don't know what I am good at. I have never really thought about it before."

Using a strength-based approach

As with Queenie, I start by asking my teen patients about their strengths. SSHADESS is an acronym for a strength-based screening approach we use in clinical settings and that I recommend to educators and health providers as well.[92] It is particularly helpful in understanding cross-cultural teens' assets and strengths as well as their challenges and vulnerabilities. While you may think you already know the answer to many of these questions, exploring aspects of the SSHADESS approach at home may be useful.

SSHADESS represents the following:

- **S** is for **strengths** or positive attributes. Asking cross-cultural teens what they perceive as their unique abilities is a fascinating way to start a discussion and can be very revealing.
- **S** is for **school or work life**. Ask what teens enjoy doing in school (or work) and if they are having any specific difficulties. Also, find out what their dreams are for the future and if they have mentors who can help them along the way.
- **H** is for **home life.** Who do the teens live with and how do they get along with them? Also, for global teens it is important to ask them what they consider to be their 'story.' More specifically, where are they or their parents from and what languages, religions, or cultures are represented at home?
- **A** is for **activities**. Ask what connections teens have to their community, including community service and extracurricular activities. Also, find out about their sleep, screen time, and social media use.
- **D** is for **diet, drugs, and alcohol use**, plus body image. In discussing this, I often ask teens about their peer

group and what kind of activities they do together. I ask what they see when they look at themselves in the mirror and if they are happy with what they see. Answers to these questions are very revealing.

- **E** is for **emotions** (including depression and suicidal thoughts). It's critical to ask young people about their mood and whether they have ever self-harmed or felt as if life is not worth living. Please be aware that simply asking the question does not increase a teen's chance of self-injury, but it may be instrumental in identifying a need and providing support.

- **S and S** stands for **sexual health and safety**. Ask who they are attracted to, what their gender identity may be, and how safe they feel in their community. Also, if they feel safe and have ever experienced violence or sexual assault. Too often these important questions are not asked out of shame or fear the teenager will regard them as impingement on their privacy. But by not asking them, we are doing our teens a disfavor, depriving them of the opportunity to open up and discuss one of the most important and scariest aspects of becoming an adult. Do ask and try again if the first attempt does not work out.

Building on strengths is the single most important thing you can do to support kids through their challenges and prevent them from engaging in high-risk behaviors. SSHADESS is organized such that it allows us to start with the issues that are easiest to discuss before moving on to the more difficult ones, including emotional life and sexuality. At the end of a clinical visit, I often circle back to a teen's unique abilities and discuss how they can continue to build on those strengths while minimizing their risk behaviors.

In sum, it is critical that we help cross-cultural teens identify and build on their personal strengths. As parents, asking kids what they do best is extremely helpful. For educators and providers, using a SSHADESS approach may provide a positive way to understand and reframe teen challenges and vulnerabilities.

Handling the inner critic

"I am ugly, stupid, fat, or..." When was the last time you yourself heard that nagging voice in the back of your head? We can all be incredibly hard on ourselves. With constant exposure to social media, pressure to fit into a peer group, demands from parents and coaches, and other stressors, teens nowadays are particularly vulnerable to self-criticism. Healthy self-esteem is therefore nothing short of a teen's armor against life's challenges. As kids try, fail, try again, fail again, and finally succeed, they develop ideas about their own capabilities. They also create a concept of self, based on their interactions with others. Kids who know their strengths and weaknesses tend to feel better about themselves and have an easier time handling conflict. Kids with low self-esteem can find small challenges to be major sources of anxiety and frustration. We know this is hard; after all, how many of us can confidently say that we are proud of ourselves and confident in our abilities?

The patterns of self-esteem start very early in life. Teens can also be sensitive to harsh or negative words of parents and others. For example, if you're excessively harsh on yourself, pessimistic, or unrealistic about your abilities and limitations, kids will mirror it. Therefore, parents and adults need to identify and debunk (or explain) inaccurate beliefs. This extends to norms regarding perfection, attractiveness, ability, and everything else. Often, kids compare their achievements to what others are doing or have done (particularly high frequency users of social media). Use a strength-based approach to develop self-esteem and keep the lines of communication open.

Strategies for building positive self-esteem

Discuss 'superpowers' or unique abilities

Have your teen make a list of their strengths or what they like about themselves. If they can't come up with strengths, ask what their friends or family members would say about them (or better yet, have them ask their friends and close family members). I have found this approach very useful in clinical, classroom, and community settings. If they have a certain skill, encourage them to develop it. For example, if they are good at coding, encourage them to join a class, club, or online course, or teach others. Supporting your teen to take on new challenges is a great way to build their sense of mastery and self-esteem. Encourage them to look back at their list from time to time to counter negative self-talk and comparisons. In addition to skills, consider the personal characteristics your kids possess that may allow them to thrive. For example, one of my sons can be particularly determined and strong-willed once he has an idea or concept that he wants to pursue. I admit I am not always patient with this; however, I realize his intense focus can also be considered tenacity, which is an important quality for adult success and will one day serve him well.

Love and accept them for who they are

Being rooted in who they really are is so important for cross-cultural teens struggling to define their identity and sense of belonging, and to get acceptance from their peers. Says Dr. Ginsburg: "Parents worry because they love. During those moments where we feel the most challenged, we can draw from our children's strengths. Teens may question who they are, but we must never question who they are. Our clarity will get them through tough times and serve as the foundation to strengthen our families."[93]

Reframe it

When you hear your child or teen put themselves down, ask non-judgmental questions that can help them check themselves. For example, if they say, "I know I'll never pass this exam," or, "I won't get into a good college or university," ask, "Please help me to understand this." Remind them of the evidence that counters their fears. Then, figure out how you can switch their sentiment to something positive or affirming such as, "I have a good chance of passing this test if I study for it," or, "There are many strong university options out there for me. There isn't one perfect school." Research shows that what we think affects how we feel and how we feel affects how we act. As such, regular negative self-talk can lead to depression and anxiety. Challenge children to find humor in the situation and see if they can laugh about it. It is all about rewiring and rerouting the inner critic!

Start writing

Journaling is a great natural counselor for kids who enjoy writing. It can help with overcoming self-doubt. Suggest to your teen that they write down their self-critical feelings and why certain statements that are worrying them may not be true. Alternatively, ask them to write down their daily experiences – what's positive and what's been challenging. Then ask them to revisit their journals a few weeks or months later to get perspective and a more balanced approach.

Get help

If your child or teen has started unhealthy eating patterns such as restricting or binging, has serious anxiety, started cutting, considered suicide, or is chronically depressed, it's high time to get professional help. Hopefully, by addressing self-doubt early on by reframing negative speak, identifying strengths, praising progress, and journaling concerns, you can help your kid to build a positive self-image and feel good about him or herself.

BUILDING RESILIENCE

Most teens face everyday challenges such as an angry comment from a sibling, a snub from a classmate, an annoying post on social media, difficulty completing an assignment on time, being late to a practice, or a conflict with a parent or coach. Some adolescents face more significant problems such as living with a chronic health issue, undergoing constant moves and family upheavals, having a close family member die, or experiencing sexual or physical abuse.

Got bounce?

According to the Australian parenting site Raising Children, resilience is the ability to 'bounce back' during or after difficult times and get back to how they felt before.[94] When a teen is resilient, they can learn from a setback or challenge and continue to thrive. Some individuals may be more resilient than others, but it is a skill that can be cultivated.

In addition to reminding themselves of their unique strengths, teens can build resilience by doing the following:

- Developing and maintaining social relationships
- Creating a good sense of self-respect
- Being resourceful

Teens with strong social relationships are much better at handling interpersonal conflicts, developing and maintaining friendships, and working in teams. To develop social relationships, encourage teens to join extracurricular or volunteer activities, clubs, or sports. When a cross-cultural teen gets involved in community activities, they have a better likelihood of developing a sense of belonging. They will also have a larger circle of individuals to trust and rely on when things are tough. Having self-respect is something that can be fostered in teens and includes being kind, accepting others' differences, and taking responsibility for their actions. A teen who has self-respect believes they should be treated respectfully by others and is less vulnerable to either being bullied or bullying others. Finally, resourcefulness is an important component of resilience and can be modeled and taught by adults. This includes setting goals, working hard, and using existing options to get things done. Another way to think about building resilience is to focus on the 7 Cs. Dr. Ken Ginsburg recommends that adults help teens develop Competence, Confidence, Connections, Character, Contribution, Coping, and Control.[95]

Resilience levels can go up and down at different times in life. In fact, your teen may be far better at handling some situations than others. Some teens manage a chronic health issue with ease but can't bounce back from a sudden move or break up with a boyfriend. With resilience, however, teens are more prepared to seek new ways to overcome problems and achieve goals. Ultimately, this is a pathway for improved self-confidence and personal success.

HANDLING FAILURE

How many of us adults (or teens) actively embrace rejection or failure? Most of us try as hard as possible to avoid mistakes, particularly big, public ones. What if we risked trying something with the knowledge that failure was a distinct possibility and continued to try on a regular basis? That's what social entrepreneur and TEDx speaker Caleb Meakins did in creating a 40-day challenge to try something new every day and embracing the likelihood he'd probably fail.

Embracing failure to create change

I was inspired by Meakins when I heard him give the keynote address at the 2019 Families in Global Transition conference in Bangkok, Thailand. I often talk to adults and teens about the importance of allowing young people to try and fail to ultimately develop resilience and create pathways to success. Too often I have witnessed young people feel crushed after experiencing a poor grade, breakup, or other setback, particularly in a university setting. Meakins spoke about creating change in the world.

As a Cross-Cultural Kid with British and Ethiopian roots, he felt a strong desire to try his hand at social innovation in his native Ethiopia instead of taking the more traditional route of becoming a practicing engineer. While deliberating his career path, he came up with the idea of having people give him a new challenge every day for 40 days (as long as it was legal) and documenting his daily trials with a hidden camera. The challenges, which range from taking a whole raw chicken to fast-food restaurants and asking staff there to cook it (answer: "no way!") to lying on the ground in a busy public metro station, are both hilarious and haunting.

The take-home message from Caleb Meakins' exploits is that we ourselves are much more aware of our own failures and rejections than the people around us. We need to challenge ourselves to get out of our comfort zones to create change and ultimately be successful by embracing failure as a natural part of the journey. The new generation of Cross-Cultural Kids have many strengths, including an understanding of cultures, sensitivity to others, and a worldview that can help them effect global change. Meakins takes the fear out of starting something new by asking us what we would do if we could try something and it was impossible to fail? The answer to this question may be our life dream or passion. Meakins' point is why not try it even if we may fail or if it didn't quite work out?

I believe we would all set more challenging goals if we adopted this mindset as it would take the fear out of failure. In Meakins' own case, he decided to return to Addis Ababa and found Bake & Brew, which serves as both a café for world-renowned Ethiopian coffee and an innovation hub for young entrepreneurs.

Caleb's story makes a good case for why parents need to stop protecting kids from failure. Instead, we need to allow young people to take risks and try new pathways in the spirit of making the world a better place. All too often, we act like 'snowplow' parents, removing obstacles in our kids' way rather than allowing them to face fear, rejection, or failure.

There are many significant global challenges out there that need to be addressed by those who are not afraid of trying. Some of the top concerns that Generation X and Millennials have today are climate change, large-scale conflict, inequality, and poverty. Our kids have creative and thoughtful ideas for approaching big issues that we adults would never envision. Let them try. And fail. And learn. And try again. After all, the lightbulb, solar panel, and airplane were all invented by individuals who dared to dream and failed many times before succeeding. Let your teen have a try at their own battles before we as adults step in to help. Stumbling comes with the territory. Sometimes it is hard to hold back, but it is important to allow teens to try.

Strategies for building resilience and handling failure

Problem solve
When you give teens control of solving their problems themselves, you're giving them the tools they need to cope better in life. Encourage your teen to think about how to problem solve instead of wishing the challenges would just disappear. Often, young people tell me they know themselves better after they have gone through a crisis. Allow them to view change as a creative way to alter the future. Finally, help teens to handle mistakes and strengthen their 'problem-solving reflexes' when they are calm, and the stakes are low so that they can flex these muscles when the stakes are higher, and they feel anxious or overwhelmed.

Keep things in perspective
When things didn't go as planned, my son's primary school teacher would ask him, "Is this a big problem or a small problem?" I remember her words to this day and think this

is a remarkably wise way of providing perspective way beyond the childhood years. Consider asking teens to put a score of 1-10 (10 being the highest) on problems and having them return to re-score the issue after a few hours or days. Also, have them focus on the facts and realities when reviewing the issue. Remind teens that in many cases problems may initially appear huge but can get smaller over time.

Celebrate the wobbles and the bounces

Often young people (and their parents) place tremendous importance on having top grades, excelling in extracurricular activities, or getting into an elite university. I remind teens that some patients of mine have had excellent grades and got into elite universities only to fall apart after getting a bad grade or experiencing rejection or break up during the first year. I also remind teens that one of the top predictors of success in adulthood is getting back up on their feet after a failure (rather than their glowing CV or the status of their university). When discussing failure in schools, I ask students to turn to each other and discuss when they failed big and how they handled it. This always leads to some humorous and heart-warming stories and lots of sharing and laughter.

Some additional questions to ask teens about failure include:

- How were you affected by the failure?
- Who or what helped you to move forward?
- What did you learn from the situation about yourself
- How can you apply what you learned to future situations

Some institutions are creating programs and courses to

help high achievers cope with basic setbacks such as Smith College's 'Fail Well' program.[96] Encourage teens to celebrate their failures and their ability to bounce back.

Get help
Handling failure and building resilience is a very personal journey that is not always linear. If your teen is not able to move forward, consider talking to someone who can help, such as a coach, therapist, or other mental health professional. Getting support on building resilience may be useful for handling chronic stress and trauma.

THE BOTTOM LINE: BUILDING SELF-ESTEEM AND RESILIENCE

- During the teen years, adolescents may struggle with self-worth and moving past mistakes and failures.

- Parents have a unique role in supporting teens through these challenges. To begin with, asking teens about their unique strengths and supporting them to develop abilities can help build self-esteem.

- Parents can also help teens reframe issues when they become self-critical and let teens know they are loved for who they are.

- To build resilience, parents should allow teens to problem solve and handle their own challenges. When cross-cultural teens have a strong sense of self-esteem and resilience, they cope better with challenging situations and navigating life's ups and downs.

Big Answers

Common parent questions on developing self-esteem and building resilience

1. **I have noticed my previously self-assured 13-year-old daughter becoming more worried about what others think of her and how she dresses and behaves. How can I help her feel more confident and secure about herself?**

   Trying to fit in and be accepted by peers is a normal part of adolescence but can certainly affect how teens feel about themselves. There are a few simple ways that you can help your daughter to feel secure and self-confident. Make sure she knows you love and support her for who she is as this is valuable for building self-esteem. Talk to her about what she thinks are her strengths and help her develop what she does best. Allow her to have moments of mastery, whether it is preparing a meal, coordinating an appointment, taking an out-of-town trip, or navigating other responsibilities. The experience allows her to try new skills and be recognized for what she does. Finally, if she is constantly worried about how she looks or behaves, it may be important for her to evaluate her friendships. Does she feel that she has friends that respect her and accept her for who she is? If not, start a discussion about the importance of true friendships and how she can develop those.

2. **When is self-confidence developed – in childhood or adolescence?**
   Self-confidence is developed in early adolescence. Parents can help teens to build self-confidence by encouraging them to build on their strengths or unique abilities, helping them redirect and reframe self-critical thoughts, and loving and accepting them for who they are.

3. **Can you build resilience? Are some people more inherently resilient than others?**
   Resilience is the ability to 'bounce back' during or after difficult times and get back to how they felt before. When a teen is resilient, they can learn from a setback or challenge and continue to thrive. Some individuals may be more resilient than others, but it is a skill that can be cultivated. To build resilience consider Dr. Ken Ginsburg's 7 Cs and help teens develop Competence, Confidence, Connections, Character, Contribution, Coping, and Control.

4. **What is the right balance between supporting our kids when they ask for help or are having difficulties, and allowing them to face uncertainty and challenge alone?**
   Allowing teens to make independent decisions and occasionally fail is an important part of growing up and becoming a successful adult. Although there is no correct answer, giving them increasing responsibility for making healthy and sound decisions while being

there to support them when they encounter significant difficulties can be helpful.

Common teen questions on developing self-esteem and building resilience

1. **How do you manage expectations from parents, teachers, and friends without putting too much pressure on yourself to be perfect?**

   A very important part of being a teen is making mistakes and learning from them, and not putting so much pressure on yourself to get everything perfect just yet. Also, chatting with family and friends if you find that you are being too tough on yourself, and getting help on how to let go just a little.

2. **How do you help a friend that thinks she's a complete failure?**

   Focusing on strengths is an important way to get people to feel good and more accepting of themselves. You may want to help your friend feel good about something that she does well, whether it is having a great sense of humor or having incredible fashion style. Also, get her to examine why she thinks she is a failure or what she may be insecure about. Finally, you may also want to make sure she is not depressed or suicidal and get an adult involved if you are worried.

3. **You make one mistake. You handle it, then comes another. How do you stop the downward spiral?**

   There is a famous Japanese proverb that says, "Fall down seven times, stand up eight." Realize that you have the power to stop the downward spiral and to get right back up again. Also, that you can talk to your parents, friends, or even a coach or counselor if you think you need help with all the issues you are facing to get back on track. You can't prevent mistakes, but you can prepare yourself for handling them. Resilience is the ability to get back on your feet after a challenge. By being able to take stock of what you learned and how you can move on from your failures, you can be prepared for all that comes your way.

4. **How do you stay positive and in control when so many things are happening around you that you can't control such as family members losing their jobs, being unable to travel, a major recession, or a global public health crisis?**

   Experiencing multiple changes that you can't control can make you feel vulnerable and stressed. It is important to stay focused on what you can control in your life. Think about keeping a journal, setting small intentions and rituals for the day, working on goal setting with a family member or friend, and staying connected with loved ones.

RESOURCES

Books

Building Resilience in Children and Teens: Giving Kids Roots and Wings (4th ed.), Kenneth Ginsburg and Martha Jablow, American Academy of Pediatrics, 2020

Websites and articles

'My 40 days - Facing the Fear of Failure', Caleb Meakins, *TedxTalks*, 2015:
https://www.youtube.com/watch?v=odcLP7gOGW8

'Resilience for Teens', American Psychological Association, 2011:
http://www.apa.org/helpcenter/bounce.aspx

The Australian Parenting Website (Department of Social Services, Australian Government): https://raisingchildren.net.au/

Families in Global Transition: https://figt.org/

"You're off to Great Places. Today is your day! Your mountain is waiting, so... get on your way!"
Dr. Seuss

IN THIS CHAPTER:
- Understand a global teen's protective assets.
- Learn key skills needed for the 21st century.
- Explore strategies for preparing teens for transition to university, work, and adult life.

Every year, June is the month when one of my favorite Dutch traditions occurs in the Netherlands. Around the country, families of graduating high school students hang enormous Dutch national flags onto the flagpoles outside their houses. They put the flags alongside their graduate's rather weathered school bag to celebrate the passing of exams and moving on to a new chapter in life. It takes a global village to raise a child, and I love that this rite of passage is celebrated in such a public way. When I pass by a home with a raised flag in my Amsterdam Oud-Zuid neighborhood, I feel a burst of emotions. I have a visceral sense of the joy and pain it took to get to this point. I imagine the countless dinner conversations, tests, performances, fights, tears, hugs, and smiles that have punctuated the long journey in their household. When I see it, the lone, fluttering bag-on-a-flag, I silently acknowledge the newly minted graduate and wish him or her all the best as they prepare to climb 'the mountain' ahead.

Raising teens and preparing them for what's next is exciting and daunting at the same time. Why don't we all 'put the flags out' around the world to celebrate our global teens' major milestones? How do we continue to uphold our global kids as they move on from one crossroads to another? How do we help our kids when there is uncertainty around us such as during the global COVID-19 pandemic? Why is having a global mindset important? What are the 21st-century skills teens need to cultivate? In this final chapter, I discuss how to prepare Cross-Cultural Kids for transition to adulthood and to thrive in our busy, modern, mobile world.

BIG QUESTIONS

Common parent questions on preparing for the future

1. How do we prepare our teen for university?

2. What are the values and skills that we can nurture in global teens to help them be successful and healthy as adults?

3. What are the job skills that a teenager needs to survive in the coming decades?

Common teen questions on preparing for the future

1. How can I set a clear path for myself that comes from knowing what I want?

2. My parents are having a hard time letting go. What can I tell them so they know I will be OK?

3. How do I prepare for being on my own without being super overwhelmed?

HELPING TEENS TO MOVE TOWARDS ADULTHOOD

For nearly 40 years my father worked as a psychiatric social worker in Delaware, my home state in the US. Growing up, I remember him helping young adults get odd jobs on weekends or summer employment like mowing the lawn, weeding plants, or painting fences. Many of these kids lived in tough neighborhoods, had difficult home lives, and no other chances to work. My father created opportunities for these troubled teens to be part of our immigrant family, share a story or two, and have a home-cooked meal. He felt it was important to give youth, especially those that had been labeled as failures and troublemakers, a chance to prove themselves. He felt they too deserved respect and love and wanted to show them that their future was bright no matter how challenging their lives had been. In retrospect, for some of these teens, spending time in our Indian-American home was surely a real cross-cultural experience. Many of these teens went on to graduate from high school, be in positive relationships, and become healthy and resilient adults engaged in the community around them. These experiences left a strong impression on me and shaped my own decision to work with young people.

Building assets for global teens

How do we create a strong foundation for children and teens to do well in life? Parents, educators, and providers often ask me this question. My response is built on my research as well as my practical experiences and what I have observed of others who work with teens. Above all, adolescents need someone who believes in them, a nurturing environment (either at home or through school or a mentor), clear boundaries and expectations (curfews, rules about using drugs or alcohol), and activities to help them use their time constructively (such as giving them work, after-school tasks, volunteer service).

Developing protective 'assets' provides an important framework for supporting teens. The main assets identified by the Search Institute, a US research group, are listed below.[97] Many of these concepts, such as building identity and providing boundaries, have been discussed in depth in previous chapters of this book.

Protective assets for adolescents

- **Support**
  Support can occur through positive family relationships and communication, but also from caring neighbors, nurturing school environments, and parent involvement in schooling (see *Chapter 13*).

- **Empowerment**
  Teens are empowered when they are valued by adults and peers. Engaging in volunteering and useful roles in the community provides them with a sense of self-worth, as does feeling safe and respected at home, in school, or in their neighborhoods (see *Chapter 13*).

- **Boundaries**
  Parents, schools, and communities can create helpful guardrails for life by establishing clear rules and consequences. Equally, positive expectations from parents and peers are critical (see *Chapter 1*).

- **Constructive use of time**
  Engaging in creative activities, with religious organizations, or in sports is important. Having time to relax and not doing anything at all is important too (see *Chapter 8*).

- **Commitment to learning**
  This includes being motivated to do well in school or work (see *Chapter 13*).

- **Positive values**
  These include a caring attitude, thinking about social justice, integrity, honesty, responsibility, and restraint (see *Chapter 14*).

- **Social competence**
  This includes planning and decision-making skills, interpersonal and cultural competence, and knowing how to negotiate with peers and manage conflicts (see *Chapter 13*).

- **Positive identity**
  When a teen feels he/she has control over things that happen, has good self-confidence, a sense of purpose, and is optimistic about the future (see *Chapter 12*).

Research shows that youths with the most protective assets are more likely to:

- Do well in school
- Be civically engaged
- Value diversity as they move into adulthood, and
- Have fewer problems with alcohol, drugs, violence, and high-risk sexual activity.

 In short, building protective assets is a pathway to ensuring our cross-cultural teens thrive. Of course, there are times when teens will have more assets in one area than another, have many skills across the board, or very few at all. Our goal as adults is to be aware of what assets our teens may have and what additional ones they need.

Rites of passage

Over the years, many communities have created specific ways for young people to take their place in the community and be supported. Initiations, life-cycle rituals, and other rites of passage allow young men and women to make the transition from childhood to adulthood. A big feature of such coming-of-age rites is their emphasis upon separation, transition, and then reincorporation into a community.

For example, in the Jewish tradition, young boys and girls celebrate their Bar and Bat Mitzvahs around the ages of 12 and 13 to demonstrate their commitment to their faith and recognize that they are now responsible for following Jewish law. After the religious ceremony, a reception is held to celebrate the young person's accomplishment, as they have often spent weeks learning and preparing for this day. In the Amish tradition, Rumspringa marks the time when young people turn 16 and are finally able to enjoy unsupervised weekends away from family. During this period, they are encouraged to try whatever they like, such as wearing modern clothing or drinking alcohol. The purpose of this is to allow Amish teens the opportunity to experience the world beyond their upbringing (rites). For many young people in westernized countries, breaking into adulthood includes obtaining control from their parents by getting a driver's license, being allowed to buy alcohol or to vote.

Adolescents who develop a relationship with an adult role model (parents or others) are more successful than their peers in coping with the everyday stresses of life. However, in our modern world, teens are increasingly growing up with less identifiable communities. More than ever, promoting healthy behaviors during adolescence, and taking steps to better protect young people from health risks, are essential for their ability to develop and thrive.

Acquiring real-life skills

The questions I get asked the most regarding transition to university, gap year, or working are almost always related to practical issues like making appointments, doing laundry, balancing finances, cooking food, and making friends. Along these lines, author and Generation Y expert Tim Elmore feels that the number one issue young people face today is that of 'artificial maturity.' He says that modern teens are overexposed to information at an earlier age than ever. However, they are gaining real-life experience far later than when they need to.[98]

When it comes to real-life experiences, the Dutch may be onto something with their concept of 'dropping.' This involves dropping off preteens or teens in the woods in the middle of the night and allowing them to find their way back in the dark, usually as a group or a pair.[99] The take-home message from this somewhat controversial rite of passage is that parents must allow teens to experience a challenge alone and problem solve for themselves. Creating situations of real-life responsibility and allowing mastery are important ways to create confidence in their abilities.

Although not as dramatic as dropping, I encourage my teen patients before they transition out of their homes to make their own doctor appointments and keep their own basic electronic health records (for example taking a picture of their vaccination records and keeping it on their phone in case of emergency). In addition, I encourage them to learn the basics of keeping and balancing a budget, doing simple laundry, or even cooking a few special dishes. One day very soon, they will have to do it all on their own.

The gift of the global mindset

What is fascinating is that with globalization, our teens are now living deep in a hybrid of languages, cultures, and traditions. Says Dr. Larry D'Angelo, the former chair of the Division of Adolescent and Young Adult Medicine at Children's National Hospital in Washington, DC, "With mobility, changing patterns of immigration, and exposure to information online and offline, we have created a global adolescent culture." Teens from Topeka to Oslo now share similar concerns about global warming, pandemics, and the refugee crisis. Increasingly, they also have similar health challenges, including vaping and body image issues.

Generation Y, also known as the Millennials, are teens born between the early 1980s and mid-1990s. They are generally described as being very comfortable using digital technology and social media. Generation Z is the group that comes after the Millennials, born between the mid-1990s and the early 2000s. They have been exposed to technology since their early childhood and have been referred to as the 'post-Millennials' or 'iGen' generation. The preteens and teens in this group have also been described as more educated, well-behaved, stressed, and innovative than previous generations. According to a 2018 US-based study by Identity Shifters, almost half of Gen Z consumers identify as a racial or ethnic minority, making them the most diverse generation yet.[100]

How do we prepare these future generations of teens that are part of this world to make the most of their cross-cultural experiences? Pediatrician and author Dr. Laura Jana outlines some important tips in her book *The Toddler Brain: Nurture the Skills Today That Will Shape Your Child's Tomorrow*.[101] In a phone interview, Dr. Jana tells me that today's youth need to have the following skills for the workplace:

- **ME** skills – learning impulse control and mindfulness.
- **WE** skills – collaborative learning and working. (Strong **ME** and **WE** skills equate to having good emotional intelligence.)
- **WHY** skills – asking about the world around them.
- **WILL** skills – self or intrinsic motivation (as opposed to extrinsic motivation alone).
- **WIGGLE** skills – my favorite – intellectual and physical restlessness.
- **WOBBLE** skills – learning from failure.
- **WHAT IF** skills – the ability to imagine the world as it should be and use imagination and creativity. According to Dr. Jana, by helping our global kids to develop these core skills, we can open the door to "a world as it could be."

Start a conversation about the future

Building on Dr. Jana's tips, the following questions may be a good way to start a discussion with a teen about preparing for the future, developing 21st-century skills, and becoming bridge builders:

- What skills do you think will be important in the future?
- What do you see yourself doing in 5 years? In 10 years?
- Do you have a passion or strength you might want to pursue?
- If you were to join a volunteer organization, what cause would you support?
- How do you think that your cross-cultural background and skills can help you to be a bridge builder, create change, and/or improve the world around you?
- What are you worried about for the future?
- When have you failed and what have you learned from it?
- How can I (or others) help you to achieve your goals?

Beacons of hope

There is so much change, uncertainty, and turmoil happening around us. Families that have lived for generations in communities are being uprooted or feeling uncertain about their future. Says author Chris O'Shaughnessy: "As the world becomes more interconnected, the challenges we face do as well. Many of the difficulties that have long been faced by the cross-cultural community have expanded into mainstream society the world over. Marginalization, exposing the vulnerable to radicalization, the increasingly disposable nature of relationships, and the ever more complex struggle to find identity are apparent all around us; and a measurable decline in empathy is fueling fears of an epidemic of loneliness."

Despite the challenges and uncertainty around us, as a pediatrician, I feel incredibly hopeful for what the future and the next generation have in store. This next generation is far more diverse than any previous generation. They have amassed incredible abilities, talents, and global prowess. I am reminded of this as I co-parent our two German-Indian-American boys, watch youths biking in my neighborhood, chat with a recent immigrant teen in the adolescent clinic, or give a workshop at a local school.

According to O'Shaughnessy, "Cross-Cultural Kids are the prototype citizens of tomorrow... beacons of hope in a world in desperate need of it." He adds, "In many ways, exploring the experience of young people who spend their formative years having to adapt to multiple cultures yields insight into the challenges we all now face. Understanding the experience of global teens reveals practical lessons in honing empathy while also fostering intercultural appreciation and understanding." I agree wholeheartedly and am proudly waving my virtual flag in celebration of all the amazing adolescents around the world. I hope you can join me in celebrating our cross-cultural teens too.

Strategies for preparing for the future

Build a life of meaning

Community service is a wonderful way to develop character and empathy. In her book *How to Raise Successful People*,[102] Esther Wojcicki, mom of three very successful women including YouTube CEO Susan Wojcicki, writes that we are happiest and most beneficial to society when we are engaged in community service that helps others. She suggests that we teach kids to find meaning and purpose through service. Likewise, holding an ordinary job such as working at a fast-food restaurant, the more unglamorous the better, provides key lessons in how to treat others and be empathetic. Educational institutions and employers are increasingly looking for kids who can manage responsibilities, are empathetic, and are exposed to the real world.

Uphold unevenness

Our kids will not uniformly excel in everything as they grow; in fact, their achievements may be quite uneven. Our challenge is to help them discover what it is that pushes them to keep learning. I found this out first-hand through my son Nick, who is a World War II buff. When he chose to focus on WWII and lessons learned as his end-of-the-year school project, his focus, creativity, and passion came alive. He and his two classmates visited concentration camp memorials, interviewed Holocaust survivors, and linked up with a local art gallery that creates mini figurines of real refugees to create social awareness. Through this project, I caught a glimpse of where my son's future interests may lie. By learning what excites them and upholding unevenness, teens can begin finding their purpose. This in turn can help them with their own career goals and propel them to a life passion that is unique for them.

Teach kids to think

What else should Generation Z focus on in the future? 16-year-old cross-cultural teen Malaika Bhayana, from Chevy Chase, Maryland, is taking a gap year and working with the European Union before starting university in the US. Malaika was born in the US, but her mother and father both immigrated from India years ago. Says Malaika: "Our standard subjects and curricula are likely going to be irrelevant in 20 years. Instead of focusing on one specific job or field, we need to start teaching kids how to think." She continues, "In Finland, kids don't start primary school until they are seven years old. These earlier years are a time for kids to explore social relationships and develop into individuals before being launched into a more formal education. This emphasis on the development of creativity and exploration skills in kids in Finland is exactly what's needed in the professional workplace in the next 15-20 years globally."

Embrace the unknown

We need to encourage our teens to step outside their comfort zone and explore the world around them. For those that are graduating from high school or university, this may include studying in a different community, region, or country. This may also include a gap year experience or a full-time job. For those who are not transitioning, this may include having a summer job, volunteering across town, or trying a class or activity they may not usually do. We never know what experiences may stick. As kids venture out of their comfort zone, we can point out the skills and strengths they are building. Finally, along with change, moves, and transition comes uncertainty. Being able to embrace this, rather than fight it, can be an important way to develop resilience and find purpose.

THE BOTTOM LINE: PREPARING THE GLOBAL TEEN FOR THE FUTURE

- Teens are more likely to thrive when family members, educators, coaches, and peers provide clear support, expectations, and opportunities.

- The most 'protective assets' for teens that have been discussed throughout this book include building identity, creating boundaries, and developing social competence.

- In addition to having protective assets, we also need to help modern teens avoid 'artificial maturity' and build real-life skills like doing finances and getting health care independently.

- Looking to the future, as Millennials and Gen Y teens reach adulthood, they will need to develop new skills to succeed in the global workforce.

- Top skills for global success include curiosity, collaborative skills, learning from failure, and imagination.

- As parents, we can also help global teens embrace the unknown, build a life of meaning, think creatively, and uphold unevenness. As author Chris O'Shaughnessy states so eloquently, "Cross-Cultural Kids are the prototype citizens of tomorrow... beacons of hope in a world in desperate need of it."

BIG ANSWERS

Common parent questions on preparing for the future

1. **How do we prepare our teen for university?**
   Allowing kids to have real-world experiences, such as managing their own finances, juggling schedules, or navigating health care are ways

for them to learn how to prepare for university and beyond. Upholding their unevenness (some teens will succeed better academically, or in other areas, than others) and encouraging them to embrace uncertainty and challenge will also help them to plot their own course.

2. **What are the values and skills that we can nurture in global teens to help them be successful and healthy as adults?**
Believing in teens for who they are, providing a supportive environment, creating boundaries and expectations, plus finding activities to help engage teens' time constructively are all important building blocks for ensuring that teens do well. Research shows that youths with the most protective factors or assets are more likely to do well in school, be civically engaged, and value diversity as they grow and become adults.

3. **What are the job skills that a teenager needs to survive in the coming decades?**
Having good emotional intelligence, being curious about the world around them, having intrinsic motivation, intellectual restlessness, and using imagination and creativity are important skills for 21st-century workers.

Common teen questions on preparing for the future

1. **How can I set a clear path for myself that comes from knowing what I want?**
Being aware of your own strengths and

challenges is helpful, as is knowing where your passions and interests lie. Try some brainstorming and goal setting with a family member or friend.

2. **My parents are having a hard time letting go. What can I tell them so they know I will be OK?**

   If you still live at home, remind your folks that it is easier to let go while you are still around than when you leave home. If you are already living away from home, remind your parents that this is an important part of you becoming an adult. Ask them to start allowing you to take on responsibilities such as managing your own finances or making appointments for your health care as ways to prove you can do this alone.

3. **How do I prepare for being on my own without being super overwhelmed?**

   Taking time now to take on real-life responsibilities such as creating your own schedule and organizing your time efficiently is important. Also ensuring that you take time for yourself and build positive ways to handle stress that work for you like regular exercise, sleep, and spending time with friends.

RESOURCES

Books

Arrivals, Departures and the Adventures In-Between, Chris O'Shaughnessy, Summertime Publishing, 2014

Grit: The Power of Passion and Perseverance, Angela Duckworth, Scribner, 2016

How to Raise Successful People: Simple Lessons for Radical Results, Esther Wojcicki, Houghton Mifflin Harcourt, 2019

The Toddler Brain: Nurture the Skills Today That Will Shape Your Child's Tomorrow, Laura Jana, Da Capo Press, 2017

Websites and articles

'40 Developmental Assets', Search Institute: https://www.search-institute.org/our-research/development-assets/developmental-assets-framework/. 40 Developmental Assets® is used with permission from Search Institute®. Copyright © 1997, 2006 Search Institute, Minneapolis, MN: www.searchinstitute.org.

'How to Prepare your Teen for the Real World', Kori Ellis, She Knows, 2011: https://www.sheknows.com/parenting/articles/847765/how-to-prepare-your-teen-for-the-real-world/

'Skills Every Child Will Need to Succeed in the 21st Century', Laura Jana, TEDx Talks, 2018: https://www.youtube.com/watch?v=z_1Zv_ECy0g

APPENDIX: SURVEY RESULTS

I conducted a ten-question survey from January to December 2019 among cross-cultural teens and their parents through international schools, cross-cultural communities, and organizations that I worked with. A total of 104 parents and 258 teens aged 12-18 years old responded and the results are presented here. Most of the respondents were from China, the Netherlands, and the UK. Half of the teens surveyed reported they had moved from one country to another during their childhood while one third had parents from different cultural or ethnic backgrounds. Nearly half of all parents reported that they had moved countries themselves or had parents from a country outside of where they were born. 70% of parents had never received information about raising or being a Cross-Cultural Kid or teen compared to 46% of teens.

Parent participants felt that the strengths of Cross-Cultural Kids were first cultural tolerance and a broader world view, followed by adaptability and the ability to speak more than one language. Teen participants saw it slightly differently, considering their strengths to be first adaptability, then speaking more than one language, followed by developing a broader world view, and travel. The top challenges that teens cited were loss of friends, followed by moving and transition.

As for general teen health issues, parents surveyed were most worried about screen time, stress, planning for the future, and building resilience. Teens reported concerns about maintaining balance, handling stress, planning for the future, and getting sleep. Although the survey is not representative of all cross-cultural teens and their parents, it does provide some valuable information about concerns from the sample surveyed. Further surveys should be done on a larger randomized population of cross-cultural teens and their parents. The specific comments and queries raised by parents and teens in the survey were used to develop the Big Questions sections in *Raising Global Teens*.

SURVEY QUESTIONS

Parent questions and responses

1. In which country or region do you currently live (n=104)?

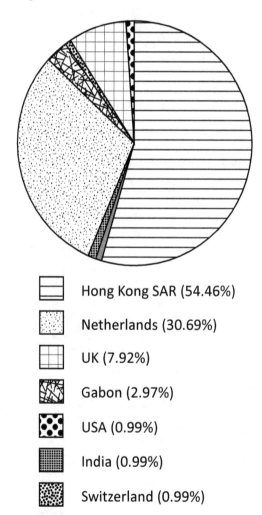

☰ Hong Kong SAR (54.46%)

▫ Netherlands (30.69%)

▦ UK (7.92%)

▨ Gabon (2.97%)

⬤ USA (0.99%)

▦ India (0.99%)

▨ Switzerland (0.99%)

⬜ France (0.99%)

2. **Have you ever discussed or received information on Cross-Cultural Kids before?**

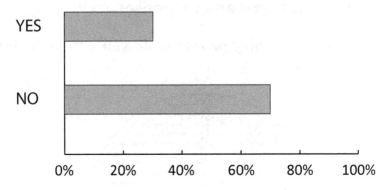

3. **Which of the following do you think are associated with being a Cross-Cultural Kid? Please check all responses that apply:**

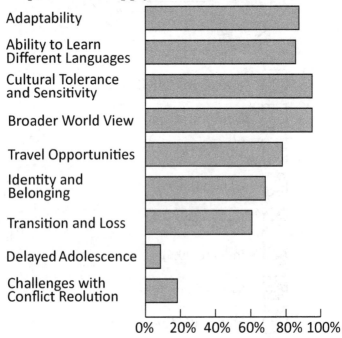

4. **Regarding your teen's general health and well-being, what issues are you most worried about? Check all those that apply:**

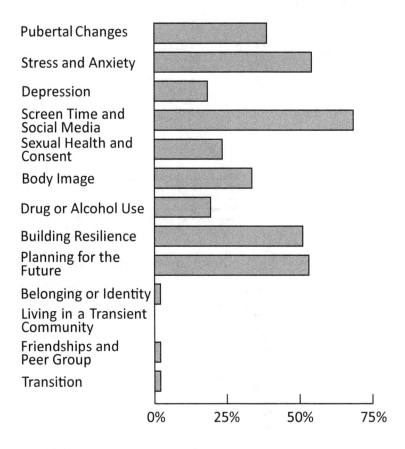

Teen questions and responses

1. **In which country or region do you currently live (n=258)?**

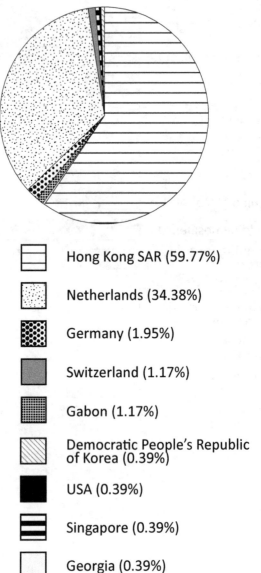

▭	Hong Kong SAR (59.77%)
▦	Netherlands (34.38%)
▦	Germany (1.95%)
▦	Switzerland (1.17%)
▦	Gabon (1.17%)
▦	Democratic People's Republic of Korea (0.39%)
▪	USA (0.39%)
▤	Singapore (0.39%)
▭	Georgia (0.39%)

2. Have you ever discussed or received information on Cross-Cultural Kids before?

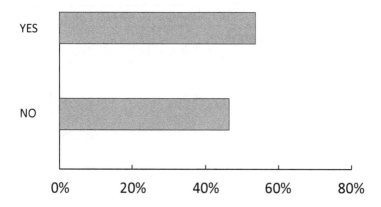

3. Which of the following do you think are associated with being a Cross-Cultural Kid? Please check all that apply:

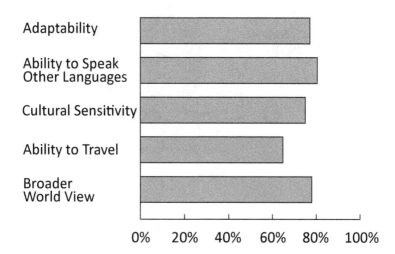

4. **Which of the following are issues or concerns as Cross-Cultural Kids? Please check all that apply:**

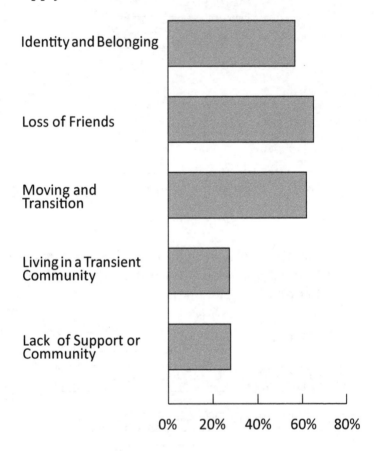

5. Regarding general health and well-being, what issues are you most worried about? Check all those that apply to you:

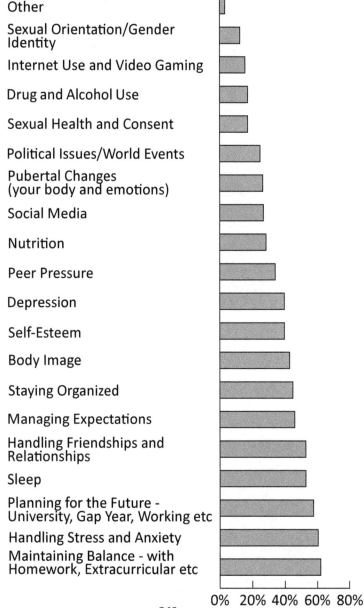

BIBLIOGRAPHY

Introduction

[1] *Third Culture Kids: Growing Up Among Worlds (3rd Ed.)*, David C Pollock, Michael V Pollock and Ruth E Van Reken, Nicholas Brealey Publishing, 2017

[2] 'Third Culture Kids: Prototypes for Understanding OtherCross-Cultural Kids', Ruth E Van Reken, 2019: http://www.crossculturalkid.org/who-are-cross-cultural-kids/

[3] Ibid.

[4] *Third Culture Kids: Growing Up Among Worlds (3rd Ed.)*, David C Pollock, Michael V Pollock and Ruth E Van Reken, Nicholas Brealey Publishing, 2017

[5] *Third Culture Kids: Growing Up Among Worlds (3rd Ed.)*, David C Pollock, Michael V Pollock and Ruth E Van Reken, Nicholas Brealey Publishing, 2017

[6] Ibid.

[7] 'Child and Adolescent Mental Health', World Health Organization, 2016: https://www.who.int/mental_health/maternal-child/child_adolescent/en/

Chapter 1

[8] 'Positive Parenting for Parents with Teenagers', Alan Ralph, Mathew Sanders, Triple P International, 2001: https://www.triplep.net.

[9] Ibid.

[10] ' "How dare you lie to me!" How to Deal with a Lying Teen', Megan Devine, *Empowering Parents*, 2019: https://www.empoweringparents.com/article/how-dare-you-lie-to-me-how-to-deal-with-a-lying-teen/

Chapter 2

[11] *Third Culture Kids: Growing Up Among Worlds (3rd Ed.)*, David C Pollock, Michael V Pollock and Ruth E Van Reken, Nicholas Brealey Publishing, 2017

[12] Ibid.

[13] 'No place to call home: Cultural homelessness, self-esteem and cross-cultural identities', Raquel C. Hoersting, 2009: https://digital.library.unt.edu/ark:/67531/metadc10991/

[14] 'Helping kids cope with cliques', Kids Health, 2018: https://kidshealth.org/en/parents/cliques.html

[15] 'Basics of identity', Shahram Heshmat, Psychology Today, 2014: https://www.psychologytoday.com/us/blog/science-choice/201412/basics-identity

Chapter 3

[16] 'Are Teenage Brains Really Different from Adult Brains?', Molly Edmonds, *How Stuff Works*, 2019: https://science.howstuffworks.com/life/inside-the-mind/human-brain/teenage-brain1.htm

[17] 'Brain Pruning: A New Theory behind Teenage Rebellion', *Rediff*, 2009: https://www.rediff.com/getahead/report/brain-pruning-a-new-theory-behind-teenage-rebellion/20090407.htm

[18] 'Understanding the Teen Brain Key for Better Parenting', Faiza Elmasry, *VOA News*, 2015: https://www.voanews.com/silicon-valley-technology/understanding-teen-brain-key-better-parenting

[19] 'Girls Really Do Mature Quicker than Boys, Scientists Find', Sarah Knapton, *The Telegraph*, 2019: https://www.telegraph.co.uk/news/science/science-news/10529134/Girls-really-do-mature-quicker-than-boys-scientists-find.html

[20] 'The Teenage Brain: The Stress Response and the Adolescent Brain', Russell D Romeo, *Curr. Dir. Psychol. Sci.*, 2013: https://www.ncbi.nlm.nih.gov/pmc/articles/PMC4274618/

[21] 'Child and Teen Brains Very Sensitive to Stress, Likely a Key Factor in Mental Illness,' *Schizophrenia.com*, 2007: http://schizophrenia.com/sznews/archives/005410.html#\

[22] 'Circulating Cortisol and Cognitive and Structural Brain Measures', Justin B. Echouffo-Tcheugui et al., *American Academy of Neurology*, 2018: https://n.neurology.org/content/91/21/e1961

[23] 'Understanding the Teen Brain Key for Better Parenting', Faiza Elmasry, *VOA News*, 2015: https://www.voanews.com/silicon-valley-technology/understanding-teen-brain-key-better-parenting

[24] 'Teen Drinking May Cause Irreversible Brain Damage', National Public Radio, 2010: https://www.npr.org/templates/story/story.php?storyId=122765890

[25] 'The Mysteriously Memorable 20s', Katy Waldman, *Slate*, 2013: https://slate.com/technology/2013/01/reminiscence-bump-explanations-why-we-remember-young-adulthood-better-than-any-other-age.html

[26] 'Adolescent Angst: 5 Facts About the Teen Brain', Robin Nixon, *Live Science*, 2012: https://www.livescience.com/21461-teen-brain-adolescence-facts.html

Chapter 4

[27] 'Puberty suppression in transgendered children and adolescents', Simone Mahfouda et al., *The Lancet Diabetes and Endocrinology*, 2017: https://www.thelancet.com/journals/landia/article/PIIS2213-8587(17)30099-2/fulltext

[28] 'Abnormalities of Female Pubertal Development', Mamie Mclean et al., *Endotext*, 2015: https://www.ncbi.nlm.nih.gov/books/NBK278950/

Chapter 5

[29] 'Study Finds Beliefs About Boy and Girl Differences Start at Early Age', *VOA*, 2017: https://learningenglish.voanews.com/a/study-finds-beliefs-about-boy-girl-differences-start-at-early-age/4043806.html

[30] Ibid.

[31] 'Stages of Adolescence', American Academy of Pediatrics, 2019: https://www.healthychildren.org/English/ages-stages/teen/Pages/Stages-of-Adolescence.aspx

Chapter 6

[32] 'Spring Fever', *Rutgers*, 2019: https://www.rutgers.international/springfever

[33] 'Sexual and Reproductive Health and Rights For All', *Rutgers*, 2019: https://www.rutgers.international/

[34] 'Could Dutch-style sex education reduce pregnancies among UK teenagers?', Tony Sheldon, *The BMJ*, 2018: https://www.bmj.com/content/360/bmj.j5930

[35] Ibid.

[36] 'The New ABCD's of Talking About Sex With Teenagers', Amy Schalet, *Huffington Post*, 2012: https://www.huffpost.com/entry/teenagers-sex-talk_b_1072504

[37] 'Start Sex Education Early, Definitely Before Puberty', Robie H Harris, *The New York Times*, 2013: https://www.nytimes.com/roomfordebate/2013/05/07/at-what-age-should-sex-education-begin/start-sex-education-early-definitely-before-puberty

[38] 'What We Can Learn From the Dutch About Teen Sex', Maia Szalavitz, *TIME*, 2011: http://healthland.time.com/2011/11/14/mind-reading-what-we-can-learn-from-the-dutch-about-teen-sex/

[39] 'Talking About Sex with Teens', *The Center for Parent and Teen Communication*, 2019: https://parentandteen.com/talking-about-sex-with-teens/

[40] 'In U.S., Estimate of LGBT Population Rises to 4.5%', Frank Newport, *Gallup*, 2018: https://news.gallup.com/poll/234863/estimate-lgbt-population-rises.aspx

[41] 'What Does 'LGBTQIA+' Stand for Exactly?', *LGBTQIA+ Info*, 2019: https://lgbtqiainfo.weebly.com/acronym-letters-explained.html

[42] 'Sexual Assault', The United States Department of Justice, 2019: https://www.justice.gov/ovw/sexual-assault

[43] 'Back to School: Talking to Teens About Sex and Sexual Assault', *Break the Cycle*, 2014: https://www.breakthecycle.org/blog/back-school-talking-teens-about-sex-and-sexual-assault

Chapter 7

[44] 'Children in a Digital World', UNICEF, 2017: https://issuu.com/unicefusa/docs/un0150335

[45] 'Common Sense Census: Media Use by Tweens and Teens', Common Sense Media, 2019. https://www.commonsensemedia.org/research/the-common-sense-census-media-use-by-tweens-and-teens-2019

[46] 'Teens, Social Media &Technology 2018', Monica Anderson and Jingjing Jiang, *Pew Research Center*, 2018: https://www.pewInternet.org/2018/05/31/teens-social-media-technology-2018/

[47] Children in a Digital World, UNICEF, 2017: https://issuu.com/unicefusa/docs/un0150335

[48] 'Effects of screentime on the health and well-being of children and adolescents: a systematic review of reviews', Neza Stiglic and Russell M Viner, *BMJ Open*, 2019: https://bmjopen.bmj.com/content/9/1/e023191

[49] 'How the iPad affects young children, and what we can do about it' (YouTube video), Lisa Guernsey, 2014: https://www.youtube.com/watch?v=P41_nyYY3Zg

[50] 'Social Media and Adolescents' and Young Adults' Mental Health', Elina Mir and Caroline Novas, *National Center for Health Research*, 2019: http://www.center4research.org/social-media-affects-mental-health/

[51] 'Teens, Social Media &Technology 2018', Monica Anderson and Jingjing Jiang, *Pew Research Center*, 2018: https://www.pewInternet.org/2018/05/31/teens-social-media-technology-2018/

[52] Ibid.

[53] 'The teenage brain on social media', Stuart Wolpert, *UCLA Health*, 2016: https://www.uclahealth.org/the-teenage-brain-on-social-media

[54] 'One in 7 Teens Are "Sexting", Says New Research', Sheri Madigan and Jeff Temple, *Scientific American*, 2018: https://www.scientificamerican.com/article/1-in-7-teens-are-ldquo-sexting-rdquo-says-new-research/

[55] 'Many U.S. Adults Sext, and It May Even Help Some Relationships', Alan Mozes, *Medicine Net*, 2015: https://www.medicinenet.com/script/main/art.asp?articlekey=189961

[56] *Plugged In: How Media Attract and Affect Youth*, Patti M Valkenburg and Jessica Taylor Piotrowski, Yale University Press, 2017: https://yalebooks.yale.edu/book/9780300218879/plugged

Chapter 8

[57] *Building Resilience in Children and Teens,* Kenneth Ginsburg, American Academy of Pediatrics, 2014.

[58] 'Treating the Lifelong Harm of Childhood Trauma', David Bornstein, *The New York Times*, 2018: https://www.nytimes.com/2018/01/30/opinion/treating-the-lifelong-harm-of-childhood-trauma.html

[59] 'Let Children get Bored Again', Pamela Paul, *Today Online*, 2019: https://www.todayonline.com/commentary/let-children-get-bored-again?cid=h3_referral_inarticlelinks_03092019_todayonline

60 'Social Class, Gender, and Contemporary Parenting Standards in the United States: Evidence from National Survey Experiment', Patrick Ishizuka, Social Forces, 2019: https://academic.oup.com/sf/article-abstract/98/1/31/5257458?redirectedFrom=fulltext

Chapter 9

61 'Any Anxiety Disorder', *National Institute of Mental Health*, 2017: https://www.nimh.nih.gov/health/statistics/any-anxiety-disorder.shtml

62 'Parent Education: Depression in children and adolescents', *UpToDate*, 2020. https://www.uptodate.com/contents/depression-in-children-and-adolescents-beyond-the-basics

63 Ibid.

64 'Anxiety disorders in children and adolescents', Shannon Bennett and John Walkup, *UpToDate*, 2019: https://www.uptodate.com/contents/anxiety-disorders-in-children-and-adolescents-epidemiology-pathogenesis-clinical-manifestations-and-course#

65 'What is self-injury?', Cornell University, 2014: http://www.selfinjury.bctr.cornell.edu/about-self-injury.html

Chapter 10

66 'Adolescents, Celebrity Worship and Cosmetic Surgery', Anisha Abraham and Diana Zuckerman, *Journal of Adolescent Health*, 2011: https://www.researchgate.net/publication/51740927_Adolescents_Celebrity_Worship_and_Cosmetic_Surgery

67 'Study Finds TV Alters Fiji Girls' View of Body Image', Erica Goode, *The New York Times*, 1999: https://www.nytimes.com/1999/05/20/world/study-finds-tv-alters-fiji-girls-view-of-body.html

68 'Maudsley Method Family Therapy', Jacquelyn Ekern, *Eating Disorder Hope*, 2012: https://www.eatingdisorderhope.com/treatment-for-eating-disorders/types-of-treatments/maudsley-method-family-therapy

69 'Overweight people are likely to own dogs that are overweight too', *Deccan Chronicle*, 2019: https://www.deccanchronicle.com/lifestyle/health-and-wellbeing/190919/overweight-people-likely-to-own-dogs-that-are-overweight-too.html

Chapter 11

70 'Substance Use', *HealthLink BC*, 2019: https://www.healthlinkbc.ca/substance-use

71 'Substance use and sexual behavior among recent Hispanic adolescents', Seth Schwartz et al., *Drug and Alcohol Dependence Journal*, 2012: https://www.ncbi.nlm.nih.gov/pubmed/22699094

[72] 'The Link Between Early Drinking Age and Risk of Alcoholism', Very Well Mind, 2019: https://www.verywellmind.com/early-drinking-age-and-the-risk-of-alcoholism-69521

[73] The Effects of Alcohol on GABA in the Brain', gammaaminobutyricacid.org, 2013: https://www.gammaaminobutyricacid.org/gaba-alcohol-effects/

[74] 'Current and Binge Drinking Among High School Students – Unites States, 1991-2015', *Centers for Disease Control and Prevention*, 2017: https://www.cdc.gov/mmwr/volumes/66/wr/mm6618a4.htm

[75] 'Binge drinking in young adults: Data, definitions, and determinants', Kelly Courtney, *Psychological Bulletin*, 2009: https://psycnet.apa.org/record/2008-18777-003

[76] 'Kids and Alcohol', Steven Dowshen, *Kids Health*, 2014:https://kidshealth.org/en/parents/alcohol.html?ref=search

[77] 'Tobacco, Nicotine, & Vaping', *National Institute on Drug Abuse for Teens*, 2019: https://teens.drugabuse.gov/drug-facts/tobacco-nicotine-e-cigarettes

[78] 'Cigarette Smokers 10 Times More Likely to Use Marijuana Daily, Study Finds', Daniel Steingold, 2017: https://www.studyfinds.org/cigarette-smokers-marijuana/

[79] 'How to Stop Teen Vaping? Try a Little Respect', *Center for the Developing Adolescent*, 2019: https://developingadolescent.org/blog/item/how-to-stop-teen-vaping-try-a-little-respect

[80] 'Quick Facts on the Risks of E-cigarettes for Kids, Teens, and Young Adults', *Centers for Disease Control and Prevention*, 2019: https://www.cdc.gov/tobacco/basic_information/e-cigarettes/Quick-Facts-on-the-Risks-of-E-cigarettes-for-Kids-Teens-and-Young-Adults.html

[81] 'How to Stop Teen Vaping? Try a Little Respect', *Center for the Developing Adolescent*, 2019: https://developingadolescent.org/blog/item/how-to-stop-teen-vaping-try-a-little-respect

[82] 'Teenage Cannabis Use Linked to Memory Problems', Kashmira Gander, *Newsweek*, 2019: https://www.newsweek.com/teenage-cannabis-use-linked-memory-problems-1433884

[83] 'Rise in Prescription Drug Misuse and Abuse Impacting Teens', SAMHSA, 2014: https://www.samhsa.gov/homelessness-programs-resources/hpr-resources/teen-prescription-drug-misuse-abuse

[84] Ibid.

[85] 'More Than One in Five Parents Believe They Have Little Influence in Preventing Teens From Using Illicit Substances', *E-Medicine Health*, 2019: https://www.emedicinehealth.com/script/main/art.asp?articlekey=170143

[86] 'Should You Drug-Test Your Kid?', Wes Boyd, *Psychology Today*, 2013: https://www.psychologytoday.com/us/blog/almost-addicted/201310/should-you-drug-test-your-kid

Chapter 12

[87] 'Symptoms and Diagnosis of ADHD', *Centers for Disease Control and Prevention*, 2019: https://www.cdc.gov/ncbddd/adhd/diagnosis.html

[88] 'Patient education: Treatment of attention deficit hyperactivity disorder in children', Kevin R Krull, *UpToDate*, 2019: https://www.uptodate.com/contents/treatment-of-attention-deficit-hyperactivity-disorder-in-children-beyond-the-basics

[89] 'Autism Spectrum Disorder: Evaluation and Diagnosis', Marilyn Augustyn, Erik Von Hahn, *UpToDate*, 2019: https://www.uptodate.com/contents/autism-spectrum-disorder-evaluation-and-diagnosis

[90] 'Helping Children with Learning Disabilities', *Help Guide*, 2019: https://www.helpguide.org/articles/autism-learning-disabilities/helping-children-with-learning-disabilities.htm

Chapter 13

[91] 'Building Success from Strengths', Ken Ginsburg, *Center for Teen and Parent* Communication, 2018: https://parentandteen.com/helping-teens-become-their-best-selves-building-success-from-strengths/

[92] 'SSHADESS Screen', *AAP*, 2014: https://www.aap.org/en-us/professional-resources/Reaching-Teens/Documents/Private/SSHADESS_handout.pdf

[93] 'Building Success from Strengths', Ken Ginsburg, *Center for Teen and Parent* Communication, 2018: https://parentandteen.com/helping-teens-become-their-best-selves-building-success-from-strengths/

[94] 'How to Build Your Child's Confidence and Self-Esteem', Monica Foley, *Child Development Institute*, 2019: https://childdevelopmentinfo.com/development/how-to-build-your-childs-confidence-and-self-esteem/#.XNqLg_ZuJPY

[95] *Building Resilience in Children and Teens: Giving Kids Roots and Wings* (4th Ed.), Kenneth Ginsburg and Martha Jablow. American Academy of Pediatrics, 2020

[96] 'On Campus, Failure is on the Syllabus', Jessica Bennett, *The New York Times*, 2017: https://www.nytimes.com/2017/06/24/fashion/fear-of-failure.html

Chapter 14

[97] 'The Developmental Assets Framework', Search Institute:https://www.search-institute.org/our-research/development-assets/developmental-assets-framework/ 40 Developmental Assets® is used with permission from Search Institute®. Copyright © 1997, 2006 Search Institute, Minneapolis, MN; www.searchinstitute.org.

[98] 'From 13 to 23: A Study in Artificial Maturity', Tim Elmore, *Huffington Post*, 2014: https://www.huffpost.com/entry/from-13-to-23-a-study-in-artificial-maturity_b_5647639

[99] 'A Particularly Dutch Summer Rite: Children Let Loose in the Night Woods', Ellen Barry, *The New York Times*, 2019: https://www.nytimes.com/2019/07/21/world/europe/netherlands-dropping-children.html

[100] 'Identity Shifters', *RPA*, 2019: https://identityshifters.rpa.com/

[101] *The Toddler Brain: Nurture the Skills Today That Will Shape Your Child's Tomorrow*, Laura Jana, Da Capo Press, 2017

[102] *How to Raise Successful People: Simple Lessons for Radical Results*, Esther Wojcicki, Houghton Mifflin Harcourt, 2019

ABOUT THE AUTHOR

Anisha Abraham, MD, MPH, is a pediatrician and teen health specialist based in Amsterdam, the Netherlands, and on faculty at the University of Amsterdam and Georgetown University Hospital in Washington, DC. She grew up in the US as the daughter of South Asian immigrants and has lived with her husband and two sons in Asia, Europe, and the US. Anisha helps cross-cultural teens manage a wide range of issues from body image to substance use, social media, and stress. She also leads seminars for teens, parents, faculty, and organizations using her 25 years of global experience as a practicing clinician, military physician, public health researcher, TEDx speaker, and health educator. She has been interviewed by NPR, CNN, NBC, Voice of America, RTHK, and The Washington Post.

For more information, see https://dranishaabraham.com/

ACKNOWLEDGMENTS

They say it takes a village to raise a child, and the same must apply to writing a book on raising them. I am grateful to many people around the globe who have supported me in completing this project. Thank you, Ajit George, for planting the seed by encouraging me to give a TEDx talk; and Ming and Wah Chen, the indomitable twins who inspired my book writing journey. I am also indebted to my fabulous Amsterdam writing group for their feedback and support over the last few years. This project would undoubtedly not have moved forward without you.

I would like to thank my wonderful publishing team who helped make this idea into a book. First, Jo Parfitt, my wise editor and publisher at Summertime Publishing who kept me moving at full speed, allowing the manuscript to come alive while patiently answering my many questions along the way. Also, Cath Brew who provided creative and beautiful images and layout, Paddy Hartnett who lent his proofreading genius, and Jack Scott who ensured the book made it to print on time.

Thanks to the many schools that allowed me to conduct the parent and teen surveys including the International School of Amsterdam, the American School of Madrid, the German Swiss International School, French International School, and the Chinese International School in Hong Kong. Also, to the wonderful experts who contributed to this book and the forewords, including Kate Berger, Malaika Bhayana, Tanya Crossman, Larry D'Angelo, Deborah Christie, Jon Fanburg, Mychelle Farmer, Preethi Galagali, Ken Ginsburg, Jeff Hutchinson, Tanya Lau, Aspen van der Hoeven, Lara Jana, Chris O'Shaughnessy, Roby Marcou, Lois van der Minnen, Cara Natterson, Allison Ochs, Mariam Ottimofiore, Jessica Piotrowski, Harshita Saxena, Tomas Silber, Maria Trent, and Ruth and David Van Reken. Thank you for your wisdom and knowledge. I also wanted to honor Caleb Meakins who was tragically killed in a car accident in Ethiopia a few weeks after we last corresponded about this book. He was a young, shining star whose life ended all too soon.

A team of thoughtful and extremely gracious reviewers around the world gave me invaluable feedback on the manuscript at various stages: Jag Bhalla, Jo Chim, Aarti Gupta, Jon Fanburg, Jeff Hutchinson, Anna Heldring, Kirsten Hawkins, Aruni John, Harshita Saxena, Melissa Strecker, Roby Marcou, Anissa Mayr, and Meena Vythilingam. Also, my fabulous teen reviewers offered spot-on suggestions, including Emma de Jong, Pauline and Jasper Kempas, plus Lucine and Ani Strecker.

A shout out to Jess Feltes for sorting out references and other pesky details in preparing the manuscript for print. Also, to Martha Bullen, Stephanie Ward, and Madhavi Sathe for their marketing and PR brilliance. Thank you to my dynamo running buddies in Hong Kong and Amsterdam who listened to my stories while keeping me sane. Also, to Debra Sequeira for her grand part in introducing me to this global adventure.

I am grateful to my sister Ajita Abraham and her family for making me laugh while providing critical feedback. To the best parents a cross-cultural teen could have, Nirmala and OC Abraham, you are my inspiration. Thank you for believing in me every step of the way.

To my sons, Nick and Kai, you remind me every day what it means to be curious and open to the world (and a humble parent) – you are the epicenter of this book. Finally, to my husband, Hannfried, who encouraged me to keep on writing and served as editor, sounding board, and co-conspirator. I am grateful for your love, patience, and infinite support. You have a very special place in my heart.

ALSO BY
SUMMERTIME PUBLISHING

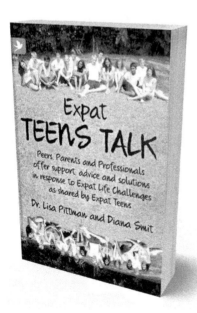

DOUGLAS W. OTA

SAFE
PASSAGE

How mobility affects people &
what international schools
should do about it

"I CANNOT
RECOMMEND
THIS BOOK
HIGHLY
ENOUGH"

THE
WORLDS
WITHIN

– an anthology of
TCK art and writing:
young, global and
between cultures

Edited by
Eva László-Herbert
and
Jo Parfitt

The
Global Nomad's Guide
to
UNIVERSITY TRANSITION

Tina L. Quick

TERRY ANNE WILSON
& JO PARFITT

MONDAY MORNING EMAILS

Six months, twelve countries, a thousand
thoughts — two mothers share the
journey of living a global life

CPSIA information can be obtained
at www.ICGtesting.com
Printed in the USA
LVHW022113091120
671185LV00016B/3027